PRAISE FOR

BRAVE NEW UNWIRED WORLD

"Courageous subject, courageous book, written by a very courageous entrepreneur."
Phil Garfinkle, founder of Picture Vision (AOL's You've Got Pictures),
adVenture Capitalist, Entrepreneur

"*Brave New Unwired World* is a mind-opener for every reader. For the ones who know all the facts, you will certainly get new perspectives on how the future might look. And for everybody else there is a huge collection of facts and thoughts presented in a fascinating way. Buckle up and enjoy the ride."
Sharon Carmel, cofounder and board member,
Emblaze Systems

"*Brave New Unwired World* offers a compelling and insightful look at the future of communication, the emergence of 4G networks, and the radical impact that new communication-based technologies will have on our personal and professional lives."
Douglas Ingram, Daedalus Venture Group

"Even people who don't venture beyond the past will be magically teleported into the future under the spell of this time-warping work. At the outer limits of our understanding of telecommunication, Lightman sets off a flare, and suddenly the last mile comes into searing focus."
Tony Dolz, director,
State of California Center for International Business Development

"A thorough and compelling study, filled with fascinating facts and personalities. Lightman knows his stuff, and *Brave New Unwired World* is essential reading for the people who will resurrect telecommunications and information technology and shape the twenty-first century."
Greg Bear, author of *Darwin's Radio,*
Hugo and Nebula award winner

"Lightman and Rojas combine a dizzying array of fields and facts to provide commentary on some of the fundamental issues that will be facing the next generations of information technology. Opinionated and thought-provoking, *Brave New Unwired World* provides a perspective that, until now, only a few have seen."
Thad Starner, PhD,
Professor, Georgia Tech, and pioneer in wearable computing

"Alex Lightman, one of the more engaging of the entrepreneurial spirits of the 1990s, has returned to the public's attention with a trenchant argument for what the future of communications will look like: It will be based on people, not places; it will be wireless; the devices will be wearable and very cheap; and the network to which they are attached will be like electricity—ubiquitous, invisible, and always on. Oh brave new world!"

Jason Pontin, editor, the *Red Herring*

"From 1G to 4G, from Moore's Law to Metcalf's Law, Lightman's *Brave New Unwired World* is worth the read just for the comprehensive historical perspective on the technological revolution over the last half of the previous century. But you get more: a thorough orientation on where this is all likely to go in the early decades of the new millennium, including not only possible roadmaps for 2.5G and beyond but also useful insights into the roles of Japan and China."

Arnold Pollard, vice-chairman, Chief Executive Group

"Lightman guides you through the jungle of wireless broadband, with an in-depth review of technologies and prevailing market conditions. From the evolution of communications and computing through their convergence, Lightman articulates how these technologies are evolving and merging to create new opportunities. It is a must-read book for anyone involved in the convergence of computing and telecommunications."

Satjiv Chahil, Chief Marketing Officer, Palm, Inc.

"Wireless is the next thing you should have understood yesterday. In this extraordinary book, rich with lucid explanations of a broad range of technology, Lightman crafts a map that will make the importance and difference of wireless make sense. If allowed by regulators, and freed from dinosaurs, wireless could fuel the next Internet revolution. This book shows how."

Lawrence Lessig, Professor, Stanford Law School, and author of *Code and Other Laws of Cyberspace* and *The Future of Ideas*

"Alex Lightman takes you on a flying tour of the Internet technologies that will shape the early part of the 21st century. He is one of the few visionaries who understand the transformational nature of the wireless Internet."

UCSD Professor Larry Smarr, director, The California Institute for Telecommunications and Information Technology

BRAVE NEW
UNWIRED
WORLD

BRAVE NEW UNWIRED WORLD

*The Digital Big Bang
and the Infinite Internet*

ALEX LIGHTMAN
with **WILLIAM ROJAS**

JOHN WILEY & SONS, INC.

This book is printed on acid-free paper. ⊗

Copyright © 2002 by Alex Lightman. All rights reserved.

Published by John Wiley & Sons, Inc., New York.
Published simultaneously in Canada.

No part of this publication may be reproduced, stored in a retrieval system or transmitted in any form or by any means, electronic, mechanical, photocopying, recording, scanning or otherwise, except as permitted under Sections 107 or 108 of the 1976 United States Copyright Act, without either the prior written permission of the Publisher, or authorization through payment of the appropriate per-copy fee to the Copyright Clearance Center, 222 Rosewood Drive, Danvers, MA 01923, (978) 750-8400, fax (978) 750-4744. Requests to the Publisher for permission should be addressed to the Permissions Department, John Wiley & Sons, Inc., 605 Third Avenue, New York, NY 10158-0012, (212) 850-6011, fax (212) 850-6008, e-mail: PERMREQ@WILEY.COM.

This publication is designed to provide accurate and authoritative information in regard to the subject matter covered. It is sold with the understanding that the publisher is not engaged in rendering professional services. If professional advice or other expert assistance is required, the services of a competent professional person should be sought.

Library of Congress Cataloging-in-Publication Data:

Lightman, Alex, 1961–
  Brave new unwired world : the digital big bang and the infinite internet / Alex
  Lightman.
    p. cm.
  Includes bibliographical references (p.) and index.
  ISBN 0-471-44110-4 (cloth : alk. paper)
    1. Information society.   2. Information technology—Social aspects.   3. Internet—
  Social aspects.   4. Wireless communication systems—Social aspects.   I. Title.

  HM851 .L54 2001
  303.48'33—dc21

                                                                    2001046682

Printed in the United States of America.

10   9   8   7   6   5   4   3   2   1

CONTENTS

PREFACE

MIRANDA: O wonder! How many goodly creatures are there here!

How beauteous mankind is! O brave new world that has such people in't!

PROSPERO: 'Tis new to thee.

W. Shakespeare (The Tempest)

I've always liked the saying,

"The best way to predict the future is to invent it,"

but have found just as much evidence to support the contention that

"The best way to invent the future is to predict it."

Congratulations. By opening this page you have become part of a great conversation. The process of improving communications that was initiated by Maxwell, Marconi, and Tesla over 100 years ago has led to a trillion-fold increase in the number of simultaneous voice calls that can be made. This amplification of human voices is probably the single most spectacular and positive human accomplishment in history. We've just started, though, and need to redouble our collective efforts to maintain this dazzling rate of improvement. What the world needs now is a simple concept to rally behind, a concept describing the next big thing in computers and communication, and in their convergence. We think it's 4G, as in "4G-ing a new world."[1]

Our purpose in writing is both to invent and to predict aspects of 4G, including the future of wireless broadband, the accelerated convergence of computers and communications, and the amazing challenges that Americans and Europeans will face from Japanese and Chinese companies. We want our readers to be first in line to stake their claim to a spectrum of opportunities, comparable to but very different in nature and technology from the Internet boom of the mid- to late 1990s. We wrote this book in a period of extreme pessimism toward high technology, especially toward the topics that form the core of this book. We, the authors, refer to this book and its message as BNUW both because it is the acronym of the title and because it reminds us to "be new" and think freshly. The boom and bust cycle will again turn itself soon to boom, and we know—to paraphrase Chairman Mao—that not only a thousand flowers will bloom, but also thousands of new companies, products, professions, and possibilities.

Though the book speaks for itself, I'd like to start with a few words about the title. "Brave New World" comes from Shakespeare's *Tempest* and is a quote from Miranda as she sees an ordinary man but thinks that he is wonderful. I think that the single most distinctive feature of the world of the future will be that humans will wear their wireless technology, and this fashionable technology will make people who see a Borg[2] thus adorned with a Head-Up Display feel what we can imagine Miranda must have felt. *Brave New World* is, of course, the name of Aldous Huxley's 1932 novel that opens with the London Hatchery where children are made. I think that wireless broadband will have a greater impact than cloning and genetic engineering, and I wanted to use the strongest and most evocative phrase for social change made as a result of embracing new technology without fear that it would be interpreted as code words for "Look—this is the future here."

"Brave New Unwired World" was the name of the wearable and pervasive computing fashion show that I produced in many cities (New York, Los Angeles, Las Vegas, London, Paris, Stockholm, Berlin, Tel Aviv, Hong Kong, Singapore, Beijing, Sydney, and Seoul, among others) that showed commercially available wireless devices from sponsors such as Motorola, Hewlett-Packard, Microsoft, and others; wearables from my company, Charmed, as well as from research labs and the U.S. military; and conceptual prototypes of every conceivable size, shape, color, core technology, and function of pervasive and fashionable computers. The BNUW shows were hard work, especially for a company in its first two years, but they made a big impact. Over 250,000 people came to the live shows, which featured professional models and production values; in addition, I'm told that over 50 million people have seen clips or images of the BNUW show in the media. If you've ever seen a model on a catwalk with a futuristic computer on her head, it's very likely it was from the BNUW show (or an imitator without regard for our copyright).

Many people (in the thousands) who came to the BNUW shows asked what it would take to make wearable computers commercially boom worldwide. This book is the answer to that question, though it doesn't have the space to deal with the BNUW fashion show. Simply search online if you want to see the clips or photos of the show.

The subtitle is "The Digital Big Bang and the Infinite Internet." Coauthor Bill Rojas and I sometimes mean different things by Digital Big Bang. Bill's view relates to the human role in the cosmos and is explained in the text. I think of the Digital Big Bang as related to my concept of the "Internet Iceberg Effect." As I said in *The Dictionary of the Future* (p. 244), "Internet connections to things, particularly sensors, that are not used directly by humans will outnumber human subscriptions, leaving 90 percent of Internet growth nearly invisible, like an iceberg."[3] In a single human life span (mine, say, starting December 5, 1961), we will have gone from only a few hundred digital devices to a few hundred billion—a burst that is big enough and fast enough to be called a big bang if anything can. There are many "little big bangs" as well, which don't make the news because we don't have a context for them. For example, China has increased its international Internet gateway capacity from 20 megabits per second to 3,257 megabits per second in less than 18 months, a fact that should stun those of us who can imagine this growth continuing, or even accelerating, as China (we predict) chooses to focus on leadership in telecommunications.

The "infinite Internet" is my phrase for the greatest invention in human history: a public utility that enables any person, place, pet, or valuable thing to access almost any information, anytime, anywhere, almost instantly, at almost no cost, with sufficient security to fairly balance most concerns. In the year of the first O. J. Simpson trial, the Internet was the only other story to get as much press, virtually all of which was good. Now, in 2002, there are fewer than 1 percent of the number of articles, most of which are pessimistic, as if something has failed. How petulant the media are with their darlings and playthings!

As of December 2001, there were roughly 600 million Internet users globally (some claim as many as 625 million), or about 10 percent of the entire world online, with as many as 180 million in the United States (just under two-thirds of all Americans). The number of Internet users has increased more than fivefold in the last two years in important countries such as China, India, and Russia, indicating plenty of room for growth in the net globally (only 0.5 percent of India, a multicultural democracy, and only 2 percent of China have access to the net) and, as BNUW will show, many technologies to accelerate this growth. Once the infrastructure for 4G proposed here gets started, mobile Internet devices costing a mere $100 (and falling down to a

few tens of dollars) will allow a greater number of users than when PCs costing $1,000 and up were mandatory. And even this isn't the limit: the Grameen
Bank in Bangladesh is making microloans so that a woman can buy a mobile
phone and then charge for its shared use, in effect allowing for the creation
of micro-telcos in millions of villages that are too small for AT&T, NTT, and
Deutsche Telekom to think about.

Although the book was written prior to the tragic yet catalytic events of
September 11, I still stand by the points of the book and see no reason to
change anything. However, as my early readers will confirm, I had an entire
section about the impact of wireless technologies on warfare that warned of
terrorist attack and the trillion-dollar impact on the U.S. stock market, but
this point is now—regrettably and sadly—too obvious to emphasize in the
text.

Amid the terror attacks and victory marches in the post–September 11
world, I do have mixed feelings that the United States will now overvalue
military technology superiority, which the country obviously has, and un-
dervalue telecommunications superiority, which, as this book indicates, the
United States has lost but could regain, if only this goal ("first in 4G") became a priority for our society. The issue of spectrum is tangled and so contentious in the United States that it will take a presidential priority to create
the context for American leadership. Despite all their other issues, Scandi-
navia, Japan, and China have exhibited brilliant public policy thinking with
respect to these matters, and the results have been companies that have grown
from small companies (Nokia) or spin-offs (NTT DoCoMo) to be among
the largest in the world in the last two decades. China, already blessed with
far more mobile users than any other nation, will add 50 million mobile users
a year, and most of these could potentially be Internet users. With $10 tril-
lion in GDP, the United States already runs a massive trade deficit in goods
with China and Japan. The nation that leads in 4G will eventually run a massive surplus in communications, and possibly even in technology and services, altering the balance of power in the age of net war.

In December 2001 a panel of 22 experts was assembled to give technology advice to President Bush—the only White House move even mildly in
the 4G direction, and one that simply doesn't compare to the life-or-death
importance given to wireless and broadband by America's big three telecom
challengers, where 4G conferences have already been held with government sponsorship. If only a tiny fraction more of the president's attention
were given to the issues raised in BNUW, especially related to spectrum use,
we might come up with a new Sputnik-like national focus. Perhaps with

just a single Kennedyesque speech (like that which started the Apollo project: "We will put a man on the moon and return him safely to earth by the end of the decade") by George W. Bush about the need to lead in the next generation of wireless communication, America could unleash a wireless broadband boom that would have a massively beneficial impact, with seven key benefits.

1. Leadership in wireless broadband could extend a bundle of communications (including radio, telephone, fax, Internet, television, and MP3), which now reach fewer than two billion people, to over four billion people by the end of the decade, allowing people who are now poor, and willing to believe that they are better off supporting (or being) martyrs to learn and earn entirely new possibilities.

2. Installation of American, or Western, equipment ties the countries that receive it more tightly into the feedback loops with the United States and the West, encouraging and facilitating communication, such as more accurate news, entertainment, and trade.

3. In case of emergency, the United States would have one more lever of influence besides massive multimonth bombing runs. Bombing runs have their place (especially if the Unites States is going to pick up the billion dollar rebuilding cost), but we might want to be able to stop communications traffic selectively, just as we minimize civilian casualties when we target more precisely.

4. I could be overoptimistic, but my own calculations indicate that after implementing most of the ideas in this book, wireless broadband business could generate $100 per month from a billion people for all-inclusive information/communication/education, or $1.2 trillion a year, plus $40 a month from another one billion people, or $480 billion a year, and $300 billion a year for consulting, integration, and related services, accounting for nearly $2 trillion annually, an amount that would be the fourth largest economy on Earth in terms of GDP. This is simply too large a sum for the United States (and Europe, Japan, and China) not to try very hard to win. I say for countries to win because governments can make or break their companies through spectrum auctions, licenses, patent protection, and even accounting changes.

5. Though it's been said before many times, true security will come to Americans from increases in the quality and quantity of democracy and freedom (including freedom of speech, association, trade, and travel). As Bernard Lewis recently put it with respect to the Middle

East, in the democracies such as Turkey and Israel, the people and the governments are both pro-American; in the nondemocracies, either the government is pro-American and the people are anti-American (Egypt and Saudi Arabia), or the government is anti-American and the people are pro-American (as in Iran and Iraq). Any lasting peace in the Middle East, or anywhere else, will be built on universal access to mobile Internet: This is the only way to reverse the process of divergence. America can no more get global public opinion on its side through bombing than Israel can get Palestinian public opinion on its side. Kill all terrorists, by all means, but make sure that there is something to increase the opportunities for work, education, entertainment, and trade for the 99.9% who will be left after all terrorists are routed. After reviewing the impact of telecommunications around the world, I'd say that getting widespread wireless Internet in, say, Afghanistan is just as important as installing a new government or building buildings, especially if numbers like $20 billion to be invested are reasonable estimates. I think at least 20 percent (and preferably 50 percent) of all foreign aid should be in the form of state-of-the-art communications, if something other than a growing number of armed welfare client states is deemed to be in America's interest. Spending $20 million on telecom out of the $100 million given to the PLO in each of the last few years could have made a big difference, as could $200 million extra in Egypt, especially if it turns out that U.S. aid money was used for weapons or sent offshore. Modern societies are built on a vast array of feedback loops, and setting up wireless broadband is the single best way to set many feedback loops in motion with maximum positive social benefits.

6. There are dozens, perhaps thousands, of technologies in company-, university-, and government-based laboratories—even in the garages of inventors—that will never see the light of day commercially unless certain other complementary technologies are also available and infrastructure prices fall enough for new offerings to be bundled. AT&T's lawyers said that the laser wasn't worth patenting because it had no conceivable use in telecommunications. Add fiber optics years later, though, and the combination created the basis for an explosion of bandwidth so great that it shattered all the forecasts based on the price for fixed-line broadband. Other massively synergistic combinations will occur only if others combinations happen first. The only way to

know is to offer everything for sale—not only individually, but in complex bundled offerings with financing options.

7. In particular, I believe that the greatest benefit of wireless broadband will be to create an infrastructure for my favorite bundled offering: wearable computers with augmented reality. I'm sure that we will see wearable and pervasive computers that eventually become roughly the size and shape of eyeglasses and allow the users to see the real world, the virtual world, or anything on the net; to "overlay" semitransparent text, graphics, and video through augmented reality; and to see through the eyes of any one of the millions of other users. At the moment, only a few dozen people have even the partial capability to do just the augmented reality overlays. Believe it or not, some of these (at Columbia University in New York, for instance) are carrying $3,000, 2-GHz laptops with two hours of battery life strapped to their backs, with $5,000 displays. The boom will happen when 4-GHz wearable computers weighing less than a pound cost under $1,000, display included, and then drop from there to mobile phone prices. Without implementation of the program outlined in this book, however, a process like this may take 10 to 20 years instead of two or three.

I want to emphasize the geostrategic relevance of expending precious political capital on wireless broadband, especially with public/private partnerships for foreign aid. If America installs equipment that helps increase India's Internet population from 5 million to 555 million in this decade, we can make a profit *and* help cement the friendship with a one-of-a-kind country, the largest democracy, and thereby earn the gratitude of a beautiful and wonderful but suffering people, who share a surprising number of the same challenges faced by Americans. A similar situation exists with China; the United States can make very low interest loans through the World Bank and Asian Development Bank. A China using American hardware and software to send a trillion e-mails a year will be friendlier to America than would a China committed to pushing American hardware and software out of Asia with its own proprietary and incompatible standards. As of December 2001, the only country in the Middle East to allocate spectrum for 3G was Israel, so America still has time to make a generous contribution to upgrading the telecommunications infrastructure for the region. If fundamentalists are going to plot, we should make sure that it's with our phones.

I think these reasons give a decent summary of what's in it for America or other countries that prioritize 4G—but what's in it for you, the reader? I admit it: Although it's written for businesspeople and engineers and scientists interested in a business-based view of the technology of the future, reading this entire book and understanding it will be tough, so what's the payoff? I think there are several good reasons to invest the five to ten hours it would take the average person to go through the book:

1. *Getting a seat in the industry equivalent of musical chairs, as entrepreneurs and investors for what could become a multitrillion-dollar industry.* My sense is that the 30,000 or so people who understand most of what is in this book will end up with most of the wealth created by 4G, leaving millions of other people to divide up the rest.
2. *Understanding the past, present, and future of the computer, communications, and high-tech industries.* BNUW deals with wireless broadband and other technologies from political, economic, scientific, technological, financial, and business perspectives, allowing for the reader to have a gestalt or "big picture" that would be hard to find anywhere else. This "big picture" can create the basis for a new dialogue.
3. *Narrowing in on the best companies, countries, industries, and technologies on which to bet your investments and your career.* My advice would be to see who starts to implement 4G first, and then go to that country, even if it means getting a work visa and leaving your home country, because the first to 4G will have an edge, and it will be important to participate as early on as possible.

That said, I hope that you will simply skip over any section that you find too technical; you can get the gist, and most chapters stand on their own, so read the book in any order, and please use it as a reference or for ideas for PowerPoint slides or business plans or reports.

Some readers might wonder why BNUW was written. The simple answer is that we wanted to send out the human equivalent of a high-frequency, highly targeted birdcall to the world. This book will find its way—perhaps through your referrals, references, gift giving, and assigned reading—into the hands of people who are willing and able to build a brand new telecommunications infrastructure, and to do well by doing good. At its core, BNUW is an open invitation to collaboration extended by the authors for tens of thousands of people to come together around the general aim of better computers and communications. The readers of BNUW might end up with a more focused goal, such as to bring wireless broadband to three billion people by the end of the first decade of the 21st century.

Finally, I've been asked who came up with 4G. My answer is that I did (there was exactly one reference on the Internet when I started; it was on a graph from a PowerPoint of a National Science Foundation with no explanation, that showed it starting after 2010). My proof is that I obtained what any person who was the first to understand 4G's importance would have: the Internet domains 4G.org and 4G.tv, as well as the first 25 or so trademark filings in the relevant categories. For the record, no government agency, as of this writing, will define it, but in its simplest sense, 4G is a suite of approaches to wireless broadband. My intention is not to own 4G in an exclusive sense, but merely to clarify its origin for historical purposes, and to have something that can be given, open-source style, to the world, rather than owned by a single person, company, or country, in just the same way that we can all use the word "Internet" because no one (yet) owns it. My intention is to make 4G to the Internet what the Internet was to ARPAnet.

If you have any comments, feel free to post comments at the 4G.org, 4G.tv, Charmed.com, or BraveNewUnwiredWorld.com web sites, or to email me directly at alex@charmed.com.

I hope that you enjoy *Brave New Unwired World,* and work to make it so.

Alex Lightman, January 12, 2002,
Santa Monica, California

Notes

1. There are no dictionary definitions for 4G as of this writing. To me, 4G stands for much more than "Fourth Generation" of wireless. 4G means broadband data transmission rates faster than 11 Megabits/second; a suite of technologies that are proven but not yet deployed to massively expand wireless communication; and a designation for future industrial and commercial clusters that deal with the final convergence of computers and communications into a single megaindustry.

2. Borg is short for cyborg and is the name used by people who wear computers all the time (vs. once in a while) for themselves. It is derived from the Borg Collective (man-machine hybrids) who menace humanity in *Star Trek.*

3. Faith Popcorn and Adam Hanft, *Dictionary of the Future: The Words, Terms, and Trends That Define the Way We'll Live, Work, and Talk* (New York: Hyperion, 2001).

ACKNOWLEDGMENTS

With respect to the research material in the book, we would like to thank the following people who helped us during the course of writing the manuscript:

We would like to thank Professor Peter Hugill of Texas A&M for providing a wealth of background information on the history of wireless communications. We would to thank Gordon Bennett for expanding the 4G portal concept for us. We would like to express our gratitude to Professor Thad Starner of Georgia Tech and Professor Alex (Sandy) Pentland for their brilliant insights on the future of wearable and pervasive computing, and for their partnership in founding Charmed with Alex Lightman. Thanks also to Professors Larry Smarr and Larry Lessig for brilliant insights into the future of the Internet.

Many thanks to David Carew of Nomura International, who provided us many suggestions regarding the viability of 4G and the strengths and weaknesses of 3G from the viewpoint of investment banking. We would like to thank Tony Corel of Squire Sanders & Dempsey for his many suggestions regarding regulatory challenges that 4G technologies will face. Many thanks to all our friends at various companies that are involved in various technologies described in this book. In particular, we would like to cite the following companies that have influenced either directly or indirectly our views on 4G: Nortel, IBM, ArrayComm, Siemens, Time Domain, RF Waves, and Gilat Satellite. Thank you, Willie Liu and others at the IEEE who help make the standards and set up the conferences that let the smartest technology researchers in the world talk with each other face to face. Thank you, Connie Hsu at Pyramid Research for market analysis relating to China. A special note of gratitude to our friends in China who have enlightened on us on China's incredible potential in telecommunications: William Krueger (Xinde Telecom), Hans So (Xinde Telecom), Kenny Wang, Fred Wang (Salon Films), and Wong Fang. China has a good chance to lead the world because it can bring forth people of your caliber.

This book represents the experience and dreams of both authors, and there have thus been many people who have contributed over the years to our ideas. Alex would like to thank

- his professors at MIT and Harvard, his fraternity brothers at Delta Tau Delta, and his employers at Reuters and IntelliCorp for many lessons in technology
- his colleagues at Charmed Technology in the United States, Europe, India, and China for their amazing brilliance and hard work in inventing, researching, building, shipping, and showing the future—we created computers as fashion, and much more (thanks to you, too, Shannon Davis, for handling everything flawlessly for years)
- the investors in Charmed Technology, especially Charles Schwab, for coming through twice when I really needed it, and for setting an example of integrity, wisdom, and how to handle decades of success with charm and grace; Phil Garfinkle for believing in the badges and Nanix; Shai Stern for brilliant work at Yazam and beyond; Michael Schwab for making it happen, and adventure travel; Tavenner Hall, both of you; Brian Jordan; Udi Shapiro, Sharon Carmel, Yaacov Ben-Yaacov, and the other brilliant entrepreneurial successes of Israel—toda and shalom; thank you all very much; the best is still to come
- his editors at Red Herring, Internet World, Field Force Automation, Intellectual Capital, and Chief Executive, who enabled him to write a complex book like this one, one column or article at a time, and partners at Penton Media, especially Megan Forrester, Steve Sind, and Michael Westcott for making it possible to do 100 Brave New Unwired World shows around the world
- his editor at John Wiley & Sons, Matt Holt, for reading his column titled "The Extinction of Profit" and making this process happen for Brave New Unwired World and The Future Engine
- his inspiring friends and acquaintances who write science fiction and make a much greater contribution than the world has ever acknowledged: Greg Benford, Greg Bear, David Brin, Vernor Vinge, Bruce Sterling, and Brian Aldiss
- his friends for decades, Tony Dolz (wireless genius), Paul Shepherd, and Rhonda Shaw, and his newer friends, Chris Harz, Kelly Carter, and Leah Thompson

Bill would like to express special thanks to the following people who over the years engaged, debated, and gave passionate guidance, helping him to develop his views on the computer industry, physics, semiconductors, molecular electronics, and nanotechnologies: Dr. Mel Pomerantz (retired from IBM Research), Dr. Ari Aviram (IBM Research and most recently Mitre Corp.), Irwin Hymes (retired from IBM), Art Bross (retired from IBM), Bill North (retired from IBM), Professor Aizawa (Tokyo Institute of Technology), Carver Mead (his advisor at Caltech), Professors Okabe and Sugano (his graduate advisors at the University of Tokyo), Professor John Ure (University of Hong Kong), Nick Donofrio (IBM), Jack Kuehler (retired from IBM), George Conrades (formerly IBM and currently Akamai Corp.), and I. Adachi (founder of Intelligent Wave, Tokyo).

Finally, both authors would like to thank their families for their relentless support and dedication over the years. Alex thanks his mother for giving birth to him 60 years to the day after Walt Disney was born, so he can pretend there is some sort of connection, and for teaching him to read anywhere, and Rauna, Turida, Vitor, and Usmar for shared blood and interesting times. Bill would like to express his deep gratitude to his late grandfather, William Benton, who loved electronics, music, foreign languages, and mathematics, and who first exposed Bill to ham radios when he was only five years old. Finally, Bill would like to thank his wife, who has always encouraged him to probe further into the realms of science, literature, religion, and philosophy.

PART I

INTRODUCTION

Time for next-generation wireless.

In a world that has grown accustomed to the rapid progress from one generation of computers to the next generation, faster and cheaper, the world of telecoms may appear one of foot-dragging reluctance. First-generation mobile (1G) was introduced in 1981 and offered voice-only handsets the size of small suitcases. Ten years later, 1991 saw the arrival of 2G wireless, offering the innovation of SMS messaging. Now 3G wireless capable of voice and multimedia on a compact handset is due take-off in 2001.

The industry has settled in to a ten-year cycle. It takes a decade to develop a new-generation system with all the phases of research, developing the technology and getting it to the standardization procedures.

It is now time to start work on the next generation.

Asiansources, January 2001, at
www.wirelesscomm.globalsources.com/MAGAZINE

PART I

INTRODUCTION

CHAPTER 1

THE PATH TO 4G

Major Technology Trends to Watch

WIRELESS TELECOMMUNICATIONS has evolved from 1G (analog) to 2G (digital) to 3G (always-on, faster data rate) since 1980, a pace of roughly a generation per decade. 3G, as we will see, hasn't delivered on its promise of wireless broadband Internet and television, leading many to ask to speed up the pace of improvement.

The timing, costs, and lack of integration in the planned Third Generation telecommunications (3G) systems have caused customers to ask for more. Bold new users are going to put pressure on the telecom industry to skip to Fourth Generation (4G) systems and deliver what had been promised for 3G by the year 2006 (at the latest) in countries with developed fiber-optic infrastructure. A later chapter presents the strengths and weaknesses of 3G systems and demonstrates that 4G is what the consumers and the investment community want in the near future: the ability to have any information at your fingertips anywhere at anytime whether moving or stationary. Knowledge of anything, anywhere, anytime: This is the beauty and attraction of broadband wireless. Contrary to what many carrier engineers have contended, it will be possible to combine ad hoc (or hot spot) networks—wireless local area network (W-LAN) antennas in campuses, neighborhoods, and shopping malls—with the public cellular networks to provide an intricate web of access points to the Internet. Further, this will seamlessly interoperate with a new wireless

Internet consisting of millions of mobile computers, sensors, and specialized devices added to the fixed PCs and servers that are connected today. Professor Hannu H. Kari of the Helsinki University of Technology has proposed that Germany could be covered by a network of W-LAN base stations as an alternative to the expensive proposition of deploying universal mobile telecommunications service (UMTS) 3G telecom infrastructure expected to cost 10,000 euros per user. This is too high: By 2005 the interest rates alone would amount to 80 euros per user per month, about half of what they now pay for service. (The euro is a little less than a U.S. dollar, though this is subject to change based on bad market changes.)

The motivations for 4G are economic, political, and technical. Following are 13 major trends that will both play a crucial role in forming a 4G cluster by making it possible for new businesses, alliances, and value chains to emerge and determine how quickly we can realize the dream of data access anywhere, anytime, at low cost.

1. *Spectrum availability.* The biggest obstacle to realizing 4G systems is making new radio spectrum available, which means new, smarter government spectrum policies. Consumer and business users hungry for bandwidth will face a great spectrum famine unless governments do something about revamping their spectrum allocations. In the United States, the military should give up spectrum or pay commercial prices for it, and the Federal Communications Commission (FCC) should take back the spectrum given to the television broadcasters, since it wasn't the FCC's or Congress's to give away. The principle of auctioning spectrum, and giving it only on payment, must be for all or for none; if for none, the U.S. government must massively increase open spectrum of the industrial, scientific, and medical (ISM) type. Space up to 1 GHz should be given to ultra-wideband (UWB) because it is a superior conveyor of wireless data, based on physics not politics, and it will be essential for emergency services such as fire and police tracking using UWB localizers that are accurate to a centimeter.

2. *Major consolidation in the cellular industry.* Cellular operators that paid enormous (if not outrageous) sums (in Europe the aggregate total is over $100 billion, with expenses up to $7 billion for a single country in one case) for limited (typically 20 MHz) 3G spectrum will be under extreme pressure to achieve profits and will further be challenged by ad hoc high-speed W-LAN technologies such as 802.11b.

3. *Technology change agents.* Ultra low-power central processing units (CPU)

and miniature software radio/radio frequency (RF) chip sets will emerge whether Intel likes them or not, and they will greatly alter the appearance of computers from a big box that sits on our desks at home or at the office to something that is small enough to take everywhere we go—thus creating the world of wireless ubiquitous computing.

4. *Convergence moves into a higher gear.* The convergence of computing and communications will find more leadership from the computer companies in the near future simply because they have a broader intellectual property base than communications companies, spanning materials research, semiconductors, microprocessors, storage, core technology and middleware, and application platforms. At the time of this writing, a number of large telecom manufacturers were actually trading at around their book value (indicating low market expectations for growth in profits) and were still in the throes of debt restructuring, mergers, employee redundancies, cost cutting—all the usual results of overspending, overforecasting, and mismanagement. Unless they miss the message of this book, in the end, computer-focused companies will dominate the merged worlds of computers and communications.

5. *Challenges to the market domination of 2G/3G handset makers.* Advances in Digital Signal Processors (DSPs), software-defined radios, and spatial antenna technologies are going to transform the massive empires of manufacturers such as 3Com, Nokia, Ericsson, and Motorola. Some companies will get bigger (an example might be Texas Instrument's DSP group); others will be rendered mercilessly obsolete; and new ones will emerge.

6. *Convergence of interdisciplinary research.* The personal digital assistant (PDA), the wristwatch, the mobile telephone, the pager, the Sony Walkman, the Sony Watchman, and all the other X-mans will converge into more universal types of devices that will adhere to open-source standards, provide broadband but with secure transmission, and be optimized to handle image, video, text, and voice. We call these devices "4G" for "Fourth Generation." Although 4G is not standardized (e.g., there is no International Telecommunications Union, or ITU, definition yet), we use the term throughout this book profusely to denote the next generation of everything in communications and computers. Examples of areas that are converging include the following:

- Embedded microprocessors. If sufficiently fast and low-power, e.g., millions of instruction per second (MIPS) at 100 milliwatts or less, chips were available, they would replace the role of field programmable gate arrays (FPGAs) and essentially become "software reconfigurable hardware" building blocks.

- Storage technologies. Scientists at IBM Research, Lucent Laboratories, and Hewlett Packard, as well as government-funded teams in Japan and Europe, are experimenting with various alternative storage technologies, including biopolymers for CDs, quantum dots, and even molecular-engineered materials. The timetable for commercialization is unpredictable in these fields, but serendipity is always looming around the corner, thus making it difficult to forecast when scientists will turn beach sand into info-sand.

- Radio frequency elements. These include RF chip sets and smart antennas and supporting infrastructure based on advanced coding and modulation methods such as Orthogonal Frequency Division Multiplexing (OFDM), UWB, and dynamic chaos. Advances in BiCMOS and silicon germanium processes will make it possible to build circuits that operate at multiples of a gigaHertz.

- Image generators[1] with augmented reality functionality. Heads-up displays and miniature video cameras with wireless transmitters will begin to unleash the hidden potential and richness of virtual reality. Image generators will include any devices for an image type such as a virtual planetarium or a portable olfactory generator that can generate images of humanly imperceptible smells, including radon and other toxic gases. Applications of image generators equipped with real-time wireless access to the Internet are broad and profound and will make for a new paradigm in the role of computing and communications in daily life.

- Life sciences applied to information processing. The emergence of image generators will enable sophisticated software methods based on genetic algorithms and adaptation, allowing us to understand the 3.2 billion base pairs that are part of every human's DNA, and possibly to upgrade one's immunity, longevity, and creativity.

- Smart wireless sensors. Millions if not billions of 4G sensors will be available in every imaginable application from remote sensing of water levels in the western provinces of China to tobacco smoke pollution detectors in public places to illegal RF signal detectors in sensitive areas such as hospital operating rooms. Every person, pet, place, and valuable thing will have a wireless sensor.

- Quantum computing. Our physical world can only begin to be explained with quantum physics, so it is not surprising that a new and important branch of computer science is quantum computing. Although a handful of laboratory experiments have verified the theoretical concepts of quantum computing, the sense in this highly specialized area of research is that big surprises are just around the corner, especially with respect to quantum cryptography. Even the National Security Agency (NSA) of the United States has been involved in this field as far back as 1994.[2] The interest on the part of the NSA is related to the exciting (or terrifying) prospects according to quantum computing theory that, bandwidth permitting, it should be possible to construct a search engine that will examine the entire Internet (mapped by IBM in 2000 and estimated to comprise more than 8 terabytes of data) in less than 30 minutes or break the toughest encryption methods used by the electronic funds networks in fewer than 5 minutes.

7. *Timing of commercial products and services.* 4G broadband wireless devices may hit the market years before the expected dates of 2007 to 2010 because the necessary components (hardware and software) are already in academic and commercial laboratories and will reach the marketplace in the next three to five years—whether the establishment of spectrum regulatory agencies and large 2G/3G service providers like it or not.

8. *Advanced interfaces.* Windows, Icon, Menu, and Pointer (WIMP) is 25-year-old technology, pioneered at Xerox Palo Alto Research Center (PARC), popularized by Apple, and standardized by Microsoft. While it might be good enough to let Microsoft bank a billion per month, WIMP isn't the best interface imaginable. Augmented Reality and heads-up displays will open up a whole new industry of extremely high-content value-added services that will challenge the traditional cellular operators and may force a restructuring of the cellular industry from large narrow-bandwidth providers to content-specific providers, as content revenues exceed revenue from just connecting.

9. *Wireless computing and networking.* In the future when a person sends an e-mail to someone, the e-mail may literally go to that person because he will be wearing a low-power mobile computer on his body (such as a wristwatch, a "smart" buckle on his belt, or a "smart" Nike shoe). The wearable computer contains basic routing protocols, making the system a "Cisco router that wore tennis shoes."

10. *The planetary grid.* The emergence of Version 6 of the Internet Protocol

(known as IPV6) will theoretically enable the direct addressing of trillions of devices. In other words, it will become possible to address directly millions of wireless sensor devices per square kilometer over the Internet. In the future, most Internet addresses will not be for humans but rather for sensor devices measuring and monitoring everything from a person's heartbeat to water levels on lakes or rivers to pollution detectors to neighborhood crime watching. M2M—machine to machine—messages will exceed B2B, B2C, and C2C messages between people combined.

11. *Strategic wireless policy.* 4G systems will challenge governments and policy makers as they struggle to balance privacy with national security concerns. Whether wiretappers at the FBI and NSA like it or not, low-power 500+ MIP chips will enable small portable devices to encrypt on the fly. It will be possible to have a wireless Voice-over-Internet-Protocol conversation in which only the two parties in the conversation know the encryption algorithm. Some governments, notably China, still prohibit telecom service providers (wireless and wireline) from encrypting anything. Such antiquated policies will probably not withstand the test of 500+ MIP processors in a wristwatch sized device. We can expect that intelligence agencies will increase their quantum computer research budgets in the hopes of maintaining an edge in the small arms race of secret mail reading, a government obsession ever since the British made sure all telegraphic submarine cables went through London in the nineteenth century. A future hacker who put a properly designed quantum computer on the Internet could, through broadband wireless links, assemble a global supercomputer based on the power of many other quantum computers and other information devices. Once broadband wireless links become readily available, the entire dynamics of controlling, censoring, storing, and retrieving information becomes a change agent for society. George Orwell never envisioned that the animals in his farm would someday be equipped with 4G infosensors that had access to the infinite Internet! Big Brother will have to contend with hundreds of surveillance-capable little brothers.

12. *Winners and losers.* The companies best positioned to reap the benefits of the previous future advances will have large interdisciplinary capabilities (sadly, thus excluding most electronics companies in the United States and Europe) or be tightly—even obsessively—focused on one or more of the technologies. Two examples of companies positioning

themselves for a broadband future directly in line with the vision outlined in this book are Sony Corporation and NTT DoCoMo. Sony has even purchased a fixed wireless license in Japan, with ambitions of operating its own "Sony Entertainment Network" in which Sony-made devices such as a new Walkman model would receive music from a wireless Internet link. The greatest challenge to telecom equipment makers will not be lack of technology for 4G, but inability to integrate all these technologies in house.

13. *Connected politics.* Finally, 4G stands for something else, the Fourth Good, or Freedom, after Liberty, Fraternity, and Equality—because 4G devices will enable people to access in a secure fashion (whether initially allowed by their governments or not) any kind of information and to contribute information back into the giant ethersphere that is now known as the Internet but is soon to transform into some much greater. Perhaps government change is the most significant likely impact of 4G, as millions of previously unconnected and uninformed residents wirelessly wise up and team up to make changes that accelerate the virtuous cycle of wireless power plays. Technologies such as augmented reality software will enhance the user experience by providing functions that the individual may not have, such as real-time language translation, dictionary look-up, and various educational and medical aids. Governments will be forced by the most informed and connected pressure groups in history to open up new spectrum and reallocate spectrum for consumer use and for unlicensed (and therefore nonmonopolistic) pupposes, bringing ever more people to the new political arena.

1.1 HOW FAST DID THE INTERNET DEVELOP?

As recently as 1980 phone conversations only traveled over copper wires and were capable of carrying less than one page of information per second. Today, a strand of optical fiber as thin as a human hair can transmit in a single second the equivalent of over 90,000 volumes of an encyclopedia. (Not that you would—a letter to the editor of *Technology Review* magazine scolded a writer who used a similar example that there were copyrights to be respected, even though the example was purely hypothetical!)

Global digital networks utilizing packet-switching technologies combine the power of these innovations in computing and communications. The Internet ties together the computing power on desks, in factories, and in offices around the world through a high-speed communications infrastructure. More than 500 million people around the world, most of whom had never heard of the word "Internet" until a few years ago, now use the Internet to do research, send e-mail to friends, make requests for bids to suppliers, and shop for cars or books. But you know this, since the odds are 99% that if you've read this far, you're an Internet user and are conscious and proud of your new Net nation.

Until recently, advances in telecommunications and computing largely occurred side by side on parallel paths. Today, nearly all advances tend to converge toward the Internet, like matter and light within the event horizon of a black hole that draws everything into it. Soon, virtually all information technology (IT) investment will be part of interlinked communications systems, whether internal to a business, between businesses, between individuals and businesses, or individual to individual, just as over 50% of all business capital expenditures are for information technology. Vinod Khosla, called the world's greatest venture capitalist by *Red Herring* magazine, believes that this investment will accelerate because each 1% increase in IT spending correlates with a 1.5% to 2% reduction in general and administrative costs. As a result, Khosla looks back 10 years and says IT spending increased from a mere half percent of sales to 3.5% of sales in the 1990s, and looks ahead to IT spending increasing further, to 10% or more of sales by the end of the decade. With over 40% of all U.S. gross domestic product (GDP) growth coming from technology, this increase should continue to drive economic growth and productivity, and thus the "greater Internet" will eventually account for a third to a half of all increase in GDP in the United States and, over time, in other advanced economies, though slowed by recession.

The Internet's pace of adoption eclipses all other technologies that preceded it. Many writers have been moved to point out the accelerating rate of adoption of communication innovations:

- Radio was in existence for 38 years before 50 million people tuned in.
- TV took 13 years to reach that benchmark.
- Sixteen years after the first PC kit came out, 50 million people were using one.
- Once it was opened to the general public, the Internet (actually World Wide Web) crossed that line in four years.

We believe that 4G-related media, including wireless TV and augmented media, will grow even faster (see far right of Figure 1.1). These statistics are even more remarkable when one considers that today the Internet is still evolving from a point of inefficiency due to the legacy of outdated telecom

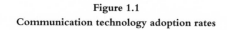

Figure 1.1
Communication technology adoption rates

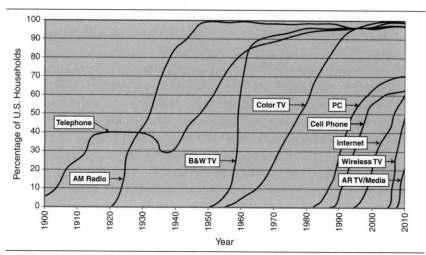

Source: 1900–2000—Adapted from *Wharton on Managing Emerging Technologies*, p. 7. Edited by George S. Day, Paul J. H. Shoemaker, and Robert E. Gunther. New York: John Wiley & Sons, 2000. 2000–2010—Estimated by Alex Lightman.
Note: AR = Augmented Reality.

networks, outdated regulatory regimes and outdated thinking that all burden the current Internet.

However its growth is measured, the Internet is expanding at a very rapid pace. Ray Kurzweil claims that the Net is growing even faster than most realize because the growth itself has a second exponent. In other words, the acceleration itself is accelerating at an exponential pace (though growth slows dramatically in countries that already have over 50% of people online).

The profound change the Internet will bring to modern business practices is a double-edged sword for emerging markets (a phrase the West uses for poorer countries that during the Cold War were called the Third World. They may be once again: Completely unwired will be First World, wired will be Second World, and nonwired Third World). Those emerging markets that start from a clear base—without adopting protectionist stances—have the potential to see their economies rapidly closing the gap with the First World economies. Those that do not become liberalized e-commerce societies will see the per-capita gap widen rapidly beyond the point where it could ever be bridged, since patents, trademarks, brands, long-term contracts, integrated supply chains, reputation, and equity markets with institutional investors cannot be built or purchased with foreign aid donations or obtained through military actions. They take decades to build and yet are so fragile they can be destroyed or discredited in a day, sometimes at the instigation of a single individual.

Government telecommunications planners must design their systems in such a way that obsolescence can be minimized and new technological advances—especially those not part of a leading vendor's offering, because they may not have the patents—can be easily incorporated into the physical, regulatory, and commercial structure. And why is this important? The info/communications system will comprise the nervous system of the 4G Society. A society with a new technology that gives a hundred-fold improvement, or can withstand quantum computer assaults on financial encryption, is a society that can maintain its growth, even as other societies, or at least their governments or industries, fall one after another in rapid succession. 4G capabilities could become a matter of wealth or poverty—or life and death—for millions in each country.

The advent of the Internet as a medium for professionals, government planners, scientists, and businesspeople to communicate and exchange ideas and information will greatly impact and accelerate the technological and social developments of the next decade. Telecommunications service providers and equipment vendors are working hard to develop and launch IP-based broadband multimedia services over the next five years. At the same time, electronic engineers, physicists, chemists, biochemists, mathematicians, and computer scientists in thousands of laboratories around the world are working nonstop to further advance the wonders of silicon chips, magnetic storage systems, and optical communications systems. It is difficult to predict where all of this is going (though this book is our best attempt), but one thing is certain: The confluence of interdisciplinary research and development will lead to surprising results that no one predicted. As a consequence we firmly believe it is increasingly possible that by the middle of the 2001–2010 decade we will have molecular-based wearable computers that can store gigabits of information all on a Star Trek–like comm badge that in turn is connected through a broadband communications link to the rest of a world filled with billions of similar devices.

While the 1996–1999 period witnessed the public emergence of many exciting startups like Yahoo!, AOL, Netscape, and Amazon.com, which grew into behemoth market-capitalized businesses, the next decade will see the emergence of companies alongside IBM, HP and Lucent Technologies such as ArrayComm, Charmed Technology, Transmeta, and Zyvex. These new companies will carry the torch further with serious intellectual property–based advances in radio electronics, wearable computing and virtual reality, microprocessors, and molecular machines that, when combined with all the wonderful advances of genetics and biotechnology, will unleash another round of technological revolution, one that will supercede all previous ones.[3]

1.2 DISRUPTIVE INFO-COMMUNICATIONS TECHNOLOGIES THAT WILL SHAPE THE NEXT 10 YEARS

The development and diffusion of new and novel technology tends to happen in bursts because major breakthroughs often require a number of previously unrelated technologies being brought together into a useful and new package. Along those lines we believe there are a number of areas to watch over the next decade, and we would not be surprised if advances in these areas create new empires run by new billionaires:

1. *Terrestrial Public Voice and Data Networks.* By 2005, most modern public telecommunications operators will have integrated their data and voice networks into a single Internet Protocol (IP) based architecture that when connected to wideband last-mile networks, such as ADSL and wireless local loop (WLL), will enable end users to access the Internet at speeds of 1.5–10 Mbps, making multimedia services a reality. Wireless television, already available on JetBlue's flights, will become as commonplace as a Walkman or MP3 player.

2. *Wireless Services.* The period from 2000 to 2005 will see narrowband cellular services upgraded to wideband services.[4] Service operators will have spent huge sums on spectrum for 3G networks but find it hard to deliver sufficient bandwidth to meet customer expectations. Most public communications service operators have already built broadband trunks consisting of fiber-optic cables and wireless links such as microwave relay stations and satellite links. 3G cellular systems such as Japan's Wideband Code Division Multiple Access (W-CDMA), Qualcomm's cdma2000, and Europe's UMTS systems will provide wideband bandwidth (384 kbps–2 Mbps) to cellular users but with certain restrictions. Broadband fixed wireless operators will begin to compete with cellular operators through the use of spatial division multiple access techniques that will enhance spectral efficiencies while providing for mobility. New types of niche services will evolve that will challenge traditional high-volume, voice-based cellular operators. The period from 2003 to 2008 will witness the marketing of software-defined radios and software radios that will be able to tune into virtually any type of modulation and coding scheme, rendering traditional 2G/3G operator business models less visible because

the inherent exclusive nature of spectrum and the subsequent high financial value of owning spectrum will be severely challenged by devices that can use almost any spectrum, and will migrate from expensive to cheap or free spectrum.

The period from 2005 to 2010 will see users demanding true broadband services where end user terminals will have guaranteed 2 to 5 Mbps bandwidth. Specialty devices will need much more than 2 to 5 Mbps, but if users can be provided a sustained throughput of 1 to 2 Mbps, a whole new world of applications becomes possible.

3. *Satellite Broadband Internet Delivery Service.* In spite of the spectacular failures of Iridium (sold for $25 million and resurrected) and ICO, satellite service is poised to provide a cost-effective solution to Internet trunking for many regions across the globe including South America, Asia, and the Middle East.

4. *Semiconductors, Magnetic Storage Systems, and Optical Systems.* Advances will occur in electronic and optical devices that will enhance the performance and throughput of communications and computer systems to help realize wideband and eventually broadband communications. Semiconductor integrated circuits will reach 2 to 5 gigabit densities and will approach their natural physical limits (as far as scientists can tell today).

5. *Microprocessors.* Advances in microprocessor architecture, digital signal processors (DSPs), compiler designs, and operating systems will make it possible to have low-power CPUs controlling everything from automobiles to consumer electronic gadgets to portable/wearable wireless information devices.

6. *Wireless Information Devices (WIDs).* NTT DoCoMo is predicting that by 2010 WIDs will become so popular that the actual penetration of mobile "phone" users in Japan will exceed 100% because people will have WIDs for everything from pet collar IDs to medical bands for senior citizens that will call emergency medical services in the event of a critical health indicator. The profit potential for market shares that exceed 100% of consumers will inspire new economic theories.

7. *New Types of Human Interfaces.* Perhaps the greatest obstacle to further proliferation of the PC has been the archaic, rather cryptic 2-D interface that users are subjected to every time they use PC operating systems. This will change as companies offer genuine 3-D interfaces that turn Internet shopping malls into 3-D experiences. Intel has long sponsored 3-D content (even paying 100% of the cost for Hollywood

movie promotions, such as the author's *Spawn* and *Xena:Warrior Princess* projects in 1998, for the movie and the television show, respectively) because 3-D, which looks better at a faster frame rate, provides a new driver of demand for greater processor performance.

8. *Wearable Computers.* Wearable computers that combine the advances of integrated circuits, radio electronics, virtual reality, and real-time operating systems will enable the construction of something that will make the archetypal Star Trek communicator, supposedly state of the art in A.D. 2400 which uses only voice and location, look obsolete by A.D. 2010. This massive improvement on the mobile phone will be a multimedia device that can access the Internet, and thus TV, radio, and computer games, via a wireless broadband link. On the way to this 4G device that is so general as to be nearly universal, there will also be novel form factors for surprisingly specific applications, such as the Charmed Badges for conferences and trade show electronic business card exchange and immediate interest compatibility alerts, medical monitoring devices that are much more narrowly focused on specific organs or even DNA sequences, and intelligent weather barometers that receive periodic weather forecasts and put "Get Umbrella by 5:30 P.M." on the To Do list.

9. *Molecular-Engineered Materials.* Molecular engineering aided by supercomputer simulations will lead to countless new alloys, composites, synthetics, and pharmaceuticals. One of the holy grails of the materials industry is high-temperature superconductors that, if ever realized and commercialized will completely revolutionize the power industry as well as countless of other industries including transportation, medical instruments, and computers.

10. *Nanotechnologies, Molecular Micromachines, Genetics, Biotech, and Molecular Computers.* Since the mid-1980s hundreds of laboratories usually consisting of interdisciplinary research teams have been pursuing alternative ways to build and assemble switching devices, logic devices, memory devices, and biochemical sensors utilizing molecular or atomic structures that, despite naysayers who attacked Dr. K. Eric Drexler (the visionary popularizer of nanotechnology), can self-assemble, replicate, and even repair themselves, as Drexler predicted. The governments of many developed countries are actively pursuing and promoting nanotechnology, including Germany, the United States, Japan, France, and England. In California alone hundreds of millions of dollars have been provided in a state-industry partnership for

a single research center. In the past 12 months a number of break-throughs have been announced around the world that are now giving credibility to the dream of molecular-based machines and computing machines. IBM spelled its name in Xenon atoms almost 10 years ago. We will see nanotechnology within our lifetime because even though some informed observers say it will take 100 years, the pace of change is accelerating so rapidly that 100 years of twentieth-century progress will happen in the next 7 to 15 years.

1.3 CAN 3G SYSTEMS DELIVER THE BANDWIDTH?

4G is a purely hypothetical term, is undefined, and no official statements have been released regarding 4G by any worldwide standards bodies. So it is very difficult to speculate. It may well be proposed by those companies that have been unsuccessful getting their Intellectual Property Rights into 3G [third-generation mobile systems].

Response by an unhappy telecom equipment maker to NTT DoCoMo's announcement to establish a $250 million 4G R&D Center; Quoted in Asiansources's online magazine

A number of large telecom service providers in Europe, Japan, and even in the United States are spending billions of dollars installing W-CDMA 3G infrastructure with the promise of 2 megabits per second data rates. Upon closer inspection, experts are realizing that 2 Mbps is not practical or achievable with the proposed 3G systems. And now, even the manufacturers of mobile base stations seem uncertain how much bandwidth their systems will deliver. Many of the bandwidth rates that have been predicted are for peak figures only under optimum conditions. Other datarate projections are pure fantasy made under pressure by engineers who need to tell management they can meet the specs promised by vendors and standards committees, based on projections made 10 years ago in an entirely different landscape with weaker computer technology.

In general, operators have been expecting to deliver between 40 and 50 kbps over general packet radio services (GPRS) from day one—roughly the equivalent to a dial up Internet connection, but this has the advantage of being packet switched, with early 3G services being expected to deliver around 300 kbps. However, Jorg Kramer, vice-president of Mannesman's Mobifunk division, predicted in 2000 that UMTS was only likely to be able to deliver between 32 and 64 kbps. According to Kramer, his company tested UMTS and found "that it will create speeds of 384 kbps, but only if you are the only person using the network, standing next to a transmitter and not moving." Now that's a breakthrough—the immobile mobile phone! You have a choice: Stand still and get your 4 MB MP3 song in 10 minutes, or move around and take a half an hour to a full hour—if you don't drop your connection, which is likely, given that coverage will be incomplete for several years. Quotes like this are nails in the coffin of 3G and spurs to the development of 4G.

These findings are supported by NTT DoCoMo's delivery of the world's first 3G service in Japan at only 64 kbps. There is clearly a very real problem in delivering true broadband (i.e., the MP3 song can be downloaded in a few minutes or, better, a few seconds, so that it seems like the radio), which conventional 3G technology as of this writing could not address.

From 2005 onward, wideband wireless technologies and 4G mobile wireless technologies will converge and give birth to a whole new range of services that will utilize next generation mobile info-com systems, which we will refer to as wireless ubiquitous computers (WUCs). We believe that a new paradigm, which we call the Wireless Information Age, will emerge sometime after 2004 as carriers begin to articulate strategies that go beyond simple mobile voice applications to provide a fully integrated bundle of mass customizable services. Full deployment of this paradigm is still years away, but this subsector is taking form, as carriers begin to create portals for their wireless data applications to unify several service offerings under one umbrella.

While some have described this paradigm simply as unified messaging, we believe the Wireless Information Age advances this concept a step further by fully integrating the wireless backbone with telecommunications and Internet infrastructure to customize the customer's demand for information, as well as aiding in the retrieval process and in deciding upon the delivery method (wireless, wireline, or cable), the format (text, voice, or video), and the browser (phone, PDA, laptop, desktop, or even paper).

Wideband and broadband wireless devices will infiltrate the mass market from 2005 onward, and by 2012, magnetics and semiconductor microelectronics will have combined with the molecular sciences and biomolecular sciences to produce miniature components the size of a sugar cube that will be able to store several terabits of information—in other words, it will be possible to carry a significant portion if not most of the world's information and content in one's wallet, and access what you can't store instantaneously through broadband wireless or wireline access.

There is a common theme from all the above, in that while there is (1) a massive consumer, commercial, and public service market for mobile Internet devices and (2) an abundance of media, information, and entertainment content that can be delivered through such devices, the limiting factor currently is spectrum availability in order to deliver affordable ultra-high bandwidth to each and every end-user.

1.4 EXIT THE 3G PAPER TIGER, ENTER THE 4G DRAGON

What if every appliance as you know it today (even air conditioners and refrigerators) were able to communicate with every other device, as well as with you and millions of service providers, all the time? Imagine if every appliance were equipped with its own intelligence, simply by communicating with a remote brain that would do the thinking for it, based on constantly updated inputs for context. Imagine everyone's laptops, phones, and PDAs all being in sync with one another as well as with those of others at all times, adjusting and delivering information to whomever, wherever, and whenever. Imagine there are no longer such things as empty vending machines—because delivery, supply, and production services always know the exact stock level—or vending machine malfunction.

We can partly deliver this capability by having a broadband wireline connection to every building and wirelessly network appliances on a local level using Bluetooth-like technology. But then what about mobile devices, such as wearable medical monitors, Walkmans, or e-Books? Wouldn't it be great if you didn't have to think about IP addresses, dial-up connections, downloading, copying files over, and all other intermediate steps? Or on a more serious note, how many lives can we save by hospitals monitoring every organ implant or fire marshals knowing the conditions and exact locations, to the centimeter, of their men in a burning building?

The smart appliances of the future will be net-enabled the moment they are switched on. Permanently. Just like when you flick the remote control of your TV today, you are not thinking about where the broadcast is coming from and on what frequency; you will take for granted the access to infinite knowledge resources as well as the ability to simply navigate through them. When you switch on your portable pay-per-view movie player, you will have the couch potato's dream of being able to watch right away anything and everything that has ever been shown in the history of cinema or broadcast news. To do all this we need the intelligent reallocation of spectrum. But there's a daunting problem yet to be solved: How do we make this pay?

The math is simple: If the network operators decide to deliver 1+ Mbps service to each subscriber, the license fee and the roll out cost alone will result in each user having to use $8,000 a year worth of service over many years, just for the operator to break even. This is if all of the current mobile phone users are convinced overnight to take up 3G services. There is no media in our history that commanded average subscription/usage fees this high, and 3G's improvements are marginal, not revolutionary.

The 3G techniques described above are not the only available technologies—or even, critics say, the best ones. One of the most vocal naysayers is Martin Cooper, who is widely credited with inventing the portable cell phone for Motorola in the early 1970s.

So we need another breakthrough. Twenty-seven years after his first invention, along comes Martin Cooper's "second ultimate solution": Spatial Division Multiple Access (SDMA). Instead of asking for infinite bandwidth, we look for better spectral efficiency. Or in Cooper's words, "There is no lack of spectrum, only a lack of spectrum efficiency."

All we need to do is to come up with a more intelligent method to reuse spectrum, not on cell-by-cell bases (which is still a homogenous broadcasting over a wide area), but on user-by-user basis. We already have substantial experience with this type of spatial technology in our wireline networks. These networks can be expanded indefinitely by merely running more lines, more bandwidth, to more terminals. The wireless equivalent of this is to create virtual wires of communications that do not interfere with each other, directed at each and every communicating device. We create a beam of communication between the base station and the user, whether he is stationary or moving.

Imagine how effective our use of spectrum would be if we could create a reliable, broadband wireless connection between any two points, and if we further imagine that independent connections could be established between the base station and two points separated by only a few feet, even though the users are sharing the same frequency, time slot, and code. The potential would exist to increase effectiveness of spectrum use by 10 million times over today's capabilities.

Once the world wakes up to the SDMA opportunity, we will have Cooper's Law on our side: Throughout the 20th century the number of simultaneous voice calls doubled every 2.5 years. If this continues, in 60 years we would have the capability of delivering the entire radio frequency spectrum today to every single individual on Earth.

Cooper also views 3G as merely a first step toward the real high-speed, inexpensive wireless communications that we call 4G. Cooper is CEO of ArrayComm, a San Jose technology company that claims its smart antennas are able to provide 1 Mbps for each of up to 40 concurrent users. The technology makes better use of the arrays of antennas found in cellular base stations. Currently cell tower base stations each contain a forest of up to a dozen antennas that are used to broadcast omni-directionally, with equal strength in all directions. But many communications and radar systems have long used similar arrays to aim their signals in particular directions. The transmissions from individual antennas interact with one another, preventing the signals from going in some directions and amplifying them in others.

The successful wireless Internet applications will change over time. Defining the content and applications that will find success over the wireless Internet is shooting at a moving target, as developments in the underlying technology will have a profound effect on what will work and what will not.

1.5 4G NETWORKS WILL USE BOTH WIRELESS AND WIRELINE INFRASTRUCTURE

In order for 4G wireless networks to be fully realized, service operators, public and private, planned and ad hoc, will need to make use of the available fixed (wireline and wireless) infrastructure in each geographic locality. In other words, broadband wireless (i.e., 4G) will need broadband fiber-optic infrastructure with high-speed IP switching in order to provide services such as video telephony, digital video broadcast, and interactive video services.

The mathematics are simple, but the implementation is very difficult: If 50 mobile 4G users were simultaneously to carry on video telephony conversations in a single cell site, the total capacity through the base station would have to be on the order of 20 to 30 Mbps, depending on the types of compression being used. Ten such cell sites in a city would require the mobile switching center to handle 200 to 300 Mbps for those calls; in other words, the mobile service provider will face the same switching challenges that a local fixed line operator would face if it offered video telephony to the home via fiber-optic and copper extensible digital subscriber line (xDSL) connections. The problem of switching the backend never goes away—it just gets bigger and bigger. Another implication is that a 4G mobile service provider will look more and more like a local telephone company because the backhaul and backend switching costs could outstrip the base station costs very quickly. The companies that continue to make high-end IP switching platforms, such as Nortel, Cisco, and Juniper Networks, will be overjoyed at the emergence of 4G wireless networks. We can expect that fiber-optic networks with Dense Wave Division Multiplexing (DWDM) will be needed in the metro network in order to cope with the exploding demand that multimedia services will require.

For the skeptics who wonder what multimedia services could become popular, one only has to turn on the TV for examples such as a psychic fortune-teller service that sends a personalized reading every morning or a personalized summary of CNN, the *New York Times,* and the *Herald Tribune* with short video clips that are available on demand. During the playoff seasons for baseball, football, basketball, and major international events such as tennis and the Olympics, one could receive customized automatic video news service.

Best of all, an entirely new type of "personalized expert advice," roughly equivalent to a video version of Keen.com, in which questions are posed and experts answer through phone or e-mail, will make doctors, lawyers, accountants, and thousands of others available instantly, without an appointment, a boon for an economy based on services like America's.

1.6 POTENTIAL POLITICAL AND ECONOMIC IMPACT OF 4G WIRELESS NETWORKS

Spectrum will become an issue as regulatory authorities wrestle with the future prospects of programmable software radios that can tune in to multiple frequency bands. The FCC has slowly come to realize the importance of software radio technology and established a formal inquiry seeking the opinions of leading experts. Service operators who have invested heavily in 2G and 3G networks will also be challenged to find ways to reconfigure their infrastructure to accommodate increasing demands in bandwidth. But don't rule out the importance of the wireline fiber-optic telecom providers because as the wireless networks mature, the traffic profile will follow the same path that has occurred in the fixed-line industry—to wit, voice traffic has been surpassed by data traffic. 2G and 3G infrastructure is not very well suited for handling mainly data traffic. Thus, the entire wireless infrastructure must be optimized for data traffic and must feed into the fixed networks wherever possible if wireless service providers are to have any hope of keeping up with future demand.

4G networks will greatly accelerate the demand for bandwidth because of higher data file transmission speeds and the ability to introduce multimedia content. Moreover, the ability to dynamically load the radio characteristics of the end user terminals combined with wideband reception/transmission will completely alter the roles of service providers and content providers and, moreover, will introduce the concept of customer location—in other words, it is not what network you are on but where you are using it that will drive many new applications. For example, one could envision a service that when you walk into Starbucks, you get "phonebucks"; by buying coffee and a bagel, you are automatically given free minutes on your mobile phone or perhaps given a discount on long-distance calls.

1.7 EARLY INVESTMENTS IN 4G TECHNOLOGY AS OF 2001

Investments Opportunity and Risk

The first investments in the embryonic 4G cluster are almost all those made by the United States, and the first list was prepared by the foresighted Daedulus Venture Group (DVG) of Lawrence, Massachusetts.

In addition to a wide range of technical challenges, there are other risk factors that could impede the growth and acceptability of the wireless systems. Although the cost is dropping, there is still a high cost benefit ratio. Prior to 2003, 4G will be considered a small-market niche that is below the 1% market share threshold of interest in manufacturing.[5] Another concern is the social acceptability of the technology, especially wearable computers, though our experience producing the Brave New Unwired World technology fashion shows is that great success can be expected if the first impressions people have of new wireless technology is that they make the user look and feel better, smarter, faster, and more connected and competent.

Wearable computers acquire all of the attributes and constraints of any wireless network. The gaps include limited bandwidth, seamless communication, and ubiquitous access. Other tough issues fall into four categories: technical, social, economical, and political. The technical issues involve protocols, mobility/disconnected operation, infrastructure maintenance, saturation, and ubiquitous access. The social issues are primarily issues involving access rights and spectrum ownership. In spite of the risk, a number of large manufacturers and investors are moving into 4G development already.

We now turn to Part II, which includes summaries of the last few decades of the wireless/cellular industry, an review of radio spectrum as a scarce resource, and an overview of 2.5G, wireless Internet services, and 3G.

Part III is the core of the book and covers pervasive computing, including the incredible shrinking computer, molecular electronics, and near term implementations of new platforms, including wearable computers and Charmed Badges. Discussions of the evolution of wearables into software for Augmented Memory and Augmented Reality, and of Badges into Info-Charm Sensors that will create a planetary computer are included, bridging current products with the visions of futurists.

Part IV goes into depth about 4G, and gives the outline of what we need to bring to market to realize the first 4G cluster, which will result from companies able to profit from making 4G handsets, infrastructure, and services accessed via 4G portals that evolve from today's portals, but which are the element that is built most closely on top of today's technology. While 4G hardware is revolutionary, 4G portals are evolutionary, and "the portal is the operating system" in 4G, so software will be more closely aligned with portals in the future than ever before, allowing selection and the downloading of applications wirelessly to a degree that is impossible today in 2001.

Part V includes case studies of Broadband fixed wireless, Japan's champions for 4G, NTT DoCoMo and Sony, and China, the chief dark horse challenger for 4G based on foresighted government, a national consensus that can be imposed like nowhere else, and the largest market for mobile Internet imaginable on earth.

NOTES

1. David Deutsch, *The Fabric of Reality* (New York: Penguin Books, 1997).

2. James Bamford, *Body of Secrets* (New York: Doubleday, 2001).

3. We will not attempt in this book to deal with the social and ethical implications of all advances in molecular information processing, but suffice it to say that if and when humans have the ability to create molecular machines that can go into the body and search and repair cancer or other damaged cells, only then will humanity be challenged to have the wisdom to use its knowledge for constructive purposes. World War I and II are not a good "credit report" for human governments, though perhaps with all this Internet information some wisdom has also been spread around, even amid all the junk e-mail.

4. In this book, we will adhere to the following definition of narrowband, wideband, and broadband:

   Narrowband: <128 kbps
   Wideband: < 128 kbps <1 Mbps
   Broadband: > 1 Mbps

5. Gartner group, 19 July 1999.

PART II

THE WIRELESS MARKET

CHAPTER 2

A BRIEF HISTORY
OF THE CELLULAR INDUSTRY—
1975 TO 2001

2.1 CELLULAR STANDARDS

Most industries have long standing agreements on the standards for the creation of products; the automobile industry is one such example. Though automobiles differ in size, color, and in other fashion-related factors, there are over 500 million cars, trucks, and buses running with internal combustion engines, with 50 million bright, shiny new ones added each year. There are a few thousand to a few tens of thousands running on various other energy sources, such as electricity or natural gas. Some experimental prototypes are even running on hydrogen. However, this overwhelming dominance of one standard was not in any sense preordained. In the 1890s, taxis run by steam and electric power competed with horse-drawn carriages. There weren't gasoline stations at every corner, and water and coal were readily available. After a decade or so, the pattern was set, and vast and powerful forces set in motion the creation of the oil, steel, and automobile industries, built around men who became modern legends: Rockefeller, Morgan, Carnegie, and Ford. These industries adopted standards similar enough for customers, suppliers, investors, employees, and journalists from 30 years ago to understand the current industry, and stakeholders today are able to guess where things will be 10 or 20 years hence, around the world.

This solid support for standards coupled with continuity is not present in the wireless industry, due in part to the difficult trade-offs in decisively choosing from among a vast armada of vendors, standards, and systems. A wireless network, unlike a car that has to work with a road that is the same everywhere, has to interoperate with hundreds of millions of other devices and thousands of interconnected networks. Before comparing 2G, 3G, and the possibilities for 4G, it's useful to give a minisummary of the elements that wireless industry executives take into consideration in selecting the building blocks of a national or international cellular system.

1. Types of basic and supplementary services to be offered to customers, which are often related to what services are offered by the leading operators. As soon as one operator offers something, most other operators are compelled to provision for the same services in the same national market.

2. Connectivity, interoperability, adaptability, and integration with the Public Switched Telephone Network (PSTN) and other mobile operators (for example, China had been using Ericsson and Motorola analog switching equipment that was not compatible, and the Ministry of Posts and Telecommunications (MPT) finally forced the two vendors to find a way for their systems to interconnect and enable roaming between operators with disparate vendor systems). In 2000 Q2, Korea and China agreed to establish roaming between their countries.

3. Growth forecasts and user-usage profiling, though these are subject to wild swings back and forth. The forecasts for per minute voice costs, wireless applications protocol (WAP) usage, and data usage, all of which were extrapolated to justify bidding up licenses, have all proven to be overly optimistic, indicating that wireless executives had too much power for their own good and got the reports that told them what they wanted to hear in the early 1990s. A decade earlier, the forecasts were far too low, costing AT&T and other incumbents to lose tens of billions in opportunity costs. With better forecasts, ATT might have used its global reach and 60 million customers to become the worldwide leader in wireless, instead of number four in the United States, after Verizon, Cingular, and Sprint, with one of the most outdated networks. At a Institute for Electrical and Electronics Engineers (IEEE) conference in July 2001 on 3G and 4G Qualcomm and NTT DoCoMo gave completely different forecasts for W-CDMA and cdma2000, hoping to create a self-fulfilling prophecy. They couldn't both be correct, but the industry is so acclimated to faulty forecasts that none of the 400

attendees bothered to question the later presenters' projections. In this environment, it's not surprising that very different choices are made, as executives try to guess which standard will win, since everyone wants to choose a winner.

4. Expected return on investments as competition intensifies. Forrester wrote a report referring to a UMTS meltdown within the next 10 years (from 2001), focusing on the average revenue per user (ARPU) measure, calculated using competitive pressures. The general conclusion was that voice revenues would drop sooner and faster than data revenues would rise, leading to revenue shortfall and losses sufficient to drive all but two operators in Europe into bankruptcy, making the task of raising funds from long term investors significantly more difficult, and putting more pressure on vendors to finance purchases.

5. Available frequency spectrum and capacity planning. It takes 10 to 20 years to plan ahead and vacate spectrum, a time frame in which handset and base station characteristics can only be guessed at, not definitively predicted. In private (and at "closed shop" conferences such as the IEEE 3G conference just mentioned) wireless industry executives will admit that they fudge the engineering reports (i.e., falsify) and claim that more spectrum is needed to initiate services than is actually necessary because they may not get another chance for another decade. It's also very difficult to plan, given that governments can also take spectrum away and give it to other constituencies for no better reason than campaign financing. President Clinton exhorted the FCC to set aside spectrum for 3G and was ignored. If the then-most-powerful man in the world couldn't influence this, lesser mortals clearly find this almost impossible to achieve. Unexpected court decisions increase the uncertainty, such as saying that Nextwave had control over spectrum that it didn't pay for, even though the FCC had auctioned it off.

6. Equipment financing. Vendor financing will be vastly more important because of the rapid rise in telecom service company debt, particularly for vendors attempting to sell systems into countries with national champions that have government support or even ownership. Ericsson had to offer 100% financing of $800 million to get the initial 3G equipment order in Germany and suffered a much greater loss in its stock price as investors worried that, once the process started, the precedent would be hard to stop. At some point, though, the money has to be re-paid, and former investors in both Lucent and Winstar will run, scream-

ing, the other way from companies that give vendor financing. Still, a $50,000 2.5G base station paid for by the carrier is probably a better deal than a $150,000 3G system with 100% financing.

7. Leased line and long-distance trunking costs. All wireless systems have to be tied into a wired network. Vodaphone and NTT DoCoMo are more vulnerable to these costs because their networks are almost entirely wireless, compared to operators that own their own wired networks. These considerations may end up driving acquisitions strategy, as predictability in operating costs and marginal costs per minute are important for quarterly earnings stability.

8. Intellectual property issues, e.g., both Korea's and Japan's selections of Code Division Multiple Access (CDMA). Since patents are for 20 years, many purchases have been delayed in part because patent issues haven't been worked out. Two examples: The European Union wanted to have the advantage of CDMA, on which Qualcomm had over 256 patents, but wanted to buy from a European supplier. Ericsson sued Qualcomm, which settled by selling its infrastructure business for over $6 billion and, more importantly, cross-licensing patents, allowing Europe to make up for a few years of delay by keeping its funds on the continent. Qualcomm has been negotiating with China for years and has been pushed into a position of licensing its proprietary algorithm to Chinese chip companies, potentially forgoing greater revenues in the long run, while the Chinese have delayed implementation of CDMA for years in order to have a better deal.

9. Government pressure, formal and informal. It's no secret that, outside of laissez-faire America, carriers are always dealing with political pressure and incentives, including tax bribes, investigations, and acquisition approvals in order to buy local. Though this strategy may give a temporary boost, it's worth noting that the leaders in wireless don't have government mandates to buy local. Part of why Nokia and Sonera are globally successful is because the Finnish market has long been wide open. Since Finland accounts for only a tiny fraction (3% or less) of Nokia's market, the company doesn't need to pressure politicians to close its market.

10. Fads and media hysteria. Though one would be hard-pressed to get an on-record admission, sometimes a certain technology gets so much hype that the press argues for or against it, and wireless executives, who have to keep their stocks growing, may sometimes bow to media exposure, which is as likely to be based on advertising as on extensive research. One

reason wireless executives have missed the threat from 802.11b is that the leading providers haven't bothered to advertise, and, therefore, media coverage in the mainstream press, as of mid-2001, was muted.

11. Personal quirks and corporate histories. Service and support is important, and some executives, having been burned, won't buy equipment from a supplier on their "shit list" at any price or for any reason. Given how hard it is to say which systems are best, executives have greater leeway to make decisions based on their emotions and then later defend these decisions with logical-sounding arguments. The British don't like to buy from Germany if they can help it, while the French don't like to buy from Britain, and China, after 100 years of good relations with Siemens, prefers to buy German when it can, while not wanting to buy American not only because of surveillance issues, but also because of military considerations. Qualcomm has an uphill battle getting China to standardize on cdma2000 because base stations are synchronized by Global Positioning System (GPS), which can be shut off or hacked (it's called Select Availability) by the Pentagon. Before passing judgment on China, it's worth noting that the European Union, America's partner in the North Atlantic Trade Organization (NATO), also doesn't trust the Pentagon with its wireless future and is spending billions to launch its own European GPS, with improvements on the U.S. system for commercial wireless. The more nations try to inject their national objectives into wireless, the less influence they actually will have and the more competition that will be created for their national champions.

Add all this up, and it's not surprising that executive choices have lead to fractured global standards. Our hearts go out to them.

Asia provides a good example of the myriad technology choices that have beset operators: Virtually every major analog and digital cellular system has found customers in Asia (see Figure 2.1).

2.2 FIRST GENERATION CELLULAR SYSTEMS: ANALOG

The concept of modern cellular communications dates back to the late 1960s (though the first Bell patents were filed too early, in 1947) when the Bell System submitted a proposal to the FCC, a system which became the first cellular, analog system: Advanced Mobile Phone System (AMPS). The key objectives of the original AMPS system were as follows:

Figure 2.1
It is a real alphabet soup in Asia

System	Frequency Used	Digital or Analog?	Countries Used
AMPS	800 MHz	Analog	Japan, China, Philippines, USA, Malaysia, Taiwan
NMT	400, 900 MHz	Analog	Thailand, Indonesia
TACS		Analog	Thailand, Indonesia, China
D-AMPS		Digital	USA, Hong Kong
PDC		Digital	Japan (developed by Japanese vendors)
GSM	900, 1800 MHz	Digital	Europe, Hong Kong, China, Taiwan, Thailand, Philippines, Malaysia, India
CDMA	800, 1900 MHz	Digital	USA, Korea, Hong Kong, Singapore, Thailand, Indonesia, Japan
Wideband CDMA	2000 MHz	Digital	Several different standards developed by NTT, Qualcomm, Ericsson and Nokia; will be deployed first in Japan, Finland, and Korea

- Large subscriber growth
- Efficient use of spectrum
- Nationwide compatibility
- Widespread availability
- Adaptability to traffic density
- Quality of service relative to fixed line service
- Affordability

Note that these objectives were quite different from those of the Nordic Mobile Telephony (NMT) initiative, primarily in terms of aiming for an international standard versus domestic standard and in terms of open standards versus ATT's desire to own and operate a proprietary system. It's important to remember that America led, and the cellular game was ATT's to lose.

By the early 1980s a number of cellular operators, newly created to gamble on the alternate cellular licenses offered to non-incumbents, installed AMPS systems in North America—and thus, the cellular industry was born.

Eventually a number of variations on the AMPS design emerged such as Total Access Communication System (TACS) from the United Kingdom and NMT from the Scandinavian countries together with Saudi Arabia and Spain, and NTT's own homegrown analog system.

By 1993 some 18 million subscribers around the world had mobile service. None of these analog systems were compatible, and they suffered from a number of problems, namely:

- Spectral inefficiency which meant that precious frequency was being wasted.
- Poor voice quality when compared to land-lines.
- Mountains of security and fraud problems (cloning cell phones and selling the imitations at a deep discount replaced drug dealing in some cities as a more lucrative activity, enough to be made into movies with the word "hook-up" in their titles).
- Difficulty of developing reliable data services, limiting the adoption by businesses whose subsidy would be necessary to fuel more rapid expansion.

A new generation of mobile phones, more efficient, secure, and digital, was essential to keep the growth going, though Jorma Ollila, current CEO of Nokia, anticipated this demand much earlier as he wrestled with what he called the Great Software Monster while managing the Global System for Mobile Communications (GSM) project and, through his success, establishing the credibility that made him the top wireless technology executive in the world.

2.3 SECOND GENERATION SYSTEMS: ADVENT OF DIGITAL CELLULAR

Vast research over a 100-year period had been carried out on radio frequency access technologies (RFAT) for military, emergency, and satellite communications systems paved the way for analog cellular to be replaced with digital cellular. Digital cellular systems incorporate advanced radio transmission and digital signal processing to provide reliable, high-quality voice and data mobile transmission with the additional advantage of security against eavesdropping and cloning, which had plagued the analog systems. The integration of low-power digital signal and speech processing subsystems coupled with an on-board microcomputer and dynamically loaded software has transformed the mobile phone into a mobile computer with speech processing. As data access and multimedia features become available, the mobile stations (which includes mobile phones) will become truly mobile multimedia information processing systems (the term often used in London, starting at Psion and its spin-off, Symbian, is Wireless Information Devices or WID).

Figure 2.2 shows the progression of the three generations of cellular systems. We are currently in the second generation, and we expect the third generation to reach the commercial market in late 2001 to 2004, depending on the region. America and Myanmar, with their shared system of measures, will probably be among the last. Although the Digital Advanced Mobile Phone system (D-AMPS) is still being used extensively in the United States and Japan uses the Japanese personal digital communications (PDC) system, the two major second generation systems competing for global market share are GSM and CDMA. Through the year 2001, according to Motorola, GSM is expected to account for 47% to 55% of new annual subscribers while CDMA will account for about 28% to 35% and analog growth will be close to nil, following in the footsteps of cable and foreshadowing the end of wireline Internet growth.

As of December 1998, there were 138 million GSM subscribers worldwide, 22.9 million CDMA users, and 32.3 million Digital Advanced Mobile Phone

Figure 2.2
Wireless technology evolution

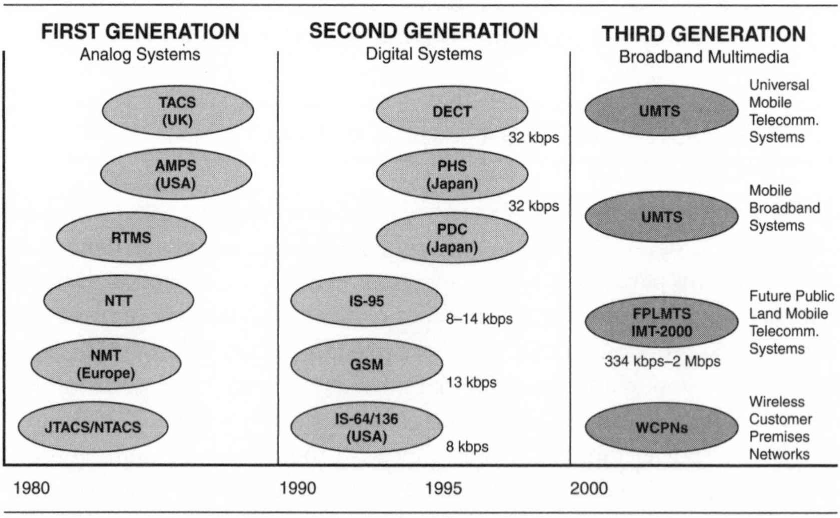

FIRST GENERATION Analog Systems	SECOND GENERATION Digital Systems	THIRD GENERATION Broadband Multimedia	
TACS (UK)	DECT 32 kbps	UMTS	Universal Mobile Telecomm. Systems
AMPS (USA)	PHS (Japan) 32 kbps	UMTS	Mobile Broadband Systems
RTMS	PDC (Japan)		
NTT	IS-95 8–14 kbps	FPLMTS IMT-2000	Future Public Land Mobile Telecomm. Systems
NMT (Europe)	GSM 13 kbps	334 kbps–2 Mbps	
JTACS/NTACS	IS-64/136 (USA) 8 kbps	WCPNs	Wireless Customer Premises Networks
1980	1990 1995	2000	

System/Time Division Multiple Access (D-AMPS/TDMA) subscribers. It was estimated in late 1999 that the digital mobile market, including Japanese personal handy phone system (PHS) and PDC users, was about 250 million subscribers worldwide.

Global System for Mobile Communications (GSM)

Global System for Mobile Communications (GSM) was developed in the early 1980s by the Conference Europeanne des Postes et Telecommunications (CEPT) and was based on technological advances at several European laboratories including those at France Telecom and Deutsche Telecom. Extensive research and discussion led to the adoption of a European standard, now called GSM, that is based on Time Division Multiple Access/Frequency Division Multiple Access/Frequency Division Duplexing (TDMA/FDMA/FDD) radio interface with a radio link bit rate of 270 kbps and the use of low-bit-rate (13 kbps) speech encoding and Gaussian minimum shift keying (GMSK) modulation. Although GSM does not represent the state of the art in terms of wireless technologies, it is nevertheless a good trade-off between reliability, complexity, and affordability. The technological choices that went into GSM resulted in a cell-site capacity within a given bandwidth similar to the existing analog frequency modulation (FM) systems. The cell-site capacity of GSM is not necessarily greater than that of analog systems, but because it is a digital technology the voice-quality is superior, data communications services are possible, and privacy and full security have become standard features (we all remember the horror stories involving eavesdropping on analog users and illegal cloning of analog phones).

Standardization Key to GSM's Success

The standardization that engendered GSM is probably the single greatest reason for GSM's success. The technical specifications for GSM Phase I comprise some 5,500 pages and have been open and available to the industry from the outset. An excellent model for cooperation between operators was created through the GSM Memorandum of Understanding (MoU) Association that helped formulate roaming and intercompany agreements. Thus, a GSM mobile subscriber could travel to any country where a GSM MoU member operator was as long as the operator had a roaming service agreement with the user's operator back at his home country.

Leading Manufacturers Supplying GSM Infrastructure Equipment and Handsets

There are many manufacturers of GSM handsets, the most successful of which are Nokia, Motorola, Ericsson, Siemens, Nortel, Alcatel, Sony, and Panasonic. The major suppliers of GSM infrastructure equipment are Nokia, Ericsson, Motorola, Siemens, Nortel, and Lucent.

DCS 1800: Extension of GSM to 1800/1900 MHz

Technology advances never stop, and the area of digital mobile communications is no exception. The key GSM manufacturers provided various extensions to the original GSM 900 MHz, which they call DCS 1800/1900 (digital communications system). DCS at 1800 MHz was developed within the European Telecommunications Standards Institute (ETSI) and was first approved in February 1991. DCS at 1900 MHz was adopted for the U.S. market. Although the air interface is essentially the same as GSM, various advances incorporated in DCS such as speech encoding and microcell technologies mean that a DCS 1800 MHz network will use more base stations than GSM 900 MHz but in turn has a higher frequency re-use pattern, which when combined with the use of microcells enables operators to handle more capacity and to provide better in-building and tunnel coverage. In terms of the central office switching, customer billing, and accounting, GSM 900 and DCS 1800/1900 systems are essentially compatible, and manufacturers are now offering DCS/GSM systems that support both a common customer and a central switching system.

For the remainder of this report GSM 1800 will be used to denote DCS 1800 since both systems use essentially the same communications protocols and since the manufacturers have accommodated the operators and have begun supplying, where practical, integrated GSM 900 and GSM 1800 equipment (i.e., dual-band systems).

Nokia Led the Way with Several Firsts

According to Dan Steinbock, "The first GSM call was made in Finland in 1991, using a Nokia phone on a Nokia network. That same year, Nokia agreed to supply GSM networks to nine other European countries. In 1994, Nokia was the first manufacturer to launch a series of hand-portable phones—the Nokia 2100 family—for all major digital standards (GSM, TDMA, personal communications networks, Japan Digital) and was supplying GSM systems to 59 operators in 31 countries by 1997. Between 1992 and 1999, the number of the world's cellular subscribers soared from 23 million to an estimated 436 million. Between 1995 and 1999, the number of GSM 900/1800/1900 subscribers increased from a few million to close to 200 million."[1]

GSM 1800 First Introduced in Asia in 1994

The first GSM 1800 license in Asia was awarded in Malaysia to Sapura Telecom in 1994. By the end of 1997 the number of licensees had grown to about 15, with Hong Kong alone accounting for six PCS GSM 1800 licenses. Although the growth of GSM 1800 licenses has been slow due in large part to the high growth of GSM 900, the key issue for operators and regulators in Asia is allocation of available spectrum because much of the GSM 900 MHz spectrum is nearly full already. We expect, therefore, that GSM 1800's role will be to serve as a cheaper alternative to existing analog and GSM 900 services. Handset prices have tended to be cheaper for GSM 1800 than GSM 900 in most of Asia. Also, operators in a number of countries such as Hong Kong and Singapore are offering GSM 1800 handsets at very attractive prices of between $200 to $300.

Japan's PHS System: The "Nine Lives Cat"

PHS is a digital mobile cellular system developed by Japanese manufacturers together with NTT DoCoMo that never really became popular outside of Japan. From 1995 to 1997, growth was robust, but when DoCoMo introduced the PDC system, PHS subscribers quickly began decreasing and virtually all the PHS operators (NTT Personal, DDI Pocket, and Astel) began losing large sums of money—NTT Personal had been losing over 100 billion yen ($909 million) annually.

Just when many industry watchers had given PHS up for the dead, it looks like the emergence of 64 kbps data transmission functionality has given PHS a second life. In mid-1999 DDI introduced higher data rate PHS handsets that could support 64 kbps and 128 kbps data rates and actually saw subscriber shrinkage slow down. Thus, Dynamic Date Interchange (DDI) Pocket was the first of the three PHS operators to start stemming the monthly decrease in subscribers and actually can look to a growing income from PHS. NTT DoCoMo PHS network had been losing subscribers every month until December 1999 when it began seeing an increase again in PHS

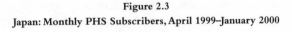

Figure 2.3
Japan: Monthly PHS Subscribers, April 1999–January 2000

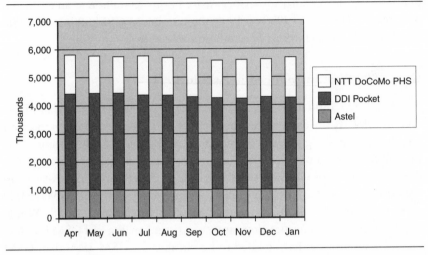

Source: MPT and TCA.

subscribers (see Figure 2.3). PHS is the closest system to 4G operating today with a plethora of devices and applications. PHS in China is widely employed and growing. Survival of PHS depends upon future spectrum assignments. The Japanese MPT may elect to allocate spectrum for a next generation of PHS because of its ability to serve some markets more effectively than 3G.

Spread Spectrum Technology: Code Division Multiple Access (CDMA)

The other competing digital cellular access technology is CDMA, which stands for code division multiple access. CDMA utilizes an advanced air interface technology known as spread spectrum that has been a core air interface technology for military communications and some satellite systems for many years and was not declassified by the Pentagon until about 10 years ago. CDMA as a consumer system was developed originally by Qualcomm, which sought to replace the AMPS 800 MHz analog systems that had been used almost exclusively in the U.S. market and had been the main U.S. system.

The U.S. FCC chose not to allocate new spectrum for digital cellular mobile radio, opting instead to open existing 800 MHz cellular bands (which were being used in analog phones) to the new service providers. The Cellular

Telecommunications and Internet Association (CTIA) in the United States was given the task of selecting a digital standard for the U.S. market and chose the digital system known as NA-TDMA IS-54 or D-AMPS.[2] The only notable example of D-AMPS being used in Asia is Hong Kong's PacLink network that was purchased by Hong Kong Telecom earlier this year for HK$3.4 billion. Hong Kong Telecom has rebranded the D-AMPS service calling it "1+1."

In spite of the fact that the CTIA had selected D-AMPS, two entrepreneurs who had founded Qualcomm persuaded the CTIA to change its selection to spread-spectrum CDMA. Qualcomm then proceeded to license its technologies to Motorola and Nortel and signed up two key U.S. operators, Sprint PCS and Prime Cellular that in 1995 together placed orders worth $850 million for Qualcomm CDMA handsets. Qualcomm then went out and secured Sony of Japan as a joint venture manufacturing partner to make the handsets. The successful rollout of the first two U.S. CDMA networks inspired other operators in the United States to adopt CDMA. By year-end 1997 CDMA accounted for 51% of the U.S. market in terms of PCS licensees, versus 28% for GSM/DCS and 20% for D-AMPS. The average number of CDMA operators per basic trading area (BTA) is 2.4 in the United States while for GSM it is 1.3. Over 83% of the BTAs have more than one CDMA operator and 48% have three or more. Thus, CDMA is positioned to dominate digital systems in the United States.

CDMA is also making serious inroads in certain parts of Asia. The first commercial launch of CDMA in the world was not in the United States but actually in Hong Kong at Hutchison Telecommunications, which rolled out its network in September 1995. The Hutchison CDMA network is actually a joint venture with Motorola, which holds a 30% stake in Hutchison Telecommunications. Presently, the Hutchison CDMA network in Hong Kong has about 300,000 subscribers. The other major markets for CDMA in Asia are Japan, South Korea, and China. As a result of strong government and industry cooperation in Korea, CDMA has become the national digital cellular standard with around 2 million CDMA subscribers. Moreover, South Korean electronics companies such as Lucky Goldstar (LG) and Samsung have emerged as major suppliers of CDMA-enabling technologies having forged various technology and licensing agreements early on with CDMA technology originators such as Qualcomm Inc. and Interdigital (King of Prussia, PA).

In 1997 the CDMA Development Group (CDU) was established to promote CDMA systems. As part of its effort the CDU created the brand name cdmaOne to refer to the first implementation of CDMA systems that are specified under the IS–95A standard. IS–95A cdmaOne systems use a spectrum of 1.25 MHz to provide a data transfer rate of 14.4 kbps.

On 8 February 1999 the CDU announced that there were 23 million cdmaOne subscribers worldwide: 6.8 million in North America and 15 million subscribers in East Asia.

NOTES

1. Dan Steinbock, *The Nokia Revolution: The Story of an Extraordinary Company that Transformed an Industry* (New York: AMACOM, 2001).

2. For the technically hungry, the D–AMPS standard employs 3 TDMA 8 kbps encoded speech channels into each 30 kHz AMPS channel.

CHAPTER 3

RADIO SPECTRUM

Managing a Scarce Resource

Wireless is all very well, but I'd rather send a message by boy or a pony.

Lord Kelvin

3.1 PRINCIPLES OF RADIO WAVE PROPAGATION

The twentieth century witnessed tremendous advances in communications and computing systems following the great communications inventions of Heinrich Hertz, Guigliermo Marconi, Nikola Tesla, Thomas Edison, and Alexander Graham Bell and the invention of the transistor from William Shockley. Using the current state of the art in fixed communications, dense wave division multiplexing (DWDM) transmission systems, it is possible to transmit up to 10 Gbps on a single strand of fiber. Countries such as China that 15 years ago had minimal telecoms infrastructure can now proudly boast that they are fast approaching the United States in terms of the scale and deployment of advanced systems. Surprisingly, the transport techniques used in modern-day fiber-optic channels are based on transmission techniques used in radio systems.

Radio communications and, in particular, digital radio communications have become necessary and critical to the world's communications infrastructure. Telecom infrastructure has incorporated microwave nodes, satellite nodes, and, now, cellular mobile nodes in response to market incentives favoring global interoperability and local land-line-like quality. In this chapter, we introduce some of the key radio communications concepts related to the impending spectrum crisis. This crisis will be exacerbated by the reluctance of governments and regulatory authorities to reallocate sufficient spectrum to more intelligently respond to the boom in wireless from areas of lower use and stagnant or declining growth, due to inertia, ignorance, and, possibly, political corruption from constituencies that find it less expensive to buy politicians than spectrum, especially when spectrum sales are rare, rigged, and unevenly regulated.

A Short Lesson in Electromagnetics

Radio transmission is based on the principles of electromagnetic radiation, which propagates as waves in free space (i.e., the vacuum). Electromagnetic waves are produced when electrons are excited at very high speeds (e.g., relativistic speeds approaching the speed of light) inside or on the surface of conductive materials. These waves were first predicted by the Scottish physicist James Clerk Maxwell in 1865 and first produced and observed by the German physicist Heinrich Hertz in 1887.

The number of oscillations per second of an electromagnetic wave is called its frequency, f, and is measured in Hz (in honor of Heinrich Hertz). The distance between two consecutive waves is called the wavelength and is designated by the Greek symbol lambda (λ). Electromagnetic waves can be transmitted by taking an electric circuit and attaching a matching antenna to it—the customary way that radio signals are transmitted and received.

Even though extremely tiny amounts of energy are being propagated in the atmosphere, modern electronic receiver circuits with a matched antenna are able to pick up or detect the signal. All wireless communication systems are based on this most fundamental and elegant principle.

One of the great mysteries of the universe is that electromagnetic waves all propagate at the same speed in free space or vacuum: the speed of light, universally denoted by the letter c. The speed of light c is approximately 3×10^8 meters/second, or about 1 foot per nanosecond (1 nanosecond or 1 ns = 1×10^{-9} seconds). In copper or fiber, the velocity slows to about two-thirds of c, changing frequency slightly. According to all physical observation by scientists thus far, it does not seem possible to go faster than the speed of light.[1] It is also possible that if something can go faster than the speed of light, we probably would not be able to detect it directly. In any event, the fundamental relation between frequency f and wavelength λ and c (in vacuum) is

$$\lambda \times f = c$$

Since c is a constant, the frequency and wavelength are inversely proportional. For example, 1 MHz waves are about 300 meters long, while 30 GHz waves are 1 cm long. Submarines use very low frequencies (VLF) for communications because only VLF radio waves can penetrate the depths of the murky ocean water.

Figure 3.1 shows the complete electromagnetic spectrum and its uses in telecommunications. Radio waves (like AM and FM radio) can travel long distances if transmitted at sufficient levels of power and can even penetrate buildings.

The properties of radio waves are frequency dependent. At low frequencies, electromagnetic waves pass through obstacles well, but the power falls off sharply with distance from the transmitting source to the order of $1/r^3$ in air (r being the radius or distance). At high frequencies, electromagnetic waves tend to travel in straight lines and bounce off obstacles. HF waves of the order of 10 MHz to 100 MHz are absorbed by rain at high frequencies. When electromagnetic waves are transmitted at high frequencies ranging from 10 MHz to 100 MHz some of them are able to reach the ionosphere, a layer of charged particles circling the earth at a height of 100 kilometers to 500 kilometers. Because of the charged particles in the ionosphere, the electromagnetic waves that reach the ionosphere are actually refracted back to earth. Under certain conditions, the waves may bounce several times off the ionosphere, a fact discovered by amateurs after President Hoover, setting the pattern for

Figure 3.1

Radio spectrum and its uses

Frequency 10^0	10^4	10^8	10^{11}	10^{14}	10^{18}	10^{22}
F (Hz)						

Radio | Microwave | Infrared | UV | X-Ray | Gamma Ray

Visible Light

Twisted Pair   Satellite   Fiber Optics

Coax Cable   Microwave

AM   FM

Maritime

TV

LF= Low Frequency
HF= High Frequency
VHF= Very High Frequency
UHF= Ultra High Frequency

SHF= Super High Frequency
EHF= Extremely High Frequency
THF= Tremedously High Frequency

foolish allocation that has been followed ever since by the United States, divided up the spectrum to give the low-frequencies to the government, the medium frequencies to business, and the supposedly worthless high frequencies to the amateurs, who've been surprisingly successful at holding on to the waves, even without an army or an intelligence agency to deploy.

Above 100 MHz, electromagnetic waves travel in straight lines and hence can be narrowly focused. The frequency range from 100 MHz to 100 GHz is called microwave. Digital cellular phones operate in the 800/900 and 1800/1900 MHz bands and thus are classified as microwave transmitters (this is why some people have raised concerns about the health hazards of mobile phones, given that no one would stick their head into a working microwave oven, nor even try to dry their poodle). Microwaves have a number of properties that affect radio transmission systems designed to use them. For example, some of the microwaves transmitted will refract off low-lying atmospheric layers and take slightly longer to arrive than direct path waves that arrive at the receiving antenna. The impact is that a time delay occurs that causes the two sets of waves to be out of phase and can create serious problems for the receiver. This problem is called multipath fading and is a problem affecting certain types of digital cellular systems such as GSM but not CDMA systems.

Digital versus Analog Radio Transmission

Trick Question: Is a digital phone really digital?
Answer: Yes and no. "Yes," in the sense that inside the phone, information is represented in digital format (e.g., 1s and 0s), but "No," in the sense that information is actually carried or transported over the air in continuous analog electromagnetic waves. Certain advanced military radar pulse systems actually turn the carrier waves off and on in a type of digital radio wave carrier "switching," but most commercial digital systems just use continuous wave (CW) radio frequency (RF) signals. Thus, only analog signals (sine waves) are used to carry information "on their backs" as they travel through the air. These analog carrier signals can carry either analog or digital information signals. The process of combining information signals on top of a carrier signal is called modulation. The difference between analog radio transmission and digital radio transmission is that, in the analog case, the analog voice signal is modulated directly onto the carrier wave, whereas in a digital system the voice signal is converted to a stream of 1s and 0s, then the stream is coded using clever mathematical algorithms that reduce noise

and interference. The coded stream is then modulated onto the carrier wave by changing the amplitude or phase of the signal.

3.2 CELLULAR RADIO AND FREQUENCY REUSE

Frequency reuse motivated the creation of the cellular radio concept. By introducing cells within a geographic area, it is possible to reuse the frequency within the service area. Cellular radio must operate in the 400 MHz to 2.5 GHz range due to the fact that the spectrum below 300 MHz is completely used up in many countries and because of physics limitations associated with frequencies above 10 GHz. For example, analog NMT 450 operates in the 450 MHz band, while GSM operates in the 900 MHz and 1800/1900 MHz bands.

Figure 3.2 illustrates the cellular radio concept. Engineers usually use hexagons for convenience when drawing a diagram of cell-site area with the understanding that a base transceiver station (BTS) is located at the center of each cell. Each mobile station (MS) (i.e., the mobile phone) then communicates with the BTS serving its cell but does not communicate directly with a central control station or with other MSs. Each of the BTSs connect to the

Figure 3.2
Cellular radio concept

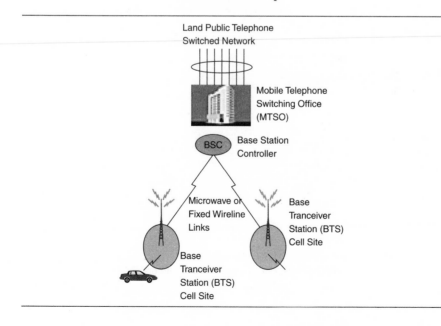

mobile telephone switching office (MTSO) via either fixed lines or microwave radio links (for example, in Hong Kong an operator such as Smartone has over 1,400 cell sites and five or six MTSOs). The MTSO comprises cellular processors and switches and associated application software and acts as the central coordinator for all cell sites. The MTSOs interface with the Public Telephone Switched Network (PTSN) company zone offices and control call processing and handle customer billing and logging activities.

Each particular cellular system can be characterized by its frequency reuse factor (see Figure 3.3), which will be dependent on the

- Cochannel interference immunity of the modulation scheme
- Diversity (spatial, time, and/or frequency), an increasingly important characteristic that tries to use the characteristic associated with multipath fading to create a form of redundancy expected to improve the quality of transmission
- Coding methods employed
- Antenna design
- Radio propagation characteristics of the environment (i.e., mountains, tall buildings, water surfaces, and so on)

Figure 3.3
Frequency reuse concepts

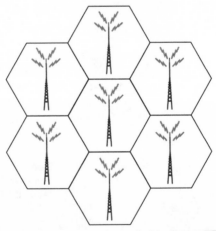

Each hexagon represents a cell site with one BTS

As an MS moves from one cell to another during the course of a phone call, the central cellular switch processor at the MTSO reroutes the call from the old cell BTS to the new cell BTS presumably without noticeable interruption. This process is called handoff. IS-95 CDMA has a feature, for example, called soft handoff. Prior to changing from the old cell to the new cell, the MS establishes a connection with the new cell. Thus, for a brief period of time the MS is communicating with two BTSs; the advantage of soft handoff is better voice quality at the outer fringes of the cell and a reduction in the number of dropped calls.

The BTS communicates with each MS via a dual channel link:

- The mobile-to-base station link is referred to as the uplink or reverse link.
- The base-to-mobile link is referred to as the downlink.

The dual channel link can be implemented as different frequencies (this is called frequency division duplex or FDD. It has one frequency but is time-multiplexed (this is called time division duplexing or TDD). GSM and IS-95 CDMA utilize FDD, while the European cordless standard digital European cordless telecommunications (DECT) and Japan's PHS use TDD.

Dynamic control of the signal power on either the uplink and/or the downlink is another important technique. Power control of the uplink tends to minimize cochannel interference within a cell site and between cell sites. Mobil stations are thus restricted to transmit at the minimum amount of power required to achieve acceptable performance within its BTS area of service. In the case of CDMA, power control is essential for proper operation.

3.3 MULTIPLE ACCESS METHODS AND MODES OF OPERATION

Since radio spectrum is a scarce resource, engineers have devised many ways to allow users to share those resources by utilizing time, spectrum band, and spatial diversities. All of these methods can be classified as multiple access schemes. There are three general classes of wireless access technologies: narrowband (below 100 kbps), wideband (100 kbps to 1 Mbps) and broadband (1 Mbps and beyond).

The main narrowband technologies are frequency division multiple access (FDMA) and time division multiple access (TDMA). In FDMA, signals from various users are assigned different frequencies and guard bands are used to prevent interference from adjacent channels. FDMA has not been practical for very large scale integration (VLSI) implementation because it requires narrowband filters that are costly to incorporate in integrated circuits.

In TDMA, user data is multiplexed into different time slots that are then grouped into frames, similar to the Internet Protocol. Interference is prevented by inserting guard time slots. GSM and D-AMPS are examples of systems that use TDMA. In the case of GSM, each time slot is 577 microseconds long and transmits exactly 156.25 bits.

Figure 3.4 summarizes some of the main characteristics of the different analog and digital systems used today. There is an item called the duplexing method that is reminiscent of the old ASCII-based communications systems in early PCs. The duplexing method or mode refers to the separation between uplink and downlink. For people familiar with satellite systems, the choice of downlink and uplink frequency, modulation, and speed can have quite an impact on overall cost of the system; thus, in all discussions on wireless access standards, the mode of operation becomes a heated subject. Basically, there are two types of modes: frequency division duplex (FDD) and time division duplex (TDD). In FDD the transmitter and receiver operate simultaneously on different frequency channels, while in TDD the uplink and downlink are transmitted on different time slots. The three key advantages of TDD are[2]:

1. There is no need for a dedicated duplex circuit, but the internal subsystems such as the frequency synthesizers, FR filter paths, and antenna switches need to be fast.
2. Battery life is increased.
3. Simplified design which lowers cost of the handset.

3.4 A SHORT HISTORY OF SPREAD SPECTRUM

In the beginning there was Noise, and God said let there be Entropy. Then, some 15 billion years later, on a small, humble planet called Earth, Claude Shannon saw that Entropy was Good and Entropy was Information, and taught us the secrets of Coding.

The first spread-spectrum patent was filed by movie actress Hedy Lamarr and George Antheil in 1941.[3] Their patent described a frequency-hopping spread spectrum method for the purpose of anti-jamming military communications, including torpedoes. Hedy grew up in Austria

Figure 3.4

Specifications of popular analog and digital cellular systems

Parameter	AMPS	TACS	PDC (Japan)	GSM-900	IS-95 CDMA
Transmission Frequency (MHz)					
Base Station Transmit	869–894	917–933; 935–960	810–826; 1477–1501	890–915	869–894
Mobile Station Transmit	824–849	872–888; 890–915	1429–1453; 940–956	935–960	824–849
Base station coverage (km)	>32	32	0.5–20	0.5–35	25
Mobile Station Transmit power (watts)	0.6, 1.2, 3.0	1.0	0.3, 0.8, 2.0, 3.0	0.125–1.0 (User); 2.5–320 (Basestation)	0.06–0.2
Duplexing Method	FDD	FDD	FDD	FDD	FDD
Multiple Access Method	FDMA	FDMA	TDMA	TDMA	CDMA
Number of Frequency Channels				124	
Channel Width (KHZ)	30.0	25.0	25.0	200.0	1,230.0
Traffic Channels per RF Channel	1	1	3	8	20–60
Total number of channels	832	1,000		125 × 8 = 1,000	60 × 5 = 300
Voice Modulation	Analog	Analog	Digital	Digital	Digital
Control Modulation **Peak Deviation** **Channel rate (kbps)**	Digital FSK ±8 10.0	Digital FSK ±6.4 8.0	—	—	—
Voice Coder	—	—	VSELP	RPE/LTP-LPC	QCELP
Speech rate (kbps)			11.2 π/4 DQPSK	13.0 GMSK	8.55 DS-CDMA
User data rate (kbps)	—	—	14.4	9.6	14.4/64

Note: FDD = Frequency division duplexing. GMSK = Gaussian Minimum Shift Keying.
DS-CDM = Direct Sequence CDMA. RPE/LPC = Regular Pulse Excitation/Linear Predictive Coding.
QCELP = Qualcomm Code Excited Linear Predictive Coding. VSELP = Vector Sum Excited Linear
Prediction.

as the only child of a prominent Austrian banker and at the age of 16 showed her flair for innovation by letting herself be filmed in total nudity in a Czech-produced film, *Ecstasy,* reportedly the first nude scene in cinematic history and an interesting precursor to Cisco founder Sandy Lerner, who became the first prominent business executive to pose completely nude (on a horse, like Lady Godiva, only with millions of dollars in personal net worth) in a major business magazine. These women knew how to inspire and enable communication, and should inspire both men and women to express themselves as they wish and think outside the box.

Hedy later married a munitions businessman, Friedrich Mandl, who aligned himself to the Nazi movement. Recognizing the danger of Hitler's ambitions to free-thinking Austrians (and not too excited about playing a starring role in the proposed Aryan breeding program), the young actress fled to the United States on a seven-year contract with Metro Goldwyn-Mayer (MGM) and changed her last name to Lamarr. Determined to repay the kindnesses shown to her by the public and to prove her patriotism, she drew upon the many conversations that her ex-husband's engineers had had concerning weapons systems. In cooperation with her friend in the U.S. symphony, composer George Antheil, Hedy came up with the idea that led ultimately to the patent filing (# 2,292,387, "Secret Communication System," patented Aug. 11, 1942) for a radio transmitter in which the transmitted carrier frequency would hop according to a prearranged, randomized, and non-repeating frequency hopping code. The actual patent that was filed made use of Antheil's knowledge of music and frequencies. A torpedo could, in effect, switch guidance frequencies as fast as Antheil could play different keys on the piano.

The history of spread spectrum and multiple-access systems is as intriguing and has often been shrouded in secrecy because it was under the control of the defense establishment. Ever since the first licensed broadcast by Westinghouse in 1920 and even before the U.S. Congress enacted the Federal Radio Commission (FRC) in 1927, the issue of frequency use interference had become an important business and military issue. Between 1920 and 1940 a number of researchers including Harry Nyquist, Edwin Armstrong, John Renshaw Carson, and R. V. L. Hartley filed numerous patents that formed the basis for the key concepts behind spread spectrum. The development of the radar in the later 1930s and during World War II also contributed greatly to the development of spread spectrum communications. In the spring of 1936 the Royal Air Force, under pressure from Winston Churchill, successfully demonstrated the first experimental coastal early warning pulse radar, and a year later radar was placed on British warships. In 1938, Gustav Guanella of Brown, Boveri and Company in Switzerland received a patent for a radar system that was "composed of a multiplicity of different frequencies the energies of which are small compared to the total energy."[4] By the end of World War II the Germans were developing a linear-FM (Chirp) radar system called Kugelschale and had discovered that bandwidth expansion without pulse narrowing could also provide for finer time resolution. World War II also spawned tremendous research activity in jamming and anti-jamming systems.

In 1948 Claude Shannon published his landmark paper on information theory. Shannon's theorems proved that there existed schemes (coding schemes to be precise) for transmitting information over a noisy real-world channel and achieving error-free transmission as long as a sufficiently high signal-to-noise ratio was available. It is hard to overstate the significance of Shannon's theoretical work because, from that day on, countless patents were filed by people using block diagrams and mathematical models that directly reflected Shannon's reasoning and logical methodology.

Shannon's work also caught the attention of the U.S. Department of Defense (DOD), and between 1948 and 1960 the DOD commissioned and generously budgeted for significant research supporting the development of anti-jamming systems and the use of spread spectrum or spreading the signal across a large bandwidth. In the mid-1950s, under the auspices of defense research, the RAKE processor was developed that used the finite time resolution capability of wideband signals to resolve signals arriving over different propagation paths, and inserted them into a diversity combiner to coherently construct a stronger received signal.[5] RAKE processors are a key element in certain commercial mobile systems such as the cdmaOne chip sets sold by Qualcomm. Another important concept in spread spectrum is the pseudo-random noise generator (PN) which was first developed by Sol Golomb while he was at MIT and refined after he joined the Jet Propulsion Laboratory (JPL) in Pasadena, California.

The notion of using coding access methods in spread spectrum is credited to John Pierce's work in 1949 (though Pierce credits Shannon for the basic idea) on deploying orthogonal functions of time. A decade later Shannon and Peirce illustrated CDMA by comparing it to a party: ". . . More and more people can come, and they would all be able to speak. If more people were there, gradually the noise would increase on each channel. But everyone could still talk, except that it might be a pretty noisy 'cocktail party' by that time." Price went on to comment that in military jargon they would describe that process as "graceful degradation."[6]

The first direct sequence spread spectrum (DSSS) systems were built in

the early 1950s, and as early as 1960, military satellite communication designers looked to DSSS, rather than TDMA or FDMA, for ways to improve
their systems. Probably the best-known military system that uses spread spectrum is the DOD's GPS. GPS systems work by synchronizing to a stream of
1023 chips with a period of 1 ms.

In the 1980s the public research papers began to proliferate on spread
spectrum systems. By 1985 the FCC gave its support for spread-spectrum in
the commercial domain and, eight years later, the Telecommunications Industry Association (TIA) adopted Irwin Jacobs's (Qualcomm) proposal for
IS95. In a nutshell, spread spectrum and CDMA came from the great minds
of the early 1900 investors, a beautiful movie star–inventor, and the Department of Defense with its many secretive programs, leading to its adoption
by industry associations and standards committees.

3.5 RADIO CHANNEL MODELING

The key promise of wireless communications is that users are free to move
and even roam into other countries. However, the radio channel provides a
more hostile environment to a transmitted signal than does a wireline channel such as copper or fiber optic cable. There are a number of phenomena
that impair the radio channel and thus present a real challenge the designers
of wireless systems:

- Additive White Gaussian Noise (AWGN)
- Radio frequency signal path loss
- Fading at low data rates
- Intersymbol interference (ISI) at high data rates
- Shadow fading
- Cochannel interference
- Adjacent channel interference

Most wireless networks operate in the microwave frequency band (1 GHz
to 1,000 GHz). At a typical transmit power of 100 mW to 1 W, a transmitter
has a coverage range of about 50 m indoors and 800 m outdoors. Users carrying their portable wireless devices and mobile phones typically walk at a
rate of 2 m/s or less.[7]

Figure 3.5 depicts a block diagram of a typical radio communication system.
The input data is modulated at baseband and then multiplied by a local oscilla-
tor to send the signal at carrier frequency. The resulting signal is transmitted over
the radio channel, which introduces noise and distortion. The receiver demod-

ulates the signal by detecting the transmitted RF signal and then deciding on the most likely transmitted sequence. The result is the estimated received data.

Noise is present in most communications systems, whether wireline or wireless. Noise, such as AWGN and path loss limit a transmitter's coverage range. Thermal noise is introduced by temperature-dependent resistive elements in the integrated circuits (IC). Human-made noise includes such sources as automobile ignitions, electric motors, microprocessors, mechanical vibrations, and spurious industrial emissions.

Many techniques have been devised by electrical engineers to overcome noise and most involve maximizing the signal-to-noise ratio (SNR) of the receiver. The obvious solution of increasing the transmitted power is not practical because of battery life and is also limited by regulators such as the FCC due to interference and health safety concerns.

3.6 ENCRYPTION IN MOBILE CELLULAR PHONES

The proliferation of international voice and data communications for private, commercial, and military applications, coupled with the widespread use of Internet technologies for information exchange, data services, and electronic commerce, has heightened the need for ever more secure, networked systems. The use of encryption in cellular phones has become political in many countries. China, for example, prohibits operators from enabling encryption on the cellular base stations, which effectively disables encryption at the handset level. The United States can't claim to be much better. The Qualcomm-led cdmaOne standard has no encryption on the voice stream, with the exception of keying PIN numbers (and that too has apparently been broken), due to opposition from the NSA. According to the intelligence agencies, villains like to use mobile phones for their illegal business transactions; thus, the rest of society should give up their privacy to enable the governments to easily listen in on their private conversations.

The European Union (EU) has implemented a more coherent and consistent encryption policy for mobile phones. GSM standards incorporate strong encryption into the handset and the base station. Unfortunately, though, since the GSM encryption scheme has been around a number of years, there are portable devices that can crack the encryption of voice streams on GSM phones if its antenna is pointed directly at someone engaged in a voice conversation. In 3G and later in 4G systems from the EU, one can expect strong encryption algorithms using keys with more than 128-bit keys.

Network security, and in particular cryptographic technologies, has now become a critical issue in the design of commercial and government networks.

Industry research firms have estimated that the worldwide demand for encryption products is over $1 billion annually and will grow to several times this. According to a survey conducted by the Business Software Alliance, over one-third of Fortune 500 companies specifically require encryption capability in their hardware and software purchases.

Cryptographic algorithms are embedded in a number of applications, such as

- Electronic funds transfers
- Internet firewalls, gateways, and routers
- E-mail and data transfer of corporate financial, engineering, and manufacturing data (the American Lawyer News Service has recommended that clients use data encryption for all sensitive e-mail communications)
- Databases
- Digital cellular phones with encrypted handset ID numbers and encrypted voice streams
- Digital voting
- Mondex smart cards and digital cash
- Electronic banking services (e.g., Intuit's home banking service)
- VSAT (very small aperture satellite) data and voice links

Data can be encrypted and transmitted over a variety of physical media including fixed line and wireless public telephone networks, digital cellular mobile phone networks (such as Europe's GSM 900MHz and DCS1800), and satellite communication systems.

Network security issues can be classified into four categories:

1. *System security and integrity.* This applies to hardware, operating system, and application software on both client and server computers.
2. *Authentication mechanisms.* These are mechanisms to ensure the identity of the user, document, application, or even a piece of source code.
3. *Access control and authorization systems.* This refers to permission that grants users access to system resources.
4. *Privacy technologies.* This means protecting the content of data transmitted over the network.

Contemporary cryptosystems are based on unique mathematical properties that can be easily exploited in either software and/or in hardware. Encryption algorithms can be classified into two broad categories: secret or shared key (sometimes called symmetrical key) and public key (sometimes called asymmetrical). Figure 3.5 provides a summary of the better-known algorithms that are in use today. Most existing or planned network security architectures for electronic commerce and other types of secure network transactions rely on a number of cryptographic technologies for data encryption, key exchange, authentication, and digital signatures. Understanding

Figure 3.5
List of contemporary algorithms

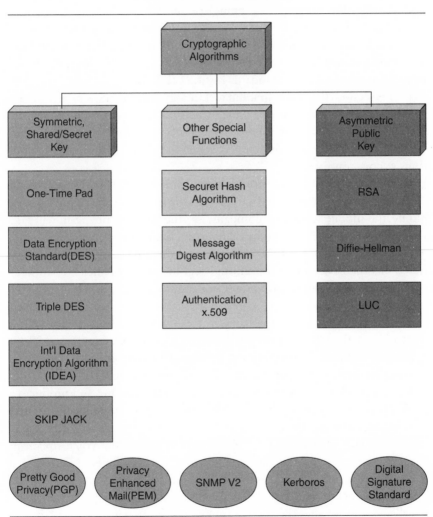

the mathematics and computational implications of these technologies is a task in itself.

Encryption in GSM Systems

One of the major drawbacks of analog cellular phones is that they can be easily cloned. Thus, the designers of contemporary mobile digital cellular phone systems, such as IS-95 DS-CDMA (direct sequence–code division multiple access) and the Pan European GSM-SFH (global system for mobile communications–slow frequency hopping) phone standard, have incorporated an encryption function for handset/user authentication and streaming of the voice signal for privacy. The GSM standard is described in a formal set of documents consisting of some 5,200 pages and is available from the European Telecommunication Standards Institute (ETSI).

In this section, the cryptographic technology used in GSM systems is described, but note that although CDMA also uses encryption technology, to date the algorithms have not been made available to the general public because it was developed in the United States and thus falls under U.S. munitions export control laws.[8]

Encryption on GSM systems is accomplished through the use of a Subscriber Identity Module (SIM) card. When the subscriber first purchases the phone, the mobile telephone company, i.e., the network operator, will set a PIN code in the SIM card of the handset. Each time the phone is turned on it will run a check of the PIN code stored in the SIM card, but it should be noted that the PIN is never transmitted over the radio channel. Network security in GSM is achieved as follows (see Figure 3.6):

1. *Authentication.* When the handset (called the mobile station or MS) is turned on, the GSM network will make an inquiry by sending a 128-bit random number (RAND) to the handset. The 128-bit RAND is mixed with the MS's secret parameter, called K_i, using a shared key algorithm known as A3. The algorithm is computed in the handset and produces a 32-bit signed result number (SRES). The SRES is then sent to the network from the MS for verification.

2. *Encryption.* GSM phones provide encryption of the voice stream to protect against unauthorized listening. The MS uses the RAND received during authentication, mixes it with K_i using a different algorithm, known as A8, and generates a new key K_c, 64-bits in length. Another algorithm, called A5, then takes the frame number and K_c to generate a 114-bit ci-

Figure 3.6
Authentication with encryption in European GSM

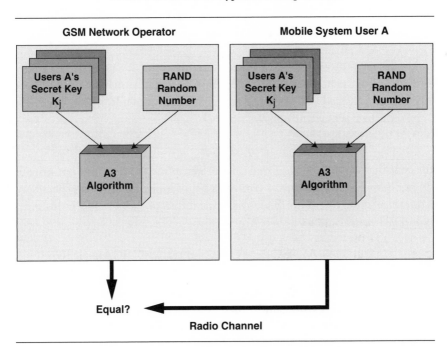

phering sequence S_2 that is then exclusively-ORed with the plaintext message.

3. *User ID protection and security management.* The secret MS key K_i is kept in the handset MS and in a repository at the network operator side. However, it is never transmitted over the radio channel. Both sides perform A3 and A8 computations. Hence, GSM security is based on shared key encryption where the distribution of the key never takes place over the radio network.

In the future it has been suggested by researchers that public key schemes should be employed in digital cellular systems to take advantage of the increases in VLSI integration.

3.7 SPECTRUM ALLOCATION AND SQUATTING

Over 30% of radio spectrum in the EU countries is owned and controlled by the defense community.[9] In the United Kingdom, the U.K. Ministry of

Defense owns 29% of the 9 kHz to 1 GHz bands, 31% of the 1 GHz to 3 GHz bands, and 38% of the 3 GHz to 30 GHz bands. We call this Military Spectrum Squatting. A number of proposals have been put forth in Europe to make better commercial use of spectrum including:

1. Co-farming—sharing the spectrum with industry
2. Having the military put its spectrum on auction and buy back what it needs, instead of expecting to get it for free while making wireless companies pay through the nose
3. Doing nothing

It seems that most Western governments are opting for the third option, but do not be surprised if industry consortia begin lobbying for more spectrum. Military planners who don't see the crucial role of the wireless industry in winning wars should read their history.

3.8 INDUSTRIAL SCIENTIFIC AND MEDICAL (ISM) BAND

There are three major ISM bands (the FCC calls these unlicensed national information infrastructure bands) that are available for unlicensed operation in the United States:

*   902–928 MHz
*   2400–2483.5 MHz
*   5150–5250 MHz, 5250–5350 MHz, and 5725–5825 MHz

In 1985 the FCC designated the 902–928 MHz and 2400–2483 MHz and 5725–5850 bands as license-free, subject to certain usage constraints such as mandatory use of spread spectrum and power limitations. The other two 5 GHz bands were allocated in 1996 after a number of petitions were submitted by companies including Apple Computer (thanks, Apple—you really do "Think Different," in this case to the benefit of everyone). Bluetooth and IEEE 802.11b systems utilize the 2.4 GHz band while IEEE 802.11a and Europe's HiperLAN 2 wireless-LAN systems are targeting the 5 GHz band. It is worthwhile keeping track of which companies oppose and support open spectrum allocations. Companies that oppose open spectrum should be boycotted or cursed, as this is the equivalent of trying to prevent communications, and few people would be excited to do business with a company that tried to eliminate the first amendment right to free speech.

AT&T opposed the FCC's decision to allocate the 5 GHz band claiming that "the increased reach that signal from U–NII devices would enjoy as a result of increased power or more directional antennas would allow unlicensed spectrum to be used for purposes beyond those envisioned by the Commission."[10] The FCC subsequently discarded AT&T's arguments and restructured the 5 GHz band to allow more ISM use. Die, AT&T, die. You had a hundred years to bring telephony to the entire world, and you didn't even try. Your day is done. Move out of the way so that other companies, with new ideas can, indeed, do more than the FCC envisions (something that, in fact, is not setting the bar very high).

The entire 5 GHz band has many uses: The 5000–5150 MHz band is used by the FAA for microwave landing systems, and the 5850–5875 MHz band is used for hearing aid devices and the planned Intelligent Transport Systems (ITS). We can expect that most unlicensed broadband wireless communications will gravitate to the 5 GHz band since the 2.4 GHz band is already quite congested. Of course, if the military were to let go of a little bit of the vast fraction of spectrum it squats on as if we were living in Burma, run by generals, things would be a lot easier.

One interesting example of an ISM service was offered by Metricom, a Silicon Valley company, until it went bankrupt. Metricom introduced an innovative wireless data packet (e.g., Internet access) service in 1994 called Ricochet. Ricochet was a wireless packet data service that operated in the ISM band at 902–928 MHz. The network was built by installing small base stations usually on lampposts in cities or inside buildings in the case of airports or shopping malls. The base stations had a range of about 0.25–0.75 kilometers and route the signal from user terminals over the same ISM band. Metricom offered its 100 kbps service in a number of cities including San Francisco, Seattle, Los Angeles, and Washington, D.C., and at various university campuses and airports around the country. Despite its failure, Metricomm did many things right technically.

3.9 COOPER'S LAW ON SPECTRUM EFFICIENCY

Martin Cooper of ArrayComm talks about his "Cooper's Law" (referred to in telecom engineering textbooks), which is based on empirical observations that for the past 104 years spectral efficiency has doubled every 2.5 years, as measured in terms of the number of voice or data "conversations" that can be transported over a communications link (see Figure 3.7).

The rate of improvement in the use of the radio spectrum has been essentially uniformly exponential for 104 years. The cumulative improvement

Figure 3.7
Cooper's Law

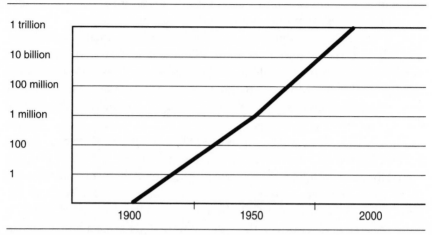

Source: Martin Cooper, Napa Valley Telecommunications Round Table, July 17, 1999.

for the past 90 years is over one trillion times (1×10^{15}) and one million times (1×10^6) in the past 45 years.

These spectacular improvements have been achieved through enhancements in four principal areas:

1. *Frequency division (e.g., FM radio).* Produced a 5 times improvement from 1955–2000, by dividing the spectrum into narrower slices.
2. *Modulation techniques.* Gave a 5 times improvement from 1955–2000, through the use of techniques such as FM, single side band (SSB), and time division multiplexing.
3. *Widening of the usable radio spectrum.* Gave a 25 times improvement from 1955–2000.
4. *Spatial division and spectrum re-use.* Contributed a 1,600 times improvement from 1955–2000, by confining the area used for individual conversations to smaller and smaller areas.

3.10 BUSINESS MODEL FOR WIRELESS SPECTRUM UTILIZATION

Let us consider in this section the classic cellular carrier business model, which might be summarized as follows:

1. Purchase spectrum (usually 10–20 MHz) either through auctions or by government bids, or, in the lucky case, as a government grant.
2. Price airtime tariffs around large volume business users.
3. Offer the minimum number of different services and pricing packages possible, given the expectations raised by competition.
4. Minimize capital expenditures (CAPEX).
5. Delay making future CAPEX outlays until absolutely necessary because of howls of outrage from customers whose calls are not getting through (e.g., the Manhattan class action suit against AT&T for poor quality that cost customers money, which alleged poor service by design).
6. Raise tariffs if the competition lets you do it (e.g., Hong Kong cellular operators tried to raise their tariffs at the same time, which brought the wrath of the regulator, Office of Telecommunications Authority (OFTA), upon them.

Competition tends to force the carriers to spend more money on infrastructure and support services. The current auctions for 3G spectrum in the United Kingdom witnessed the bidding price blow through the 1.7 billion pound level and eventually ending up in the 4–6 billion pound stratosphere per carrier, even though the new entrants from outside were limited. Spectrum has become exceedingly expensive in many markets, and not available at all in most others.

There are a number of technology trends that could radically alter the business models of present-day carriers and possibly render them altogether obsolete. The following emerging technologies, in particular, are going to play significant roles in the next generation of wireless systems and depending on their confluence could very well have a critical impact on the types of services that consumers will expect:

- Short-range spread spectrum wireless systems such as Bluetooth
- Major advances in storage technology, which will make it possible to actually store large control programs and data in portable devices
- Spatial technologies such as smart antennas
- Software defined radios and software radios that will be able to send and receive multiple protocols
- Broadband wireless systems that will deploy spatial technologies in order to provide transmission rates above 1 Mbps to every wireless user

- Novel form factors for Wireless Information Devices that will be able to send and receive multi-media data and will be dynamically programmable by the service provider
- Wearable computer devices that will become as natural to wear as a watch or piece of jewelry is today

NOTES

1. Physicists such as Steven Hawking believe that radiation may be able to travel faster than the speed of light for very short periods on the surface of black holes.

2. Vijay K. Gorg, *IS-95 and cdma2000* (Englewood Cliffs, N.J.: Prentice Hall, 2000).

3. Marvin K. Simon, *Spread Spectrum Communications* (New York: McGraw Hill, 1994).

4. Savo Glisic in Marvin K. Simon, *Spread Spectrum Communications* (New York: McGraw Hill, 1994).

5. Ibid.

6. Ibid.

7. If the user were to travel at very high speeds, there is the risk of relativistic effects such as the Doppler shift that can complicate the design of the radio channel.

8. In the early days of GSM, Motorola had a fully functional product ready for the market but was held back by about one year because the U.S. government would not allow the company to export the GSM phones with on-board encryption functions; the effect of this ludicrous situation was to give Nokia, Ericsson, and Siemens a major head start on penetrating the European and Asian GSM markets, and potentially costing Motorola and other American companies tens—possibly hundreds—of billions in potential market value that accrued to less fettered Scandinavian, Asian, and Continental European manufacturers.

9. *Book of Visions 2000*, study sponsored by the European Commission under the Wireless Strategic Initiative (WSI, 2000).

10. Bennet Z. Kobb, *Wireless Spectrum Finder: Telecommunications, Government, and Scientific Radio Frequency Allocations in the U.S., 30 MHz–300 GHz* (New York: McGraw Hill, c. 2001).

CHAPTER 4

DIGITAL SIGNAL PROCESSORS

4.1 INTRODUCTION

Digital signal processing (DSP) is the changing or analyzing of information that is measured as discrete sequences of numbers. DSP is different from plain old ordinary digital processing in two respects:

- Signals come from the real world. This intimate connection with the real world leads to many unique needs such as the need to react in real time and a need to measure signals and convert them to digital numbers.
- Signals are discrete. This means that the information in between discrete samples is lost.

The advantages of DSP are common to many digital systems and include:

- *Versatility.* Digital systems can be reprogrammed for other applications (at least where programmable DSP chips are used) and can be ported to different hardware (for example, a different DSP chip or board level product).
- *Repeatability.* Digital systems can be easily duplicated and do not depend

on strict component tolerances. Digital system responses do not drift with temperature.

- *Simplicity.* Some things can be done more easily with digital than with analog systems.

DSP chip sets can be sold as complete packaged chips or as cores that are embedded into a larger chip set, such as a mobile phone chip set. DSPs are typically high-density, high-speed, programmable integrated circuits that utilize mathematical algorithms to transform analog signals into digital streams. Some of the applications of DSPs include:

- Digital filters
- Speech analysis
- Image processing
- Oil exploration

Market Size

In 1999 the worldwide DSP market was nearly $4.4 billion.[1] As broadband communications markets continue to grow, DSP technology providers such as Texas Instruments and Lucent are well positioned to continue benefiting from the robust demand.

Similar to the business model for microprocessors, success in the DSP segment is achieved by winning designs with major original equipment manufacturers (OEMs), such as networking and cellular giants, and then sustaining the customer relationship for as long as possible.

However, since the DSP code is still largely written in assembly language, dependencies have been created on DSP instruction set architecture (ISA), conveniently compelling customers once they get started to keep using the same supplier so that the customers can reuse the legacy code.

Nevertheless, new competitors could begin to make inroads over the next two years, depending on how the market is viewed. According to senior analyst for In-stat's Logic Group Max Baron, "DSP offerings at different levels are evolving rapidly as companies like Mysticom, DSP Group, Infineon, LSI Logic and others introduce their intellectual property. In System on a Chip (SOC), however, newcomers to the market have been faced with the daunting task of convincing tool vendors to support them and OEM designers to try them out. . . . With the advent of easier to use hardware and software design tools, additional DSP core products could very well begin to eat into the long-held bastion of the traditional suppliers."

4.2   PROGRAMMING DSPs

DSPs can be controlled with a native operating system, and entire libraries for implementing many functions are available for the major DSP chips on the market. Operating systems on DSPs are used when the task to be performed is very complex because the programmer may need to control the allocations of system resources (RAM, etc.) and to perform multitasking, where several tasks take turns executing. Some engineers actually write their own DSP task-switching or job allocating operating system and certain companies offer prewritten operating systems that execute on DSP processors.

These companies describe their products as real-time operating systems. What "real time" means can be debated, but it normally means that the maximum time for the operating system to respond to an external event is known. The calculation for measuring this time involves adding together interrupts, response time, task-switching time, and other processor and operating system benchmarks. Real time also usually means fast. Embedded CPU or DSP tasks often require a real-time response time. Prices and features vary. Most manufacturers charge for purchasing their development environment, which allows you to develop code that will run on their operating system. Some companies also charge a fee for each product you build that includes their operating system software. This is usually called a target fee or run-time license fee. Some operating systems have no run-time license fees. Some companies include the operating system source code for free, while others may charge extra.

Company Profile: Texas Instruments (TI)

Texas Instruments (TI) is the world's leader in DSPs. Dominated by TI, Lucent, Motorola, and Analog Devices Inc. (ADI), which collectively hold over 95% of the market, the DSP arena has been polarized. The market is characterized by four vendors who comprise most of the market and by multiple vendors at the low end who are trying to break in. TI had 47.1% of the merchant DSP market in 1999, followed by Lucent with a 26.1% share, Motorola with 14.5%, and ADI with 7.6%.

TI has announced two new DSP cores, one offering performance applications and the other setting ultra-low power records. These new cores are targeted at consumer and broadband communications infrastructure applications from digital voice and data, to audio and video while maintaining software compatibility with previous generations of TI DSPs. TI's new TMS320C64x DSP core is the company's fastest DSP chip to date. Some of the key features of the DSP are as follows:

- Clock speeds of up to 1.1 GHz.
- 9,000 million instructions per second (MIPS) performance (10 times the DSP performance of the TMS320C62x).
- Very long instruction word (VLIW) Architecture. Quad 8-bit/dual 16-bit instructions enable nearly nine billion, 8-bit multiply-accumulate cycle (MAC) operations per second; special-purpose instructions improve data flow, reduce code size in memory, and accelerate key application tasks such as error correction, bit manipulation, motion estimation, and compensation; target markets include broadband communications infrastructure and precision imaging (medical, security, and TV-quality networking applications).

TI's other new DSP chip is the TMS320C55x DSP core that slashes power consumption considerably:

- 0.05 mW per MIPS.
- 800 MIPS performance at 400 MHz.
- Scalable instruction word length reduces code size by 30%.
- Advanced power management design techniques automatically power down inactive peripherals, memory, and core functional units for minimal power consumption.
- Dual-MAC architecture doubles the number of instructions per cycle while reducing power per function.

Target markets include battery-powered applications, including music, photography, and medical applications such as hearing aids, as well as cell phones. TI's C54x is used in 70% of the world's cell phones. TI's integrated development environment, eXpressDSP Real-Time Software Technology, supports the new C64x and C55x DSP cores by providing a complete, open DSP software environment with the tools and software to begin development today. Some of TI's major OEM customers are Cisco, Ericsson, and Nokia, each of which buys TI's DSP cores.

NOTES

1. Cahrers In-Stat Logic. Available at www.instat.com.

CHAPTER 5

2.5G SYSTEMS

An Interim Solution

5.1 INTRODUCTION

The challenge for operators is to migrate to new technologies that enable new services and generate additional revenues. Unfortunately, the morass of technical issues associated with migrating from an existing system to a new one makes the process very challenging and risky for the operator. Figure 5.1 highlights the major migration paths that are available post-3G harmonization by the ITU, ETSI, and various national standards bodies.

Japan's PDC is worth mentioning because (1) it has already achieved data rates of 32 and 64 kbps so in a sense PDC was 2.5G and (2) NTT DoCoMo and Japan Telecom will migrate PDC to W-CDMA while KDDI will upgrade to cdma2000. In actuality, NTT DoCoMo will not "migrate" but instead will operate the two networks side by side until it can safely move its PDC customers over to its 3G network. This process may take one to two years according to NTT executive's public statements.

5.2 GSM AND GSM PHASE 2, 2+ VAS

GSM Phase 2 and Phase 2+ are still considered 2G but did provide a number of new and useful messaging and wireless data functions to the GSM standard (see Figure 5.2). Most GSM Phase 2/2+ systems offer some combination of the functions listed below:

- Voice mail
- Remote voice mail
- Multiparty calling and three-way party calling
- Cell broadcast
- AoC information (cost information)
- Real-time advice of charge (AoC) information
- Short message services (SMS)
- Internet messaging service
- Data transfer—asynchronous and synchronous
- Facsimile services
- Prepaid SIM cards
- Secretarial services
- Informational services
- Mobile commerce and transactional services
- Expansion of SMS and cell broadcast with advertising revenues

Cell Broadcast and Short Messaging Services (SMS)

Cell Broadcast provides a new opportunity because the operators can get advertising revenues from content suppliers. In the United Kingdom, OnetoOne is promoting cell broadcast STD discount zones because it intends to compete directly with British Telecom (BT) long-distance business. Thus, OnetoOne users are being sent subscribers trunk dialing (STD) numbers over the air (these are like area codes in the United States) where they can call at competitive prices relative to BT's fixed line calls. In the United Kingdom, local calls are metered, which presents a potential arbitrage opportunity for cellular operators. The motivation for Cell Broadcast in Hong Kong is quite different: customer loyalty programs and generation of advertising revenues.

The GSM technical specifications provide 1,000 logical Cell Broadcast channels that subscribers can tune in to. For example, it is not inconceivable that media and news firms can sign up with an operator to provide English and local language alerts. From the operators vantage point, it is more economical to utilize Cell Broadcast (one to omnipoint) rather than doing only point-to-point SMS transmissions; of course, SMS is marketed as a fee service whereby the user is charged for each message sent.

Most of the GSM equipment manufacturers are now developing products to the new GSM Phase 2++ specification that, among other things, defines a programming interface for the SIM card. It is not inconceivable that with the new spec, operators might be able to turn some of the cell broadcast

Figure 5.1
Wireless technology evolution path

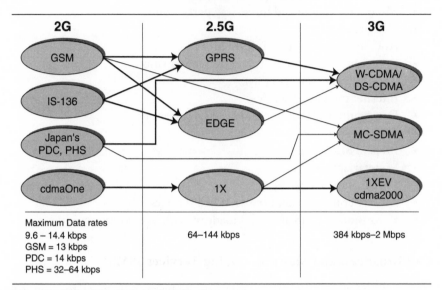

Source: Dr. Howard Xia, Vodaphone; Nokia, Siemens.

channels into paying channels. However, for the time being, Cell Broadcast is treated as a free service to the subscriber.

Handset capabilities have various limitations when it comes to cell broadcast. For example, the Nokia 6110 handset can have the user program up to 10 channels to "listen" to. Some manufacturer's models do not provide for multichannel reception, which means that the user can only tune in to one channel at a time.

Battery life is an important issue when evaluating the benefits of Cell Broadcast. The GSM Phase 2 document specifies a method for reducing battery life wear-down as a consequence of continually receiving cell broadcast messages. Essentially, the technique calls for sending a message beforehand to notify the handset to ramp up the power for the receiver.

Prepaid or Stored-Value SIM Cards

Prepaid service is not without its own technological choices: Operators have to choose between stored-value SIM cards versus network-stored value SIM cards. Initially, all the operators have started with stored-value SIM cards in

Figure 5.2
GSM 2G and 2.5G functions and services

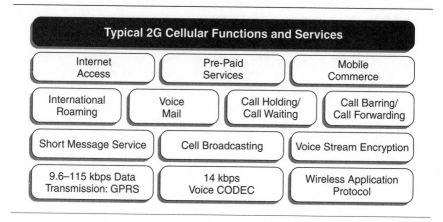

which the user's balance is actually stored in the SIM card; the motivation was to build a prepaid solution quickly at lower cost in order to grab market share. The major drawback is integrity of the balance update—similar to what happens when a banking ATM machine has to abort a transaction due to insufficient cash.

In some countries prepaid service is the norm; in both Italy and the Philippines, for example, more than 55% of the subscribers use prepaid cards. In Italy one can go to virtually any newspaper stand and purchase a recharge card. The issue of privacy is important with respect to prepaid cards because in Italy, for example, one must show a credit card or adequate proof of address to sign up for a prepaid card. In Hong Kong and Japan, prepaid cards are completely anonymous; although in Japan, due to a high-profile criminal hijacking in which the suspect used a prepaid card, the law enforcement agencies are trying to ban prepaid cards.

Mobile applications are virtually limitless once the handset can be dynamically programmed with SIM cards, part of the reason this is a $4 billion industry in Europe, led by Gemplus, Schumberger, and Oberthur.

5.3 GPRS and EDGE: 2.5G Systems

General packet radio services (GPRS) is a circuit-switched cellular migrate solution developed by ETSI for operators who currently are running GSM 900/1800 networks and want to provide an interim solution (call it 2.5 G) to begin creating demand for wireless data applications.

GPRS offers air interface transfer rates up to 115 kbps, subject to mobile station capabilities and carrier interference. In the initial release GPRS uses GMSK, the same modulation scheme as GSM. The subsequent system called enhanced data rates for GSM evolution (EDGE) uses a new modulation scheme—eight-phase shift key (8PSK).

As shown in Figure 5.3, GPRS is actually an overlay system over a GSM network and introduces new network processing nodes such as the serving GPRS support node (SGSN) and the gateway GPRS support node (GGSN) to create a packet-switched network on top of the GSM voice network. The radio modulation used in GPRS is the same as in GSM, but GPRS employs enhanced coding schemes and time-slot aggregation, which are software-controlled from the base station (meaning that handsets do not need to be replaced) to achieve a maximum capacity of 171 kbps. In practice, the actual capacity is more like 50 kbps due to time slot aggregation and requirements to have more signaling (or backhaul communications).

The key drawbacks of GPRS are as follows:

1. GPRS is not an elegant solution and actually introduces architectural inefficiencies in the backhaul that will make scaling difficult. One of the great achievements with fixed-line communications has been the

Figure 5.3
General packet radio services (GPRS)—The concept

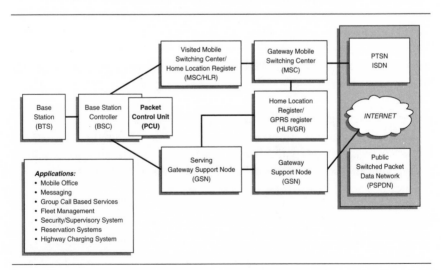

Source: Siemens.

ability for carriers to figure out ways to increase switching capacity. Wireless network designers have similar challenges.

2. If the overall cell load approaches 80–85%, the entire system will bog down.

3. Cell size diminishes as user data rates increase in GPRS, and depending on the coding scheme used, the effective cell size can decrease by as much as 82% of the original size.

EDGE provides significantly higher data rates (11.2–59.2 kbps per time slot that in a multislot configuration translates to over 384 kbps) than Phase I of GPRS by reusing GSM carrier bandwidth and time-slot structure to provide an efficient way of increasing bit rates. From a carrier's perspective, the main drawback of EDGE is the requirement to replace all base stations and handsets with EDGE-compatible systems—a massive expense, especially for a system that is seen as temporary and transitional. EDGE is a viable migration path for TDMA, GSM, and IS-136 networks. In contrast to GPRS, which requires upgrades to the core network only, EDGE requires that both handsets and the core network be modified to accommodate a new radio interface (8PSK) that can provide three times more data capacity per time slot of GPRS (see Figure 5.4). New coding schemes have been developed to accompany the 8PSK, but their drawback is an increased signal-noise (S/N) ratio, meaning that the cell size is significantly reduced as compared to GPRS or GSM. The cost to upgrade a 2G system to EDGE is not insignificant and must include allocations for the following:

1. Handsets need to be replaced, and since most operators are subsidizing handsets, the cost will be on the order of $100–$200 per subscriber.

2. The front end of the base station has to be replaced depending on the modularity of the vendor's design. Nevertheless, we are talking about costs on the order of $100,00 per base station. If you are AT&T Wireless with 10,000 TDMA base stations you might think twice about this cost, weighing carefully whether narrowband (100 kbps) services really can generate enough additional revenue to justify the capital expenditures.

3. More backhaul bandwidth will be needed, which must be purchased from network owners that may be owners (NTT for NTT DoCoMo) or competitors, leading to higher prices than in a totally free market.

4. Extra network elements need to be added to the mobile switching center.

Figure 5.4
Radio interface features

System	Feature	Description
EDGE	Channel Bandwidth	200 KHz
	Access Scheme	Time Division Multiple Access
	Time slots	8
	Speech Frame Length	4.615 ms
	Speech CODEC	Adaptive Multi-rate (AMR)
	Data Rate	384 kbps maximum
	Modulation	GMSK and 8-PSK
	Handoff	Hard
	Timing	Asynchronous

Source: Ericsson ITU.

5.4 TECHNOLOGIES FOR MOBILE STATION GEOLOCATION AND E911

Prompted by the success of 911 services for fixed telephone users and the growing number of mobile users in the United States (44 million to 67 million between 1996 and 1998), the U.S. Congress has mandated that the FCC insure compliance with regulations regarding a mobile service called Enhanced 911, which require mobile service providers in the United States to equip their infrastructure (by October 2001) with the ability to locate a stressed mobile user calling 911 to within 125 meters. As a consequence, the U.S. operators have invested considerable money and time in selecting their own technological solutions to the E911 mandate, though most operators did not make this deadline.

A number of E911 location determination technologies (LDTs) were being considered by the operators. Operators are free to choose their implementation, including assisted-GPS location, network-based methods such as radiolocation measurements by the base station, hybrid methods where the mobile station and the base station are used, and, finally, mobile station based methods. CdmaOne systems operators should find it rather straightforward to do geo-location because cdma base stations already use a GPS pilot signal to synchronize their internal clocks. Thus, the cdma base stations can send simplified GPS signaling to the cdma phone.

CHAPTER 6

THE WIRELESS
INTERNET MARKET

6.1   MIGRATION OF 2G AND 3G CELLULAR SYSTEMS

As Figure 6.1 shows, the industry generally expects to see a gradual migration from second generation (2G) services, such as GSM and TDMA, to 3G services.

The Promise of the Wireless Internet

The seductive lure of the wireless Internet is that it will combine the best of both worlds, mobile voice and data. The Internet will be brought to a new audience, becoming a ubiquitous phenomenon, and the mobile handset will assume a much greater role in our lives. As a result, a far greater proportion of GDP will revolve around mobile communications. In a recent note, the Global Mobile Commerce Forum commented that consumer brands such as McDonalds and Reebok view mobile communications as their main competitor for leisure spending.

We are already beginning to see new mobile Internet portals emerge as well as the start of intense innovation in devices such as mobile phones and handheld computers. Over the next decade we expect that a new industry focused on mobility and the Internet will emerge that results in a massive dislocation in the power of current clusters related to wireless, Internet, and

Figure 6.1
Subscriber growth during migration from 2G to 3G

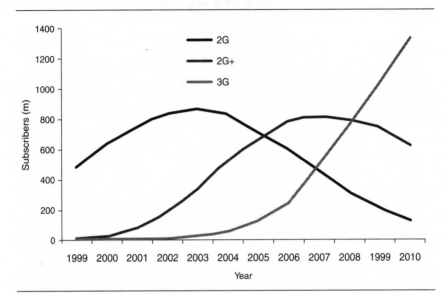

Note: Enchanced second-generation subscribers also use 2G, and 3G subscribers also use 2G+ and 2G.
Source: Ovum.

other technologies, perhaps even automobiles, if telematic excellence becomes the key basis for differentiation (not a prediction, just to make the
point that, once a shift this big stars, it doesn't have clear boundaries).

As Figure 6.2 shows, within three to four years more mobile phones will
access the Internet than personal computers.

The capabilities and limitations of the PC as an interface have defined our
whole perception of the Internet, when the Internet is about boundlessness.
The services that have succeeded on the Internet to date have done so because they are well suited for delivery over this media.

The extension of the Internet to the mobile devices is providing a new
channel for the distribution of existing Internet services but also bringing to
the fore a whole new range of Internet services. The ability of the mobile device to deliver personalized, location-sensitive content and applications to
users when and where they want them will open up the door to services that
were previously either impossible or impractical.

Furthermore, the use of mobile Internet devices for bandwidth-hungry
data services, including video and entertainment, will have a corresponding

Figure 6.2
Number of mobile internet subscribers to overtake fixed Internet subscribers

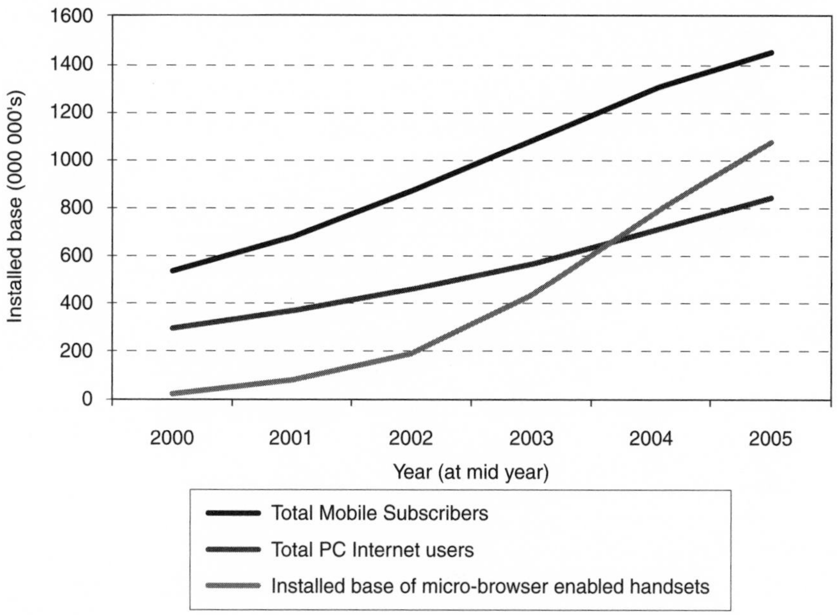

Source: Ovum and OC.

impact on the value proposition for operators, who will increasingly seek alliances with media companies and content providers (see Figure 6.3).

6.2 SUN JAVA, IBM, INTEL, AND QUALCOMM'S BREW

You can expect IBM, Intel, Sun, Qualcomm, and others to start vying for technology mind share in the wireless data area. Intel and Qualcomm in particular have a great deal at stake in the future 3G and 4G markets. Intel realizes, after the emergence of Transmeta whose market capitalization was worth over $1 billion, at one point, that low-power computer chips are critical to the success of wireless ubiquitous computing and that if they do not offer solutions, other competitors will. Thus, Intel is pushing hard to make its Xscale (formerly known as StrongARM) processor the core to the platform of choice for wireless data systems. Other major players are preparing to enter this market, including IBM, which has given a free ride to Intel for decades, through purchases, investment, cooperation, and not competing as hard as it could be for Intel's business, though signs indicate that this is about to change.

IBM has a treasure chest—no, make that a warehouse—of technology for 3G and 4G to draw upon.

1. *Silicon germanium process.* IBM is manufacturing various RF chips with this technology including 802.11b chip set for Intersil. In June 2001 IBM announced that it had built a prototype silicon germanium transistor that could switch at 210 GHz, far above anything else in the industry today.
2. *Low-power microprocessors.* This is an area where IBM has not really flexed its muscles but could in the next two years.
3. IBM has been making subsystems for both of the two leading wearable computing companies, Via and Xybernaut, as of mid-2001, and has an extensive research and development (R&D) program in pervasive computing, though to date it makes a bit too much of a Linux watch that just tells time.

Figure 6.3
Voice versus data revenues

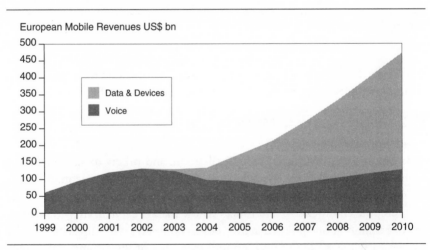

Note: The data and devices figures in this chart do not include access to WAP services via a circuit-switched voice connection, or SMS revenues, but do include machine-to-machine data traffic revenues.

Source: Nomura research.

4. IBM is integrating 802.11b functionality into some of its new laptops, manufacturing the antenna into the frame to have the Personal Computer Memory Card International Association (PCMCIA) or PC card slot.

5. IBM actually makes and sells its own GPS chip set and can be expected to continue development on its own internal RF design capabilities.

NTT DoCoMo is working with Sun Microsystems to incorporate JAVA in all of its future 3G i-mode phones, which, when combined with another feature that NTT DoCoMo is incorporating—GPS, will provide the platform for a whole range of location-based services.

Qualcomm has released its Binary Runtime Environment for Wireless (BREW) software platform, which is designed to act as a sort of application programming interface (API) on wireless data systems such as mobile phones. BREW takes up about 20 KB of memory and supports applications written in C++, a kind of object-based extension of the C programming language. Qualcomm claims that BREW applications use roughly one-fifth the memory space of Java-scripted subroutines and is offering BREW as a complement to Java. Qualcomm offers BREW at no cost to carriers, developers, and other partners in an attempt to win industry support. Interestingly, BREW is being targeted for the Japanese and Korean markets ahead of the United States. BREW runs currently on the Qualcomm cdmaOne chip set, and the company is planning to port it to other mobile manufacturer's chip sets. It is too early to make a call on the battle between Java and BREW, but one could argue that what the industry really needs is a complete real-time operating microkernel for 3G and 4G systems (see a later chapter on the importance of real-time operating systems in the 4G world), though these memory-conserving enhancements are steps in the right direction and magnetically attract ever more software developers into the wireless world.

Mobile e-Commerce

Mobile commerce combines SIM card software programming with SMS and cell broadcast, thus enabling operators to offer a new array of services. A GSM MoU Mobile Commerce Forum for operators and manufacturers that meets regularly in Europe has already been formed.

In Hong Kong, SmarTone, Hong Kong Consumer Subscriber Line (CSL), and Hutchison are all pursuing mobile commerce service offerings. Our view is that SmarTone and Hong Kong CSL are probably three to five months ahead of Hutchison. Nevertheless, Hutchison has been closely following the U.K. mobile commerce pilot that was carried out by Cellnet and Barclays Bank.

Within the GSM camp there are two different schemes being developed for mobile commerce. The first one is the specifications included in GSM Phase 2+ that stipulates a SIM card toolkit and programming interface. SIM cards are being developed by companies such as GEMPLUS and Schlumberger that will have CPU, RAM, volatile memory, and even ROM onboard the chip.

We expect, therefore, SIM card manufacturers to begin to play a pivotal role in the development of future mobile communications similar to the role that Intel has played in the development of the PC.

Manufacturers such as Nokia are not happy with ceding so much control to the SIM card manufacturers and, as a consequence, are developing an alternative approach—wireless access protocol (WAP). WAP allows the manufacturers and operators to place control programs and applications on the mobile handset's on-board CPU(s). Software can be loaded at production time, at the customer service center, or even via the radio interface of the cellular network.

6.3 MARKET FOR LOCATION-BASED MOBILE SERVICES

In the United States location-based services are receiving increased attention, especially in the retail sector, as a number of portal sites and shopping mall management companies are offering retailers the chance to beam advertisements and information to shoppers's cell phones as they near or enter the shopping mall premises. According to Cliff Raskind,[1] a senior industry analyst at Strategy Analytics, location-based services in the United States will reach $7 billion by 2005.

Location-based services actually were introduced in Japan and the United Kingdom ahead of the United States. One of the large mobile service providers offered a double phone package that enabled, for example, a wife to buy a mobile phone for herself and another one for her husband. Then, during the day and most likely at night the wife could check up on her children or her husband by dialing a special number that would tell her the cell site location of the other mobile phone or phones. The answer to the question "Honey, where are you now?" can become a rather incriminating experience for the wireless user who is unaware that he or she is being watched by a spouse's new invisible eye.

NOTES

1. Planet IT (December 12, 2000).

CHAPTER 7

THIRD GENERATION
(3G) SYSTEMS

As plans move forward, European business leaders and politicians could barely stop gloating [about 3G]. For once, the Old World appeared to be leading the U.S. in the development of an important new technology. Mobile telephony, they said, would create a brave new wireless world and perhaps even give birth to an economic miracle. President Clinton warned that unless U.S. tech companies quickly got involved in 3G, there would be a wireless gap . . .

Wall Street Journal, 5 June 2001, p. 1

7.1 EXECUTIVE SUMMARY OF 3G

1. European operators spent far too much money on 3G spectrum because spectrum efficiency in 3G is not much improved over 2G systems, indicating a gap between engineers and executives, who should have more prudently factored technology issues into their bids.

2. The only winners in the 3G auction mania in Europe were the government tax collectors (the United Kingdom Labour party won a landslide victory in 2001 in part because its budget had a nice windfall), but this was done at the expense of the financial health of the wireless operators whose debts have skyrocketed, leading to deterioration in their bond ratings and facing class action law suits by disgruntled shareholders, all of which distract from building new networks.

3. The Japanese government did not take an ax to the balance sheets of its champions as did European governments, but essentially gave away the spectrum to three national operators: Japan Telecom, NTT DoCoMo, and KDDI. Despite the hype, NTT DoCoMo stunned the industry when it announced just prior to its 3G commercial launch in May 2001 that it would only do a soft launch with 4,500 subscribers and hinted that the "real" launch might have to be delayed by one to two years. One of the reasons for 3G pessimism in Japan is that the W-CDMA system

from NTT DoCoMo is not able to deliver an average throughput per user above 64 kbps. It is like installing DSL for 10 times the price of a dial-up line and then learning that the real data rate was maybe 3 times the dial-up line's capacity.

4. China will have to reconsider its strategy of adopting Time Division-Synchronous Code Division Multiple Access (TD-SCDMA) and possibly wait for 4G systems that really can deliver on promises made for 3G but undelivered of mobile data rates greater than 1 Mbps per user, or greater than 40 Mbps per cell.

5. Our impression is that 3G systems are waystations rather than destinations and will be a short-lived migration path from 2G and 2.5 systems to 4G, if at all. We expect that most operators will end up upgrading their systems to GPRS and a more limited number to EDGE. In general, Europe and Asia will convert from GSM (Global Standard for Mobile communications), whose widespread adoption has given them the lead in wireless technology, to W-CDMA (Wideband Code Division Multiple Access). In North America, CDMA (Code Division Multiple Access) networks, such as Sprint's and GTE's, will also migrate to W-CDMA. But TDMA (Time Division Multiple Access) systems, such as AT&T's and Southwestern Bell's, plan to go to EDGE (Enhanced Data Rates for Global Evolution). Presently, a number of mobile carriers around the globe are in the process of upgrading their GSM networks to GPRS and EDGE. EDGE employs a totally different modulation scheme, Eight-Phase Shift Keying (8PSK), which requires a 7 to 10 dB higher signal-to-noise ratio (SNR), leading to a factor of 5 decrease in average cell size. The theoretical maximum data rate of EDGE is 384 kbps as compared to W-CDMA's much faster 2 Mbps (we must note though that the aggregate cell capacity of W-CDMA with 10 MHz of spectrum is 3.8 Mbps).

7.2 IMT-2000 3G CONCEPT

International Mobile Communications in the Year 2000 (IMT-2000) is the ITU blanket name for the third generation of mobile radio systems. The stated performance objectives for UMTS/IMT-2000 systems are to feature high-speed data transmission, Internet access, wireless packet data, and various multimedia services. In terms of capacity, UMTS/IMT-2000 systems are supposed to provide voice and low-rate services as well as high-speed services up to at least 144 kbps in moving cars, 384 kbps while walking, and up to 2 Mbps when standing still or inside a building with a picocell base station.

The goals of UMTS/IMT-2000 are lofty, but the problem is that European governments decided to turn 3G into a taxation rape, plunging the 3G operators into an abyss of debt with little or no hope of ever recovering its investments in spectrum, at least not with the 3G technology on offer in 2001.

7.3 SPECTRUM AUCTION INSANITY IN EUROPE!

Auction prices for 3G spectrum in Europe reached astronomical proportions. Finland was the first country to license 3G operators in March 1999, awarding four licenses out of an initial 15 applications to existing operators Radiolinja (first in 2G), Sonera, Telia Mobile, plus Suomen Kolmegee. Finland set a good example, which was ignored, by foregoing its powers of coercion and giving away 3G licenses. The United Kingdom, followed by Italy and Germany, and then the rest of Europe had auctions for 3G spectrum. The United States followed suit with its own madness for 2G spectrum on January 2001. When it was over, EU operators had paid over $100 billion for the 3G spectrum (see Figure 7.1). Now they will have to dish out another $100 billion to build out the network. On 5 June 2001 the *Wall Street Journal* ran a front-page article "How Europe Tripped Over a Wireless Phone for the Internet—User 'WAPathy' a Concern." It is not surprising that EU telecoms stocks were down 60% from their peak some 13 months earlier or that the financial institutions were talking about downgrading EU telecom operator bonds and that shareholders of those companies were talking about class action suits.

These outrageous fees had the effect of driving up the cost of 2G spectrum in the United States (see Figure 7.2). According to the *Wall Street Journal*, worldwide telecom debts have reached a staggering $650 billion including those from fiber-optic operators, many of which are bloated with excess

Figure 7.1

House of horrors in Europe

EU Operator	Amount Paid for 3G Licenses (US$ in billions)	Outstanding Debt (US$ in billions)
Vodaphone	17.30	9.33
France Telecom	19.84	50.88
British Telecom	14.50	40.70
KPN	7.55	19.50
Deutsche Telecom	13.48	48.34

Source: Advantis; *Wall Street Journal,* June 5, 2001.

capacity. If they can't make money now, it will be even more difficult when competition from computer companies and technologies, quietly evolving within the unlicensed band or the military, are brought to market by small, aggressive, debt-free, high-tech-driven newcomers.

7.4 THE LOOSE FEDERATION OF HARMONIZED UMTS/IMT-2000 3G STANDARDS

One of the great euphemisms of the IMT-2000 movement was the adoption of the term 'harmonization'. The ITU was deeply involved in the process of developing uniform specifications for the 3G systems under the title of IMT-2000 within the framework of Future Public Land Mobile Telecommunications Systems (FPLMTS). The principal political purpose of ITU in proposing IMT-2000 was to harmonize allocation and use of radio spectrum worldwide. However, due to political and vendor lobbying, at one time there were at least seven different air interface standards being proposed, and after two years of political maneuverings no one dominant air interface emerged. In the end, only two options were filtered and five major systems resulted for the IMT-2000—this process of having competing systems and then adopting them altogether is called harmonization. Each of these systems differs in terms of the radio interface (timing, modulation, power control, handoff, etc.).

UMTS is the European version of IMT-2000 and is touted as a migration

Figure 7.2
Relative costs of new 2G and 3G spectrum

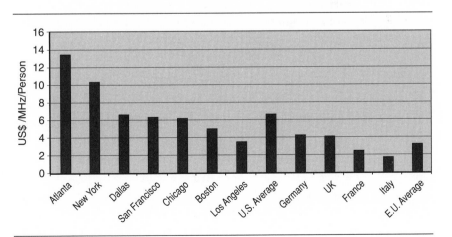

Source: Nomura International.

path for GSM systems (in Western Europe up to 70% of adults now use a GSM phone). The GSM operators in Europe have selected TD-CDMA as the air interface. In the United States, the CTIA wants to make UWC-136 the migration path for IS-136, and cdma2000 the migration path for IS-95 and a wideband packet CDMA (WP-CDMA) system.

The harmonization was necessary because of the contentious arguments that arose over 3G. Probably the most heated debates were between NTT DoCoMo with its W-CDMA system and Qualcomm with its cdma2000 system, and between Ericsson and Qualcomm concerning CDMA patents. Qualcomm needed better international lawyers to argue its case, just as it needed better PR people through most of the 1980s, because it owned much of the core technology but didn't protect it as well as it could have, and certainly didn't have the government officials going to bat for it as its rivals did. We would have preferred that if the United States had a trade dispute it used its political capital to protect wireless (a trillion dollar value added, over 1% of the value of the entire wealth in the United States) instead of bananas, a far less strategic resource.

Roughly analogous to the Beta versus VHS standards wars, the W-CDMA versus cdma2000 war has its technical arguments and of course its political/intellectual property aspects. Qualcomm has not been perceived to offer low royalties, and the Japanese felt that it was better to use a system in which they had a significant amount of intellectual property. The Europeans, of course, wanted to make sure that GSM operators could migrate as painlessly as possible, and thus, began in 1998 to 1999 a foray of vendors, governments, and standards bodies trying to persuade each other that their home-grown system was superior. (As if the market had nothing to say on the matter.) So much for claims about rampant capitalism. Socialism still rules European telecom.

Although, surprisingly, Japan played virtually no significant role in the development of GSM systems, its giant firms are like sumo wrestlers itching to take on middleweight boxers in Ultimate Wrestling and are actively involved in the development of 3G systems. In early 1997 Japan selected CDMA as the national digital 2G standard. Immediately following the announcement by the MPT in Japan, two operators, DDI and IDO, confirmed $3 billion capital expenditure commitments to roll-out cdmaOne in late 1998 and early 1999. However, NTT announced that it would go with its W-CDMA system for 3G. In other words, even in Japan there was no harmonization as different operators backed different horses. A number of companies including Ericsson and Nokia were working closely with NTT DoCoMo on the latter's 3G W-CDMA system, so it should not be a surprise that the two vendors ended up on the side of the NTT DoCoMo camp when the standards wars erupted in 1999.

If that were not enough, China, which had agreed to let China Unicom install cdmaOne systems, suddenly did a policy U-turn and declared that Unicom did not have permission to install cdmaOne. When all the 3G smoke cleared, we were left with the following outcomes:

1. Ericsson and Qualcomm settled their dispute when Ericsson acquired Qualcomm's technology business unit and its patents in CDMA for over $6 million.
2. China's MII declared the Chinese Academy of Sciences and Siemens' TD-SCDMA the standard for China.
3. NTT DoCoMo stuck to its guns and kept its W-CDMA standard basically intact while KDDI was forced to follow Qualcomm and Motorola because its 2G system is cdmaOne.
4. The ITU and ETSI agreed to adopt three CDMA radio transmission technologies for CDMA and two technologies for TDMA systems:
   - IMT-2000 CDMA Systems:
     Frequency Division Duplex (FDD)/Direct Spread (DS). W-CDMA (e.g., NTT DoCoMo, Ericsson, Nokia). The W-CDMA standard became unified through the cooperation of a number of organizations including ETSI, TIP1 (USA), Association of Radio Industries and Business Telecommunication Technology Committee (ARIB/ TTC; Japan), and TTA (Korea) through the auspices of the 3G Partnership Project (3GPP). The operators also played an important role in the harmonization process through their own association which they called the Operators Harmonization Group (OHG): This group of operators represented carriers who were using a myriad of 2G standards including GSM 900/1800, PDC, IS-136, and IS-95.

     Frequency Division Duplex (FDD)/Multiple-Carrier (MC). cdma2000 (Lucent, Motorola, Qualcomm).

     Time Division Duplex (TC). TD-CDMA/TD-SCDMA (People's Republic of China) ETSI worked closely with Siemens and the PRC's MII to harmonize the two systems for inclusion in the family of IMT-2000 systems. TD-CDMA refers to the UMTS terrestrial radio access (UTRA) that had been promoted by the ETSI.

- IMT-2000 TDMA Systems

    Single Carrier. Enhanced Data rate for global evolution or enhanced data rate for GSM evolution (EDGE)

    Multi-Carrier. Digital European cordless telecommunications (DECT).

3G thus is not a single standard or technology but an umbrella term for a variety of approaches to bringing high-speed Internet services to cell phone networks. In most cases, 3G will come from updates and upgrades to current systems, which differ from continent to continent and from country to country. Most 3G networks will start off as hybrids, with new capabilities added gradually as demand dictates.

The differences between the three CDMA systems deal with the intricate details of the radio modulation and overall radio interface systems as well as with various details about how base stations communicate with each other and with the mobile handset (see Figure 7.3). Both the cdmaOne and W-CDMA systems are optimized for a mix of voice and data users. The peak data rate is limited to reserve capacity for voice users. Mixed power and rate control are used to maximize overall system capacity.

The three CDMA camps had been in disagreement over certain critical technical issues for a long time regarding things such as chip rate and synchronization versus asynchronous operation of the base stations. The NTT DoCoMo-led W-CDMA camp wanted a chip rate of 3.84 Mcps (mega chips per second) while the cdma2000 camp needed a rate of 3.6864 Mcps, which would make cdma2000 upwards compatible with cdmaOne 2G systems.

Although it appears that there is not much difference between the two chip rates, the fact is that existing cdmaOne systems need to be able to migrate to cdma2000 systems, and the only way to do this is to have the cdma2000 systems operate at a multiple of the cdmaOne chip rate which is equal to 1.2288 Mcps (i.e., $3.6864 = 3 \times 1.2288$). If the ITU had selected a single rate that was not a multiple of 1.2288 Mcps then cdmaOne systems would be rendered non-upgradable; thus, there is an element of politics involved even down to the esoteric choice of the chip rate—another example of why it's so tricky for wireless execs to choose their allies and systems.

As shown in Figure 7.3, another subtle but critical feature of the North American cdma2000 system is the use of GPS for the synchronization between base stations. The W-CDMA system from Japan does not use GPS and is a very important feature for the Japanese. Why? Because if a country is dependent on the GPS system to run its entire cellular network then they could

Figure 7.3
Comparison of IMT-2000 3G CDMA-based radio transmission schemes

System	Feature	Description
W-CDMA	Spectrum	5 MHz
	Duplex mode	FDD
	Spread Spectrum	Direct Sequence
	Chip rate	3.84 Mcps
	Modulation	QPSK/BPSK with HPSK spreading
	Speech CODEC	Adaptive Multi-rate (AMR)
	Timing	Asynchronous (synchronous mode supported)
	Power Control	Fast open loop and closed loop power control at 1600 Hz
	Handoff	Soft/Softer
	Network signaling	Phase 1: GSM/MAP
		Phase 2: ANSI-41
cdma2000	Spectrum	5 MHz/1.25 MHz IS-95 overlay
	Duplex mode	FDD
	Frame Length	5 or 20 ms
	Speech CODEC	EVRC and Selectable Mode Vocoder (SMV)
	Spread Spectrum	Multicarrier
	Chip rate	3.6864/1.228 Mcps
	Modulation	ZPSK/BPSK with QPSK spreading
	Timing	GPS synchronous
	Power Control	Fast open loop and closed loop power control at 800 Hz
	Handoff	Soft/Softer
	Network signaling	Phase 1: ANSI-41
		Phase 2: GSM/MAP
UTRA/TD-SCDMA	Spectrum	5 MHz/1.6 MHz
	Duplex mode	TDD
	Time slots	15
	Spread Spectrum	TDD
	Modulation	QPSK and/or 16 QAM
	Chip rate	3.84 Mcps
	Power control	100–800 Hz
	Timing	Synchronous
	Handoff	Hard/Baton
	Network signaling	Phase 1: GSM/MAP
		Phase 2: ANSI-41

Source: Ericsson, ITU.

be held hostage to GPS politics in the future, and thus choice of a system rests on how well Japan's military and intelligence communities get along with Americans, which in turn ties technology to volatile events, such as how the prosecution of a Marine who rapes an Okinawan teenage girl is handled (sadly, not a rare source of tensions). It's easy for Americans, who have not experienced foreign invasion or occupation for over a century, to dismiss Japanese and European fears (only Pancho Villa dared try in the twentieth century—he went into New Mexico before it was a state, shot up a town, then bolted before sunset), but Japan has been occupied by the U.S. military since WWII, even though U.S. bases in other areas, notably the Philippines, have been closed. Korea, facing a fierce, erratic foe across the DMZ, has different strategic motivations and wants to be tied into U.S. military systems. Japan is more ambivalent about this. Though the book *A Japan That Can Say No* was a bestseller, there was no Korean counterpart. Military control is one of the reasons that the Chinese standard, TD-SCDMA, does not use GPS timing although generally this is not mentioned in any "official" documents. Very senior officials admitted this to us, and we passed it on to Paul Jacobs at Qualcomm during Red Herring's Venture conference. His response was to say the Russians had had the same complaint, but that it could be handled. We don't know how this legitimate concern can be overcome, and thus cdma-2000 will have a very hard time of it and not meet projections for international uptake (recall how fast Nokia's GSM was adopted).

Think of it like a marathon race through a California forest where runners are allowed to use GPS to find their way. However, if they are foreign, they must carry a uniformed member of the military on their back, and if they complain about the burden, he will shut off the GPS (or put a blindfold on) and get the runner lost.

For the GSM manufacturers, their key interest has been (1) to replace the TDMA radio interface with a wideband CDMA radio interface and (2) to maintain the existing back-end of the GSM standard which includes roaming and various enhanced services.

7.5 W-CDMA 3G NETWORKS DO LITTLE TO IMPROVE SPECTRAL EFFICIENCY

Apart from the enormous sums spent on 3G spectrum, cell site capacity is a major issue for 3G, as the total available data rate per cell does not exceed 3.9 Mbps, thus making even the provision of a few hundred kbps per user a very costly proposition.

3G networks should arrive in Europe in 2002 and the United States in

2003. Unlike the previous two generations of cellular networks, 3G systems have been designed specifically to carry data as well as voice. Carriers promise downloads approaching 2 Mbps—twice as fast as wired broadband services, and fast enough to bombard cell phones, handhelds, and laptops with video, music, and games. But there is a growing chorus warning that 3G will not be all it's cracked up to be, and, in fact, the consensus is building that 3G operators will not be able to promise or count on revenue related to less than 100 kbps per user, meaning that it will not significantly improve on 2.5G GPRS/EDGE systems. This is like saying you can get a Toyota Corolla for the price of a Corolla, or for the price of Ferrari, but it's called Ferrari-Cola because Toyota licenses the brand name. Which do you choose? Probably the Corolla. However, what if you had already contracted to buy the Ferrari-Cola because your trusted advisors told you it would perform even better than a Ferrari because that's what they thought would allow them to keep their positions? To come back to wireless, it might seem, given that 3G doesn't offer compelling return on investment (ROI) position with respect to 2.5G, that if you were faced with the decision, you wouldn't proceed.

What if you had already sunk billions into 3G licenses and had promised shareholders and governments? You might, like the townspeople in the parable of the Emperor's New Clothes, then pretend you see the clothes or the ROI, and just build your network and hope for better advice in the future or simply sell your company and get a golden parachute, leaving the investors to eat the billion dollar mistakes.

Figure 7.4 compares the maximum capacities or data bit rates that 2G, 2.5G, and 3G cell sites can support. We can see from this chart that 3G CDMA systems really do not improve spectrum efficiency at all. In fact, the use of TDD is a rehash of the 2G GSM systems. The reason we are facing a bandwidth choke point now is that time division multiplexing has already yielded about as much extra spectrum as we can ever expect using this suite of algorithms. We can't make more time by making ever-bigger watches with smaller and smaller increments marked off. We need more watches, newer watches, and watches run as one of many downloadable applications run on computers rather than gears and springs.

Shannon's Law teaches us that there is only so much information that can be delivered in a given bandwidth with a given SNR, and we are now approaching his theoretical limit. The total bandwidth of a 3G base station is 3.9 Mbps, which translates to 3.9 Mbps/5Mhz to yield 780 kbps per MHz. A typical GSM base station can support 40 simultaneous users for 1 MHz of spectrum or 40×13 kbps $= 532$ kbps per MHz of spectrum. Hence, the capacity

Figure 7.4

Performance comparison of 2G, 2.5G, and 3G systems

Performance	3G W-CDMA (3.86 Mcps)	GPRS	EDGE
Carrier Bandwidth (MHz)	5.0	0.2	0.2
Peak Downlink Data Rate Per User (kbps)	2,000	128	384
Actual capacity available to each user (kbps)	100	170 raw, average 128	200–240
Number of Spatial Channels	1	1	1
Number of Carriers per 10 MHz spectrum	2 (TDD)	50	50
Spectral Efficiency bps/Hz/cell	0.1	0.18	0.18

Source: ArrayComm.

improvements from 3G cannot justify the huge costs associated with spectrum auctions and network build-out. The executives who admit this will be remembered with respect for a long time to come, though they will probably be terminated or leave to pursue other interests.

One of the key parameters that greatly impacts the business model is the spectral efficiency of the wireless system. In the case of 3G W-CDMA, it is estimated to be no more than 0.1 bps/Hz/cell, which, practically speaking, means that that total throughput of a cell base station will be less than 4 Mbps so that each user in a cell must share the bandwidth. CDMA was selected by the ETSI for 3G because it is very tolerant of noise and difficult to intercept or interfere with although it uses a lot more spectrum than the signals alone require.

Ironically, governments charge billions more for security on one hand, and then insist that this security be easily defeated by anyone with a badge on the other hand, leading to security lapses so that more spectrum is called for in the next iteration. What a racket. Too bad RICO (racketeering and organized crime statutes in the United States) don't apply to governments. Then the operators could get their money back without legal recourse if their system security is weakened or compromised by government entities or their contractors.

W-CDMA and CDMA are based on a technology known as spread spectrum. Older cellular technologies such as GSM and TDMA use a variant of the approach taken by ordinary radio stations—namely, they divide the radio spectrum into narrow frequency bands. To add capacity, these networks can interleave several phone calls on each frequency channel, but there is a tight limit to how many users can share a channel before the signal quality suffers. CDMA, on the other hand, assigns each phone call a particular code. Multiple radio signals can then share a fairly wide range of radio frequencies. Each phone will pick up the transmissions intended for it by watching for its code. In some implementations of spread spectrum, the transmitter and receiver hopscotch among frequencies in a prearranged sequence.

Although spread-spectrum systems have their inefficiencies—with all the overhead to determine which messages are going to which phone, they tend to use a lot more bandwidth than the signals alone require—they are very tolerant of noise and are difficult to intercept or interfere with. CDMA uses channels 1.25 MHz wide in the 800 MHz or 1.9 GHz bands. W-CDMA channels are 5, 10, 15, or 20 MHz wide in several bands located around 2 GHz, which allows for faster data rates and more users.

Though 3G has been promising a 2 Mbps connection (just type "3G" and "2 Mbps" into the Google.com search engine and see for yourself that it's still being touted this way, though cheerleaders, red-faced, have admitted that this just isn't so). In fact, this describes a raw data pipe that is shared among all the users on a 10 MHz radio channel in one cell. If there are many users in your cell using serious business applications, downloading large files, streaming multimedia, or anything else 3G is supposed to deliver, then the data rate will drop sharply for everyone. The only remedy, using conventional wisdom, is to have fewer people allocated per base station, i.e., build more of them. In fact some industry players have proposed surrounding us with small picocells placed every 10 meters. This obviously has an economic limit, and it is for this reason that NTT DoCoMo of Japan, the world's first to commercially roll out a 3G trial in June 2001, is taking a pragmatic approach. They are only promising 64 kbps commercial service at launch (much more expensive 384 kbps "showcase professional" service will be selectively offered to a small number of users only).

NTT DoCoMo shows a sound strategy for next-generation telecom success: Promise only what you can deliver, but get out there first, even with a small group, and start gaining real-world experience with paying customers before making big boasts and promises. And be smart enough to base your operations in a country with a strategic national plan to lead in wireless, thereby getting spectrum handed over for free and saving the time and distraction in hundreds of little ways compared with companies in continental Europe and the United States, where there are thousands of petty tyrants in multiple agencies of government.

3G networks will offer just over 1 Mbps when the entire overhead is taken into account, but that's not 1 Mbps per user because the bandwidth will be shared among everyone in a particular cell (the geographical areas covered by a single cell tower), which could be dozens of people at a time on each channel. Users should expect 64 kbps from 3G networks at best, a privilege for which they will unhappily have to pay a handsome premium, or get subsidized by an operator eager to buy market share, dot-com style. Although quite an improvement on current wireless networks, 3G, at least as of mid-2001, is only marginally faster than an ordinary modem and hardly enough to justify all the futuristic claims made for the networks.

When we consider that Microsoft spent $1 billion to promote a major product like Windows 95, an amount that was seen as excessive, the $100 billion spent on 3G seems like a big rip-off. At least Microsoft stakeholders got the Rolling Stones singing "Start Me Up" and Jay Leno making software jokes. With 3G there's not even a T-shirt or trademark to build a brand around. All this sets the stage for something better: 4G, coming sooner than 2010 as had been predicted by the National Science Foundation and the head of Qualcomm.

First, though, let's look at what 3G networks will need, even if they are to be used as transitional systems, much less if they are supposed to prosper for the 20-year license periods.

Figure 7.5
Architectural concepts of IMT-2000 networks with IP fixed line backbones

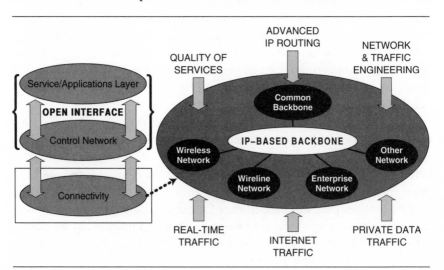

Source: Ericsson, Pyramid Research.

7.6   3G NETWORKS WILL NEED BROADBAND IP FIXED INFRASTRUCTURE

A number of telecom makers and mobile service providers have teamed up to form an industry consortium called 3G.IP that has the mission of developing a common 3G network architecture strategy for backhaul and mobile switching centers (see Figure 7.5 and Figure 7.6). A common architecture is sorely needed in order to tap and leverage the awesome firepower of the application development community, including software and content. NTT DoCoMo has been one of the most aggressive service providers in this area because of its insistence on using an Asynchronous Transfer Mode (ATM) switch architecture in which base stations will have an ATM-compatible

Figure 7.6
3G.IP network reference model (early 2000)

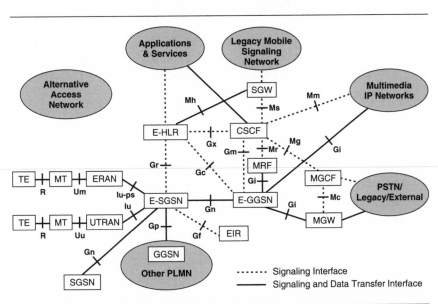

Note: TE = Terminal Equipment. MT = Mobile Termination. ERAN = EDGE Radio Access Network. EDGE = Ehanced Data rates for Global Evolution. UTRAN = UMTS Radio Access Network. UMTS = Universal Mobile Telecommunications Services. E-HLR = Enhanced Home Location Register SGSN Serving GPRS Support Node. GPRS = General Packet Radio Service. GGSN = Gateway GPRS Support Node. PLMN = Public Land Mobile Network. PSTN = Public Switched Telephone Network. CSCF = Call State Control Function. EIR = Equipment Identify Register. MRF = Multiple Resource Function. MGW = Media Gateway. IP = Internet Protocol. E-SGSN = Enhanced SGSN. E-GGSN = Enhanced GGSN. SGW = Signaling Gateway.

Source: www.3GIP.org

port. In the case of 2G GSM networks, the backhaul accounts for roughly 9% of the total capital expenditures, but in a 3G network this proportion could double to 20%. As Tom Peters might put it, "BACKHAUL MAT-TERS! A LOT!" Ask the next wireless exec you meet (or the team at the next financial meeting, if you are an exec) what proportion of expenses is for backhaul. It'll probably be higher than you thought in either case.

Moreover, even if the capacity of 3G base stations was not an issue, the ability for the backhaul to scale up with user demand is going to make the mobile service provider look more and more like an Internet Data Services provider than a traditional wireless operator. Put another way, wireline companies that are laying dense wave division multiplexing (DWDM) metro networks may want to consider getting more involved with the cellular business because they start off, potentially, with a 20% cost savings. We would not be surprised to find companies like MCI WorldCom in the 3G or future 4G wireless businesses since they will be increasingly advantaged, in an era when cost-cutting is king.

PART III

PERVASIVE COMPUTING

CHAPTER 8

THE INCREDIBLE
SHRINKING COMPUTER

8.1 FIFTY-THREE YEARS OF ELECTRONIC COMPUTER TECHNOLOGY

Do you know how many microprocessors your new car has? There are likely more than twenty. Some experts are predicting that each car manufactured in 2006 will have over 100 microprocessors. Embedded microprocessors made by companies such as Motorola and Advance RISC Machines (ARM) are used to control everything from electronic dashboards, ignition systems, fuel control, and exhaust systems.

It has been a little over 50 years since the first large scale electronic computer, the Electronic Numerical Integrator and Calculator (ENIAC) was built at the University of Pennsylvania, and it has been over 53 years since Shockley, Brattain, and Bardeen invented the germanium transistor at Bell Labs (see Figure 8.1). The ENIAC computer contained some 18,000 vacuum tubes and could perform a decimal arithmetic function in about 0.5 milliseconds. In those days several companies, such as Raytheon and RCA, had projects trying to develop electronic computers out of vacuum tubes. ENIAC was the only one that really worked. Who would have imagined that in just 50 years the ENIAC, which required the space of a large room to house and the electrical power of a small town to operate, could be reduced to a silicon chip the size of a thumbnail?

In the spring of 1947, Thomas J. Watson Sr. set out to prove that IBM could build the best scientific computer, and by the end of that year, IBM engineers completed a million dollar machine called the Selective Sequence Electronic Calculator. It was 120 feet long, had 12,500 vacuum tubes, and 21,400 mechanical relays.[1] It was the first computer to actually run on software and clearly represented the "start of the art." In 1947, *Time* magazine carried an article on the transistor invented by William Shockley et al., which a meticulous competitive analysis manager at IBM noticed and sent a memo to Thomas J. Watson saying, "The transistor may have application to our business." In the early 1950s a Japanese company named Sony Corporation invented the transistor radio that used silicon transistors because germanium supplies had been completely depleted during the Pacific War. By 1956 the price of a transistor was around $16.00 and was being used mainly for hearing aids. But Pat Hagerty, factory chief at a little known company called Texas Instruments (TI), believed he could get the price down to $2.50. He convinced the company to spend $2 million on designing a transistor radio targeting the mass consumer market. The gamble paid off and TI captured the transistor radio market in the United States. IBM, led by Thomas Watson Jr., asked TI to manufacture transistors in volume to bring the price per unit down, and IBM committed to purchase large quantities. The punch card system designers at IBM protested the use of transistors and refused to use anything except vacuum tubes. Finally, an insightful Watson Jr. issued a memorandum that said, "After October 1, we will design no more machines using vacuum tubes."[2]

What began was a 10-year-long battle against competitors such as Univac, Sperry, and Control Data to develop transistor-based computers. Texas Instruments further transformed the industry when it developed the first workable integrated circuits (ICs). In the early 1970s two companies, Intel and IBM Corporation, developed separately another milestone in the industry—the microprocessor. Intel, under the leadership of semiconductor pioneer Andy Grove, began manufacturing the humble 4-bit microprocessor which when combined with what was state of the art at the time, 1k DRAM chips, was used to construct the personal computer such as the Apple computer.

IBM built a multibillion dollar empire from its mainframe systems by outdesigning, outselling, and out-servicing its rivals. In 1980, IBM established a special team to develop the personal computer that, if combined with its own microprocessor technology, would have allowed IBM to offer a personal workstation that was compatible with its mainframe systems. Unfortunately for IBM, the U.S. Department of Justice's 10-year antitrust lawsuit against IBM prevented the company from cross-subsidizing the personal computer by implementing a common reduced instruction set computer (RISC) architecture across all computer platforms. IBM had to select a non–IBM operating system, and although it could have chosen UNIX from Bell Labs,[3] it decided to use the DOS operating system running on Intel's x86 microprocessor. IBM owned up to 25% of Intel's stock at the time, so they were slightly biased towards Intel. And that was how Bill Gates and Microsoft were given the clear runway with which to launch their business! It is terribly ironic that in 2000 the same Justice Department, but different people, pursued the behemoth Microsoft "monster" that it had actually helped to create two decades earlier. One has to wonder if these antitrust market interventions are really worth the tax payer's money, given that each intervention has the potential to create a new monopoly.

Data communications and voice communications have been undergoing their own sort of revolutions, capitalizing on advances in semiconductor and optical technologies. Another important area for technological progress is the field of communications software and internetworking. In the early 1970s, Bell Labs began perfecting its early versions of the UNIX operating system, which was developed for the purpose of providing network control function

Figure 8.1
Fifty-three years of electronic computing, 1948–2001

Prepared by Aaron Leventhal for Alex Lightman.

over networks such as the Public Switched Telephone Network (PSTN). DEC PDP minicomputers were the select choice of UNIX programmers, and many universities bought DEC's computer including the following on VAXes. UNIX Internetworking research at Bell Labs inspired another break-through in the industry but this time at IBM labs—the RISC, though RISC actually was independently developed at IBM Research Labs and by David Patterson at the University of California at Berkeley. The concept of RISC was to design a compiler that is optimized for the higher-level languages and is cognizant of the underlying central processing unit's (CPU) capabilities. Then it would be possible to design a CPU that was simpler, consumed less power, and could actually run the source code faster. In other words, the RISC concept was based on the notion that silicon wafers are best utilized if the physical layouts on the chip are structured and well-organized so that electrons do not have to travel in circles to get the job done. This concept was promoted heavily by Caltech's Carver Mead,[4] who argued that Intel's "spaghetti design" was not exploiting silicon properly. Thus, microprocessor and chip design, in general, began to take on an artistic challenge as well. IBM, led by Dr. John Cocke, proved Carver Mead's hunches about structured de-sign right when it demonstrated that the experimental RISC chip could run mainframe code faster in emulation mode than could the mainframe CPU.

In the mid-1970s another important and critical development took place. As Bell Labs was putting connectivity functions into its operation system, UNIX, university labs such as Caltech, Stanford, Berkeley, Carnegie Mellon, MIT, and others wanted to exchange chip designs via their computer work-stations. The U.S. government's Defense Advanced Research Projects Agency (DARPA) came to the rescue when it helped fund what later became the predecessor to the Internet when it designated a company called Bolt Beranek Newman (BBN) to implement the network. That is how the Inter-net was born. Some 25 years later the general public gets introduced to the Internet, and the stock boom on both NASDAQ and other OTC exchanges literally mesmerize the world. The UNIX computers of the mid-1970s at those DARPA-funded projects used a communications protocol called Inter-net Protocol that, unlike IBM's Systems Network Architecture (SNA) proto-col, was open to the public and subject to debate and further refining.

Thousands, millions, and now billions of transistors integrated on silicon chips and placed into various electronic and telecommunications products have become the workhorses of the digital age. The economies of scale of the Internet has further enabled hundreds of millions of people to get con-nected, searching and retrieving information (and viruses too). The process of progress then continues because as people learn more they will invent more and on and on the process continues.

In summary, the pace at which the vacuum tube from the early 1920s and 1930s became the transistor became the transistor radio became the silicon integrated circuit became the microcomputer became the digital cellular phone today will be greatly accelerated in the next 10 years. When combined with the fabulous advances taking place in materials science, in the biomedical sciences, in genetic engineering, and in quantum information theory and quantum cosmology, we must turn to science fiction set in the far future for predictions and descriptions of the society post-2010.

In the remainder of this chapter we are going to introduce a number of fundamental as well as empirically verified axioms or "truths" about information processing, storage, and communications. The key message is that physics and information processing are two sides of the same coin! The physical universe and information processing are connected by a quantum mechanical umbilical cord that most likely cannot be severed. By looking at certain axioms of the IT industry, we will search out clues to determine where the next breakthroughs will come from and how it will impact communications, computers, and information and media.

8.2   THE TRANSISTOR AND MOORE'S LAW

If the past five decades are any indication of the technological prowess of the information technology (IT) industry, then it is beneficial to ask what may lie ahead for computing. What are the fundamental physical limitations? What are the manufacturing limitations? What is theoretically possible that the industry has not even approached yet? In this chapter, we are going to take a closer look at the key technical drivers of the microelectronics and computer industries in order to build a platform for discussion of future trends. The form factors, power requirements, and functionality of 4G communication systems will be largely determined by the advances in integrated circuit design and manufacture as well as software advances.

The transistor has been the workhorse of the industry, and although there are a number of variations involving different semiconducting materials, transistors all have certain commonalities. They are three terminal devices and can serve as a switch or as an amplifier. Figure 8.2 presents a field effect transistor (FET); the three terminals are called the source, the drain, and the gate. If the voltage on the gate is zero, very little current will flow from the source to the drain. However, if the voltage is increased above a certain threshold, the current will begin to flow from source to drain proportional

Figure 8.2
Conventional three-terminal, two-state transistors

Conventional *Micro*electronic Transistor: A *Bulk-Effect* Switch and Amplifier

- Schematic of nMOS transistor: metal contacts (green) printed on surface of selectively "doped" silicon semiconductor (yellow and orange)

- **Transistor "Off"** P semiconductor insulates and blocks current flow between "source" and "drain" contacts

- **Transistor "On"** Current flows between "source" and "drain" when a positive charge is applied to the "gate"— polarizes carriers and opens "channel" (blue arrows)

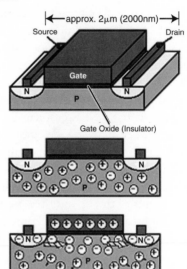

Source: Mitre Corporation.

to the square of the gate voltage (i.e., amplification). This is how the FET can be used to act as a switch. Most transistors used in microprocessors and dynamic random access memories (DRAMs) use complementary metal–oxide semiconductor (CMOS) or metal-oxide-semiconductor FET (MOSFET) transistors built on top of a silicon substrate. High frequency radio chips may also use gallium-arsenide bipolar CMOS (Bi-CMOS) transistors, the latter of which is a combination of bipolar junction transistors (BJT) and CMOS transistors.

In 1967 Gordon Moore of Intel noticed that chip density basically doubles every 18 months and that performance increases 35% during the same period. This empirical observation is known as Moore's Law (see Figure 8.3) and has been valid for 30 years and shows signs of continuing at least for another decade.

In fact, in the 50 years since the invention of the transistor in 1947 by Bell

Labs, microelectronics progress has proceeded at an exponential pace fueled by a 15% yearly miniaturization rate, inducing almost 30% cost decrease and 50% performance improvement in electronic function each year.[5]

A lot of people confuse Moore's Law to mean that performance doubles each generation. This is not accurate, for it is the density of the transistor count that is the fundamental factor that, in turn, leads to performance increases. When we are talking about microprocessor designs, the chip, software, and compiler architecture play especially significant roles in determining performance improvements.

Moore's Law:
Semiconductor transistor density doubles about every 18 months. In fact, in the 50 years since the invention of the transistor in 1947 by Bell Labs, microelectronics progress has proceeded at an exponential pace fueled by a 15% yearly miniaturization rate, inducing almost 30% cost decrease and 50% performance improvement in electronic function each year.

Economic Corollary:
Price elasticity: For every 1% drop in price, demand increases 1.5%.

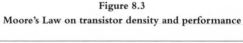

Figure 8.3
Moore's Law on transistor density and performance

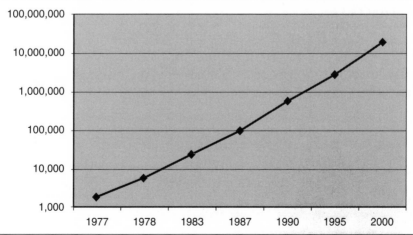

And the Bad News Is the Corollary to Moore's Law:
The Economic Version

All the spectacular growth of the semiconductor industry comes with a high price in terms of dollars and the environment: It now costs in 2000 over $2 billion to construct and tool up a wafer fabrication facility, which means that only the very, very large corporations have any hope of funding new semiconductor manufacturing lines. It is not surprising that giants like IBM, Siemens, Motorola, and Toshiba often team up to share the costs for memory and logic fab facilities. The environment is not being helped by semiconductor plants because they often have to use very dangerous and highly toxic chemicals for lithography etching and processing. Some futurists believe that the day will come, with the assistance of molecular biologists, when computer and memory chips will be fabricated using biochemical processes that are more friendly to the environment.

Corollary to Moore's Law
The capital investment required for semiconductor production doubles with every generation of technology.

8.3 COMPUTER STORAGE TRENDS

Ruettger's Law

Michael Ruettger was the long-time CEO who grew storage leader EMC to a market value comparable to that of IBM. The authors chose this name in his honor, as no previous popular name existed. Ruettger's Law tracks the spectacular growth of storage requirements in modern-day society. The law can be stated as follows:

Ruettger's Law:
Companies and governments double their storage requirements every year. Price elasticity: for every 1% drop in price, demand increases 4%.

In conversation with the authors, Ruettger pointed out that some medical records such as image data can't be compressed. Furthermore, by law in the United States, all medical records, text, and image must be stored 10 years and shared with 36 different entities (insurance, Centers for Disease Control, state, federal, etc.). These legal requirements also apply to image data such as that from MRI, computerized tomography, X-Ray, ultrasound, and any 3-D versions of those.

If we consider the impact of Metcalf's Law and Gilder's Law (Chapter 9) with Reuttger's Law, we can quickly come to the conclusion that storage requirements will continue to grow and grow and will keep the compression researchers employed for years to come.

8.4 MICROPROCESSOR TRENDS

Microprocessors are used in everything from rice cookers to automobile ignition control systems to mobile phones to Internet servers to supercomputers. In their brief 30-year history, these computer chips have seen their performance improve 25,000 fold over the first commercially marketed microprocessor, the Intel 4004, released in 1971 and was 4 bits wide. Microprocessors and programmable digital signal processors (DSPs) have also become the workhorses of mobile cellular phones and other types of wireless data devices. By most estimates, mobile phones and automobiles represent the largest markets for embedded processors.

The improvements in microprocessor performance over the past 30 years have come from four principle areas:

1. Dramatic advancements in semiconductor tooling and manufacturing, which have consistently enhanced reliability, shrunk the minimum feature sizes of transistors, and improved their switching speeds (meaning higher density—Moore's Law)
2. Innovations in circuit design methods (on-board cache, flash memories, synchronous DRAMs (SDRAMs), internal clocks, better synchronization schemes)
3. Innovations in the architecture (pipelined, superscalar, and parallel methods)
4. Innovations in software optimizing compilers

According to the Semiconductor Industry Association in its annual roadmap, by 2006 the high-performance microprocessors may reach an internal clock frequency of 3.5 GHz, featuring 200 million transistors with 0.07 micron fabrication dimensions on a chip measuring about 5 square centimeters and consuming over 160 watts. The peak performance of such processors may reach 10 Gigagflops.

Currently, the major microprocessors on the market today would include:

- Intel Itanium 1000 MHz processor
- Intel Pentium III 500–800 MHz x86 Instruction Set
- IBM/Motorola PowerPC 32/64-bit microprocessor unit (MPU) and microcontroller variations from Motorola
- Sun Sparc 64-bit
- Alpha 64-bit MPU (developed originally by DEC and then DEC was merged with Compaq and then in June 2001 Compaq shut down its own CPU development and sold Alpha to Intel)
- HP Spectrum Processors
- MIPS
- ARM (micro-controller)
- Transmeta 128-bit VLIW processors

8.5 THE QUEST FOR THE COMPUTER HOLY GRAIL—LOW-POWER CPUS

Do you know why IBM's stock has done so well in 2001 while most of its competitor's stocks sank to alarmingly low values? Answer: IBM has, through its mainframe servers, reduced the footprint needed to run the equivalent of hundreds of UNIX/Linux servers, thereby reducing the monthly electric power and rental costs for the burgeoning data centers needed to house the endless Internet servers. IBM did this by pulling a very old rabbit out of the hat—its 25-year-old Virtual Machine operating systems technology that enables a server to run independent, complete images of an operating system simultaneously without needing separate hardware. Hardware and software architecture can greatly affect the performance of a computer. How fast the system clock is does not give much insight into the complete system performance.

If an investor were to ask us which technology could change the entire industry in one fell swoop, our answer would have to be ultra-low power CPU chips. IBM recently announced that it has improved its chip fabrication process to reduce CPU power consumption by up to 90% as compared with an Intel. Without such chips, nothing remotely resembling our vision for 4G can be achieved because for computing to become ubiquitous it must be wireless, allowed to be on all the time, and it must not be subject to California-style electric power outages. The Intel empire could clearly be at risk because a small elite team of chip designers could design a chip that uses 1/100 or even 1/1000 the electric power than today's Intel Pentium fried-egg cookers consume. If Intel engineers can appreciate that axiom, they just might become motivated enough to invent the ultra-low power chip. In our view, the current microprocessors have become very complex and that complexity is fine for servers, supercomputers, and high-end desktops but is not well-suited for wireless ubiquitous computers (WUCs). Thus, we believe that a totally different stored-program simplified software and hardware architecture is needed for WUCs. Moreover, the ratio of hardware to software should be in favor of software so that the computing and communications capabilities of WUCs can be reconfigured dynamically by downloading software from a web server or from the service provider's web server. Thus, the industry's trend towards hotter and hotter chips has got to be reversed if WUCs are to populate and prosper. It is worth reminding ourselves that when the ENIAC computer was built half a century ago, the lights in the entire town would dim when the vacuum tube contraption was turned on. Thomas J. Watson Jr.'s greatest achievement in IBM perhaps was buying a Sony transistor radio and showing it to his computer engineering team, which stubbornly wanted to continue spending millions on the state-of-the-art (at the time) vacuum tubes, and then shifting to transistors.[6]

One such candidate for future ultra-low power chips may be stacked computer architectures. Stacked machines do not need to be pipelined for arithmetic and operands since the operands are made immediately available in the top of the stack-buffer registers. If an on-board RAM memory is available then pipelining can make memory access completely hidden. Philip Koopman has shown that stacked CPUs can do context switching for interrupts in zero time because no registers need to be saved. Early evidence suggests that stack computer programs can be 2.5 to 8 times smaller than complex instruction set computing (CISC) programs and another 1.5 to 2.5 times smaller than RISC computer programs. The size of the program can become an issue for WUCs. More research needs to be done on stack compilers, but proponents of this architecture believe that it will be possible to make them as efficient as register-based CPUs.

The company or companies that succeed in developing and manufacturing ultra-low power chips will own the microprocessor industry—without question. If a chip can be powered with a few hundred microwatts, it might be possible to power the chip without a battery because the AM radio signals could provide sufficient energy to at least turn on some of the circuits. For those operators which sold their AM radio stations to minority radio station programmers thinking that AM radio was a dying technology, there may be regrets.

Case Study: Transmeta Corporation

One company that has created quite a stir in the market is Transmeta Corporation, which came out of its five-year self-imposed secrecy in 2000 and announced a chip set based on very long instruction word (VLIW) architecture—another kind of holy grail of the industry but more geared to supercomputers and servers. Transmeta was started in about 1995 and, unlike most Silicon valley startups, did not issue a press release, announced no products, and did not even have a public relations department until January 2000 when the super secretive company finally announced its first two chips based on its Crusoe processor design. The company was initially funded with $12 million by several people including Paul Allen, Microsoft's cofounder, and George Soros. The company employs Linus Tovalds, creator of the Linux operating system. By the end of April 2001 the company had secured its second round of financing to the tune of $88 million from America Online, Gateway, Compaq Computer, Sony, and several Taiwanese electronics firms.

The company filed its first patents in 1996 and 1997, describing a process called code morphing that "provides a microprocessor which is faster than microprocessors of the prior art, is capable of running all of the software for all of the operating systems which may be run by a large number of families of prior art microprocessors, yet is less expensive than prior art microprocessors." The company released details of its architecture in January 2000, which is based on simple, high-performance, low-power VLIW engine with an instruction set that bears no resemblance to that of x86 processors. Transmeta has developed a software layer that implements what it calls code morphing, which converts x86 instructions into the hardware engine's native instruction set. This concept was researched quite extensively at IBM Watson Labs in the mid-1980s as an extension of the research that led to the PowerPC architecture. The current Crusoe processor uses roughly one-quarter of the logic transistors required for an all-hardware design (e.g., Pentium III) of similar performance.

Transmeta has introduced an advanced form of power management which it calls LongRun. Intel has introduced its own power management system called SpeedStep in its mobile Pentium-III chips. SpeedStep has two modes: low-power and high-performance. It switches the CPU from one to the other based on whether AC power is available. Transmeta's LongRun, on the other hand, dynamically selects from as many as 16 voltage and speed levels.

Thus, the Crusoe processor is very-low power (typically one-eighth that of comparable x86 chips) and makes it extremely attractive for mobile Internet and wearable computer applications. In principle, the VLIW engine inside the Crusoe processor can execute any instruction set including x86 and IBM PowerPC instructions as long as the compiler support is there. It is not surprising that Transmeta has chosen IBM to manufacture the chips. S3's Diamond Multimedia group has said that it plans to ship a Transmeta-based (TM3120) Web tablet running at about 400 MHz. The alliance with IBM could lead to further windfalls for Transmeta especially if IBM chooses to manufacture Transmeta's chip with IBM's new silicon on insulator (SOI) process.

A Closer Look at the Transmeta Architecture

The first implementation of the Transmeta architecture (see Figure 8.4) utilizes two inter units, one floating-point unit, a memory load/store unit, and a branch unit. The Integer Register file has 64 registers. A Crusoe processor instruction word, called a molecule, can be 64 bits or 128 bits long and contains up to four RISC-like instructions, called atoms. All atoms within a molecule are executed in parallel, and the molecule format directly determines how atoms get routed to functional units, which in effect greatly simplifies the decode and dispatch hardware. The fundamental difference between the Crusoe concept and other superscalar out-of-order x86 processors, such as the Pentium II and Pentium III processors, is that the latter need to use a separate hardware unit called the In-Order Retire Unit, which adds a lot of hardware complexity (see Figure 8.5). In those processors the In-Order Retire Unit is necessary because the dispatch unit reorders the microoperations as required to keep the functional units busy. In the Crusoe processor the retiring process is carried out in a middle-software engine that runs on a read-only memory (ROM) and is actually a virtual machine that translates the x86 instruction stream in real-time.

As can be seen in Figure 8.6 the Transmeta chips are significantly smaller than their Intel counterparts because the x86 instruction set is quite complex and requires that the decoding and dispatching hardware comprise large quantities of logic gates, which in turn leads to large heat dissipation. A number of companies are using Transmeta chips in laptops (e.g., Sony, which is also an investor in the company). Overall, we believe that the Transmeta approach may have more application to servers than to WUCs because being

Figure 8.4
Parallel execution in the Crusoe processor

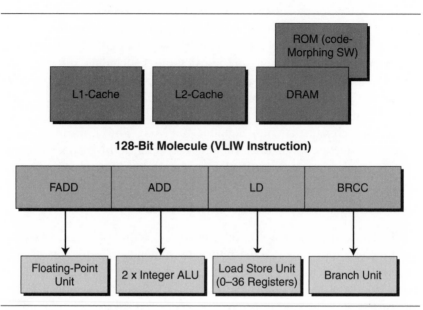

Source: Transmeta Corporation.

forced to run Intel-compatible code is already a bad starting point for achieving truly mobile wireless computers. We can expect that Intel, IBM, Motorola, and others will look for ways to really get into low-power, mobile computing, which targets power consumptions of a few 100 milliwatts or less.

8.6 THE ROAD AHEAD: 2001–2010

Various technological advances have conspired to sustain the validity of Moore's Law, and together these advances have been behind the successes of the computer industry and, in a large way, the communications industry. The 1980s and early 1990s witnessed the unleashing of computing power to individual users's homes and office desks. The proliferation of second-generation digital mobile cellular systems has highlighted the tremendous potential of wireless communications. The combination of ultra-fast PCs, multimedia mobile phones, and other devices will herald a potent mixture that will drive unstoppable demand for bandwidth.

It is difficult to envisage all of the types of consumer and industrial multimedia devices that will become available over the next decade. As Figure 8.7

Figure 8.5
Conventional superscalar out-of-order CPU

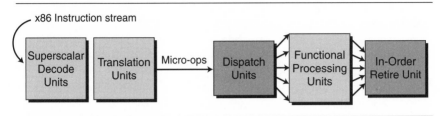

Source: Transmeta Corporation.

Figure 8.6
Comparison of chip sizes

	Mobile Pentium II	Mobile Pentium II	Mobile Pentium III	TM3120	TM5400
Process	.25 micron	25 micron shrink	.18 micron	.22 micron	.18 micron
On-Chip L1 Cache	32 KB	32 KB	32 KB	96 KB	128 KB
On-Chip L2 Cache	0	256 KB	256 KB	0	256 KB
Die Size	120 mm²	180mm²	106mm²	77mm²	73mm²

Source: Transmeta Corporation.

shows, integrated circuit density will continue to grow, enabling many new types of applications. Every person, every car, every truck will use these devices, and they will become as common as the plain old telephone.

MOSFET and CMOS transistors can scale down to ever and ever smaller dimensions, but most scientists believe that at dimensions smaller than 0.1 micron (1000 angstroms = 100 nanometers) the MOSFET no longer functions in a fashion suitable for switching or amplification because of various microscopic effects such as thermal noise, tunneling, and heat dissipation. Heat dissipation and cost of manufacturing are believed to be the most serious obstacles to using conventional transistors beyond the 0.1 micron range.

Over the past three to five years a number of conferences have been held to investigate alternative technologies and solutions to help sustain Moore's

Law for another 10 to 20 years. Some of the challenges and their proposal that have been submitted include:[7]

Challenges:

- Lithographic techniques for 100 nanometer-scale transistors or other switching devices.
- Cost and lack of competitive differential with each subsequent generation of lithography.
- Functionality inflation. As soon as a new Pentium processor is on the market, software operating systems and applications, through terribly inefficient design, tend to squander the improvements in the hardware by gobbling more and more memory. Some people have even applied the term Parkinson's Law (originally, that work expands to fill the time available) to describe how "software expands to fill the memory available." Companies like IBM and Hewlett Packard have understood this

Figure 8.7
The U.S. Semiconductor Industry Association's IC technology roadmap

	1997	1999	2001	2003	2006	2009
Technology Generation						
DRAM (half-pitch)	0.25	0.18	0.15	0.13	0.10	0.07
MPU (gate length)	0.20	0.14	0.12	0.10	0.07	0.05
DRAMs						
Samples	256 Mbit	1 Gbit		4 Gbit	16 Gbit	64 Gbit
Production ramp up	64 Mbit	256 Mbit	1 Gbit	1 Gbit	4 Gbit	16 Gbit
Logic transistors/cm2						
MPUs (millions)	3.7	6.2	10	18	39	84
ASICs (millions)	8	14	16	24	40	64
Frequency (MHz)						
Transistor speed	750	1,250	2,100	3,500	6,000	10,000
Across-chip Speed	750	1,200	1,400	1,600	2,000	2,500
Voltage	1.8–2.5	1.5–1.8	1.2–1.5	1.2–1.5	0.9–1.2	0.6–0.9
Packaging (pins/balls)						
MPU/MCUs	600	810	900	1,100	1,500	2,000
ASICs	1,100	1,500	1,800	2,200	3,000	4,100
Wafer Size (mm)	200	300	300	300	300	450

Source: SIA.

issue for quite some time, and that is why they devote substantial resources toward realizing optimizing compilers that take advantage of the new features of each iteration of the microprocessor.

Alternative Potential Solutions

- Multilevel logic. Numerous research projects exist that are looking at ways to have more than two switching states in a device. For example, resonant tunneling transistors offer the possibility of multilevel functions, but the research is still in its early stages.
- Parallel architectures and new circuit design methods. One should never abandon the possibilities in improving performance through ingenious circuit and architectural innovations. Parallel computing designs could give further life to microelectronic systems by not using redundancy to achieve overall system performance improvements.
- Nano-electronics and molecular electronics. The subject of a later chapter, the promise of integrated billions of devices in a square centimeter is inspiring chemists, physicists, biochemists, and material science specialists to explore ways of fabricating alternatives to the field effect transistor and the bipolar transistor using pure or hybrid approaches employing molecular or atomic structures. This is clearly the long-term direction of the industry, but it will take another 10 to 15 years before the supporting infrastructure can be built up. Nevertheless, if you have a son or daughter attending a university, it would not be a waste of time for them to study condensed matter physics, biotechnology, or molecular engineering because these fields will be the future.
- Interconnect technology. IBM has made a significant breakthrough with its SOI and copper-wiring technologies, the latter of which can improve the performance of chips by 20 to 40% depending on the function.
- New materials. Organic alternatives to silicon and gallium arsenide (GaAs) is gaining a lot of interest because of the potential to reduce the exploding costs of semiconductor fabrication (the economic version of Moore's Law).
- Self-organized structures and self-assembly. The possibilities here are virtually limitless as know-how from the biotech industry slowly gets transferred to the microelectronics industry. For example, one could imagine using DNA/enzymes/proteins to mark or locate structures on a substrate to enable controlled deposition with very fine precision.

Current lithographic and chemical techniques are not selective but operate more as a blanket approach, similar to spraying water on a forest fire from an airplane.

- Optical and opto-electronic devices. Although a large part of new research capital in optics has been devoted to fiber-optic transmission, one should not rule out the potential of novel optical components in microelectronic chip applications. Optics may be the best way to access quantum computer systems or molecular-scale devices as opposed to using conventional metal interconnect and wiring schemes.

- Sensors. The field of sensors is so rich and broad that it takes a four-inch book to just catalog all the different types. In our vision for 4G, smart wireless sensors will become an integral part of the future "Infinite Internet" providing data to people, anytime, anywhere.

- Micromachines. They hold a lot of promise in realizing special components for future microelectronic systems such as microactuators for medical uses (e.g., ear implants).

- Quantum computing. Many researchers believe that someday it will be possible to build machines with quantum computing subsystems. The theoretical work in quantum computing is quite active, and in the last two years experimental verification and simple prototype demonstrations of a small number of molecules working on quantum computing principles have inspired the computer research community to press on with this tantalizing field. If we were to put a time frame on it, we would say between 2010 and 2020 viable systems could be developed that would probably be commercialized as hybrid systems interfacing through wires or optics to conventional silicon circuitry. Governments are also supporting this field wholeheartedly because of the vast and disruptive potential of quantum computing in communications, cryptography, and search engines, just to name a few applications.

- Environmental concerns. The semiconductor industry uses many very toxic and lethal chemicals that are far from being environmentally friendly. Perhaps, through the use of water soluble biochemicals and self-assembly, someday we will be able to "grow" our circuits in a flask.

8.7 THE PETAFLOP COMPUTER BY 2010

The U.S. President's Informational Technology Advisory Committee has named supercomputing as one of three key areas to be supported by the federal government. In particular, it has made the realization of the petaflop computer a goal to be reached by 2010. If one wanted to make a petaflop computer out of the state of the art in 2006, it would take over 100,000 CPU chips and would require the power of an entire building at 15 MW.[8] NASA's Jet Propulsion Laboratory (JPL) has a research project that is studying an alternative approach to building the petaflop computer by combining several different technologies including holographic memory, cryogenic memory, optical interconnects, semiconductor memory, and picosecond superconducting switching devices. JPL estimates that the refrigeration costs associated with using cryogenic components would be a small fraction of the total cost of the system, and given the huge power consumption that conventional semiconductor processors would require, it seems a very viable approach. The JPL research team is exploring novel computer architectures such as multithreading that can be used to maximize the performance of the system. Although this research is still in its early stages, the goal of building a petaflop computer is lofty and could result in a number of useful innovations.

If low-power CPU chips could be developed that consume much less power than today's microprocessors, the architecture of the petaflop computer could be greatly simplified.

NOTES

1. Thomas J. Watson Jr. and Peter Petre, *Father Son & Co.* (New York: Bantam Books, 1990).

2. Ibid, p. 229.

3. IBM has actually developed, jointly with Bell Labs, a version of UNIX that ran on the mainframe.

4. An author (Rojas) had the honor and opportunity to have Carver Mead be his undergraduate advisor from 1977 to 1981.

5. D. Bois, *Future Trends in Microelectronics,* ed. S. Luryi, J. Xu, and A. Zaslavsky (New York: Wiley, 1999).

6. For anyone who was a ham radio operator before solid state radios became popular, those old pictures of vacuum-tube radio equipment still can bring out the goose bumps. There was something very romantic about watching a tube short-wave radio turn on, glowing and pumping out watts from the antenna.

7. P. R. Jay (Nortel), "Considerations Beyond Moore's Law." In *Future Trends in Microelectronics: The Road Ahead,* (New York: Wiley, 1999).

8. M. Dorojevets et al., "RSFQ Computing: The Quest for Petaflops." In *Future Trends in Microelectronics* (New York: Wiley, 1999).

CHAPTER 9

THE POWER OF THE NETWORK

9.1 METCALF'S LAW

Robert Metcalf, the inventor of the Ethernet (another great invention from the most famous research trust fund of all time—Xerox PARC) and 1981 founder of 3Com Corp. (Santa Clara, California), discovered a fundamental characteristic of networking that is usually named after him:

> *Metcalf's Law:*
> The "value" of the network is proportional to the square of the number of people or processors connected to the network.

Metcalf's Law has manifested itself in the grandest of ways: As George Gilder points out in his book *Telecosm,*[1] between 1989 and 1993, the percentage of America's computers on LANs rose from less than 10% to more than 60%. As scientists, engineers, and businessmen got connected the quantity and quality of information improved dramatically because of the feedback loops created by the ability to post opinions in user groups. Large projects such as the Human Genome Project are benefiting enormously because of the wide reach of the Internet as a medium to disseminate and assimilate relevant genome data and analysis.

Lessons from the Last Thirty Years of Networking Research

Thirty years of networking and telecommunications research have taught the IT industry important lessons. Jim Kurose[2] summarizes the major lessons that have been learned over the past 30 years:

- *Importance of the "right" service architecture.* The startling success of Internet applications such as the Web and Internet audio illustrate the importance and potential of rapid, widespread network application deployment. This quick deployment was possible because these applications were built at the edges of the network, utilizing existing network services. Difficulties in adding new telephone-based services, which require modification of the subnet infrastructure, provide a counterpoint. Thus, defining a minimal but sufficient set of subnet services to allow future, yet-to-be-discovered applications to be built and deployed is a critical research issue. What are the right subnet services for future applications that are likely to require mobile, real-time, and group communication?

- *Multiservice network architectures.* New service models are being defined, but specific mechanisms and protocols are needed to provide applications with differing performance and reliability requirements with different classes of service. Although much research has been accomplished in this area, a complete network architecture has yet to be fully demonstrated. At the transport level, how does one provide for the different reliability needs of different applications? At the network layer, how are calls with differing or multiobjective cost functions to be routed? At the link level, which packet scheduling disciplines are appropriate? How does the mobility of an endpoint change the architecture? Also, how should an application specify and characterize its traffic load and service requirements?

- *There will never be enough bandwidth.* Bandwidth, like computing power, has historically been consumed as fast as it has become available. Scarce bandwidth means contention and congestion.

  To what extent must resources be explicitly reserved to provide the appearance (to the application) of congestion-free communication? To what extent can statistical multiplexing gains be exploited within/among the various classes of traffic? To what extent should congestion be avoided (via resource allocation and call blocking) versus reacted to (via congestion control)? Is it possible that optical networks, with their potential of almost limitless bandwidth, will relieve the bandwidth crunch?

- *Importance of scale/interoperability.* Widespread access to the Internet has contributed significantly to making the Internet the valuable resource it is today. The importance of the "scalability" of network protocols and architecture has been recognized for many years for subnet services, such as routing and name serving. It is also true, however, for end-system protocols, which may have to accommodate a large number of users (e.g., reliable multicast) or a large number of connections (e.g., an information server). Scalability will thus continue to be a critical concern in the future.

Protocols define the manner in which different entities interact. How should fundamentally different networking technologies (e.g., ATM and the Internet) with different protocols interact/interoperate to provide seamless end-to-end transport service? Even within a given architecture, how do different versions of the architecture interact (e.g., int-serv and non–int-serv networks) operate? How can legacy systems be accommodated?

- *Reliability.* The telephone network has been engineered with reliability as a primary concern. Redundancy, network monitoring, and network management play key roles; yet we read stories of spectacular telephone and computer network failures. As software plays an increasingly important role and as network control becomes increasingly sophisticated, software reliability/verification/testing and automated network management become increasingly important.
- *Security.* Researchers have provided the fundamental building blocks (e.g., public key cryptography) with which an amalgamation of both application- and network-related security concerns (e.g., secure transaction technology, router authentication) can be addressed, but these components have yet to be assembled into a cohesive, encompassing security solution and have not yet been deployed in a widespread manner.
- *Evaluation Methodology.* As network control mechanisms become increasingly complex and their scale larger, evaluating these control mechanisms becomes increasingly difficult. Traditional evaluation methods have included implementation/experimentation, simulation, and analysis. Experimental networking must evolve into a more rigorous experimental science, with rigorous, repeatable large scale implementations, measurements, and experimentation. One critical problem in experimental network evaluation methodology is that the only

large scale, "live" environment for experimentation is the Internet it-self—a production network with little monitoring capabilities. New simulation technology is needed to handle network sizes that are measured in the tens and hundreds of thousands. Analytic techniques are needed that can model realistic traffic mixes and a large number of connections in a network (multinode) setting.

Peer-2-Peer (P2P) Computing—Capitalizing on Metcalf's Law

By enabling millions of computer users to search for files and transfer them from one desktop computer to another, the balance of power shifts from the commercial interests that now dominate the Internet to the individual.

New York Times June 29, 2000

P2P software takes the idea that the Internet is for sharing to new levels. P2P has been described as "an anarchistic threat to the current Internet" (David Streitfeld, *The Washington Post,* July 18, 2000, p. A1), and Marc Andreesen has called P2P software the most important thing on the Internet in the last six years (when Netscape was first released) and a "benevolent virus." Ian Clarke, the creator of FreeNet, says, "People should be free to distribute information without restrictions of any form."

P2P can be seen as a type of network in which each workstation has equivalent capabilities and responsibilities. This differs from client/server architectures, in which some larger or more powerful computers are dedicated to serving the others. P2P systems generally involve these key characteristics:

- User interfaces load outside of a web browser.
- User computers can act as both clients and servers.
- The overall system is easy to use and well-integrated.
- The system includes tools to support users wanting to create content or add functionality.
- The system provides connections with other users.
- The system supports "cross-network" protocols like extensible mark-up language-remote procedure calling (XML-RPC) for electronic services and electronic fulfillment (such as digital media distribution).

P2P networking will also be especially applicable to wearable computing and networking, as users will need to locate specific kinds of digital data without having to use unsophisticated search engines that generally return many more irrelevant results than relevant ones.

COMPANY PROFILE: Entropia Inc.

Entropia, Inc., (www.entropia.com) is a startup company that is all about peer-to-peer supercomputing. The company is privately held and is head-quartered in San Diego, California. It has Professor Larry Smarr, head of Cal (IT)^2, known for the Supercomputing Center at the University of Illinois at Urbana-Champaign, on its Scientific Advisory Board.

Entropia is creating the world's largest Internet- and Enterprise-distributed computing service by converting the idle time of PCs into large-scale computer power via the Internet. Internet- and Enterprise-distributed computing are being embraced widely by industry leaders as the most intel-ligent form of peer-to-peer computing. By downloading Entropia software called Entropia 2000, from the company's Web site, people and organizations can contribute their computers' otherwise wasted processor time to impor-tant projects that significantly accelerate progress and production in the med-ical, scientific, research, and entertainment industries.

The company's flagship product Entropia 2000 snaps into any PC and connects it to a global Entropia computing grid of more than 100,000 PCs in more than 80 countries. The software allows researchers in business and academia to tackle complex computing tasks by taking advantage of idle PC resources across the world.

In November 2000 at the Supercomputing 2000 conference in Dallas, Texas, the company announced a collaboration with the National Compu-tational Science Alliance[3] and the National Science Foundation's (NSF) Na-tional Partnership for Advanced Computational Infrastructure (NPACI).[4] As part of the agreements, Entropia will donate 200 million CPU hours to the PACI program, creating the largest computing platform ever offered to its national academic user community. The Alliance and NPACI are both part of the National Science Foundation's Partnerships for Advanced Computa-tional Infrastructure Program.

This partnership will serve one of the largest communities of nationally distinguished computer and computational scientists and researchers. En-tropia's donated resources are comparable to 10 years of output from the largest computational systems currently available to academia. These 200 million CPU hours will be utilized by projects jointly selected by both En-tropia and the PACI program. Current scientific research projects supported

Figure 9.1
Entropia used the Internet to achieve 1 Teraflop

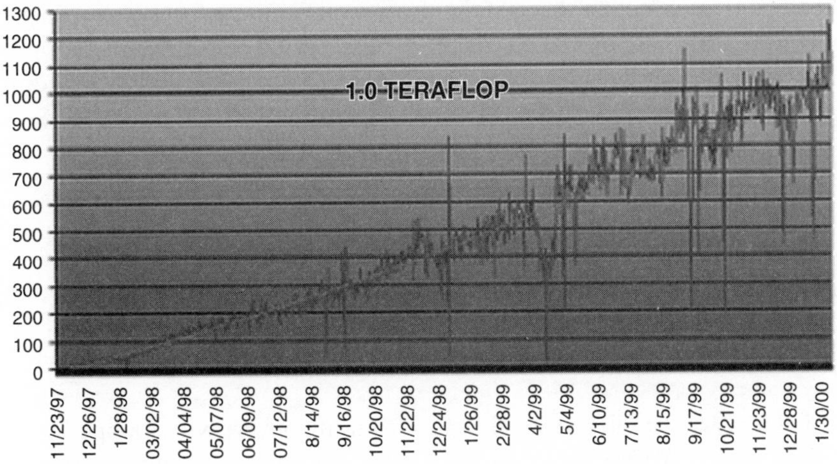

Source: www.entropia.com.

by the PACI program include bioinformatics, protein folding, telescience, multiphysics simulations, and scalable visualization rendering.

Through this new collaboration, Entropia will deploy its Node Server at the leading-edge sites of the Alliance, the National Center for Supercomputing Applications (NCSA) in Urbana-Champaign, Illinois and of the NPACI, the San Diego Supercomputer Center (SDSC) in San Diego, California. This deployment will also mean access to Entropia's global network of PCs. Both NCSA and SDSC have been leaders in providing national access to innovative high performance computing architectures for 15 years. Entropia's donation extends this tradition to a planetary architecture.

Entropia's Internet experiment is a good example of the power of Metcalf's Law (see Figure 9.1). The company used 100,000 PCs in over 80 different countries to collectively calculate the Great Mersenne Prime (2^P-1) Search (GIMPS) and found the first million digit prime number.

Gilder's Law of Telecosm

George Gilder has made the observation that bandwidth will become an abundant resource almost to the point that many companies will waste it. The reason for the spectacular growth in wireline bandwidth really is predicated on profound advances in fiber optical transmission. The current state of the art enables transmission speeds of up to 320 gigabits per second on a dual fiber, but that is still far short of the theoretical maximum of 25 terabits per second. Gilder has pointed out that in fact bandwidth capacity in fiber optical systems has grown at a pace two to three times faster than growth in computing power (as measured in Millions of Instruction Per Second (MIPS):

Gilder's Law of Telecosm
Bandwidth grows at least three times faster than computer power.
Corollary: Network traffic in bits doubles every one hundred days.[5]
Price elasticity: For every 1% drop in price, demand increases 2.5%.

Gilder's Law applies to wireless spectrum in concert with Cooper's Law (see section 3.9). Otherwise, government policy and inefficient use of spectrum tends to restrict bandwidth growth. Another point worth mentioning is that wireless systems today have a significant amount of computing power that is usually camouflaged in the form of digital signal processors. For example, even though a GSM phone transmits data or voice at a maximum of 13 kbps and GSM GPRS can transmit at 165 kbps, the on-board baseband processor is carrying out all sorts of computations including encryption/decryption, coding for modulation, voice recognition analysis, and so on. Do not be fooled by the small size of the digital mobile phones—they are the Trojan horse of the communications industry, and with 4G systems the personal communicators will function more like a computer than a phone.

Notes

1. George Gilder, *Telecosm: How Infinite Bandwidth Will Revolutionize Our World* (New York: Free Press, 2000).

2. Jim Kurose, "Future Directions in Networking Research," Association of Computing Machinery Computing Surveys (December 1996), 28A.

3. The National Computational Science Alliance is a partnership to prototype an advanced computational infrastructure for the twenty-first century and includes more than 50 academic,

government, and industry research partners from across the United States. The Alliance is one of two partnerships funded by the National Science Foundation's Partnerships for Advanced Computational Infrastructure program, and receives cost-sharing at partner institutions. The National Science Foundation also supports the National Partnership for Advanced Computational Infrastructure (NPACI), led by the San Diego Supercomputer Center.

The National Center for Supercomputing Applications is the leading-edge site for the National Computational Science Alliance. NCSA is a leader in the development and deployment of cutting-edge high-performance computing, networking, and information technologies. The National Science Foundation, the state of Illinois, the University of Illinois, industrial partners, and other federal agencies fund NCSA.

4. NPACI unites more than 45 universities and research institutions to build the computational environment for tomorrow's scientific discovery. Led by UC San Diego and the San Diego Supercomputer Center (SDSC), NPACI is funded by the National Science Foundation's PACI program and receives additional support from the State and University of California, other government agencies, and partner institutions. The NSF PACI program also supports the National Computational Science Alliance led by the University of Illinois. For additional information about NPACI, see http://www.npaci.edu.

5. Some, like technology writer Jeff Hecht, say that network doubling is a myth, and has slowed down in any case because of recession. However, the authors believe that this pace is possible for 4G if this book's agenda is implemented.

CHAPTER 10

MOLECULAR-SCALE ELECTRONICS
AND QUANTUM COMPUTING

Now is life very solid or very shifting? I am haunted by the two contradic-
tions. This has gone on forever; will last forever; goes down to the bottom of
the world—this moment that I stand on. Also, it is transitory, flying, di-
aphanous. I shall pass like a cloud on the waves. . . . But what is light?

January 4, 1929
Virginia Woolf in her personal diary

10.1 INTRODUCTION

Much of the success of the microelectronics industry in the past two decades
can be attributed to improvements in design methodologies, manufacturing
control, and precision. The advent of very large scale integration (VLSI)
would not have been possible without the huge investments in materials research that led to such achievements as ultra-high quality silicon crystals,
high-purity (99.999% pure) materials, high-resolution resists, rugged insu-
lating and passivation thin films, highly-precise etching techniques, and
high-resolution lithography tools. The ability to collect and analyze the materials processing data has also played an indispensable role in the development of microelectronic chips.

Future computer technology will be greatly affected by advances in materials research across many industries including the fine chemicals, biotechnology, energy, transportation, and aerospace industries (see Figure 10.1).
Aerospace-related materials in particular have cross-industry promise over
the long-term in manufacture of new materials such as exotic drugs, diamond crystals, and metals. The manufacture of certain drugs can be greatly
simplified in the zero-gravity (or microgravity) environment of outer space
because constituent molecules, i.e. proteins, enzymes, and hormones, can be
easily assembled without sticking to each other, in contrast to the gravity-

126

Figure 10.1
Advanced materials

Inorganic Materials	Metals	Composites
• Ceramics	• Amorphous	(Polymers) Metals
• Metals	• Superconductors	(Ceramics)
	• Semiconductors	• Reinforced Plastics
	• Pure Metals	• Reinforced Metals FRM
	• Alloys	• Carbon-Carbon Fibers
	• Intermetals	• Ceramic Matrix

Ceramics	Synthetic Organics	Biomolecular Materials
• Glasses	• Hydrocarbons	• Carbohydrates
• Crystallized Glasses	• Organic Superconductors	• Nucleic Acids
• Monolithic Crystals	• Amines, Dyes, & Salts	• Lipids
• Crystal Mixtures	• Synthetic Polymers	• Amino Acids
	• Organic Halogens	• Proteins

plagued Earth's surface. This highly specialized area of research is not limited to the United States and NASA. For example, Fujitsu, Hitachi, Mitsubishi Heavy Industries, and other Japanese companies have been studying microgravity manufacturing of biomolecular materials since the late 1980s.

10.2 THE PHYSICS OF DEVICES AT NANOSCALES

Currently, the state of the art in semiconductor VLSI manufacturing is 0.18 micron dimensions allowing the manufacturing of 256 megabit and 1 gigabit chips. The resolution and tolerances needed to fabricate these dense circuits are rapidly approaching 100 to 1,000 angstroms.[1] The technical hurdles that have to be overcome in future VLSI fabrication include:

- Total wiring length is becoming a problem. In current microprocessors the total wiring length is now on the order of kilometers per square centimeter.
- Interconnectivity complexity—typically one new interconnect layer is added every three to four years.

- At minimum feature size of sub-100 nm (0.1 micron), wires no longer behave like wires and instead begin to take on nonlinear properties.
- Total power consumption will make dynamic charging schemes impractical, and it may be necessary to employ on-chip wireless communications methods such as electronic polarization of nanostructures.
- Insulation between devices (cross-talk, tunneling problems).
- Electromigration.
- Diffusion and implantation control.
- Failure of semi-classical Boltzman transport equation. Below 100 nm devices behave more like quantum transporters, and the phase of the wavefunction begins to become important.
- Line-width control (250 to 500 angstroms).
- Defect-free design methodologies will need to be replaced with redundant architectures such as HP's massively parallel Teramac project.

Another complication is if too many transistors are put on a custom chip, then the total length of time for the signal to travel inside the chip can become a limiting factor. Thus, shrinking the transistor so that one can cram more circuits is not necessarily the optimum path in the future. We should consider that every mechanical system, and we can include living cells in this category, has its naturally optimum size. Microprocessors are no different. Future designs, especially for WUCs, will need to make trade-offs between the number of transistors and complexity and power consumption.

The theoretical and modeling challenges are no less significant. Simulation tools such as SPICE have to be modified to deal with quantum effects. At a few hundred angstroms the linear dimension begins to approach the mean-free path of the information carriers—electrons, holes, phonons, and quasi-particle excitations. Beyond these dimensions, the sizes of components are comparable to interatomic distances, which means that the behavior of such information devices can usually only be modeled with quantum mechanics. The quantum-mechanical characteristics of molecular-scaled or atomic-scaled components, passive or active, suggest the concept of the quantum component or cell.[2] In a quantum-scaled system, switching and storage can no longer be treated as classical processes but rather must be reformulated in the framework of quantum-mechanical and quantum-statistical probabilities, taking into account, among other things, interactions within the molecular/atomic passive and active devices themselves.

10.3 THE ROLE OF MOLECULAR-ENGINEERED MATERIALS

Molecular sciences (e.g., atomic physics, quantum chemistry, biochemistry, biotechnology, polymer science, and so on) present vast potential, albeit extremely challenging, to develop novel computer elements with the earth-shaking possibility of self-assembly. Computer-aided chemistry makes use of innovative computer graphics, large data bases of chemical formulas, and numerically intensive supercomputers to assist chemists in the design, visualization, and synthesis of organic materials and processes. The ability to catalog large numbers of complex chemical structures is making it possible to assemble complex molecules from smaller components (see Figure 10.2).

10.4 QUANTUM DOTS AND SINGLE ELECTRON TRANSISTORS

Quantum dots are molecular arrays in which individual electrons can be trapped in specially formed island-like structures measuring roughly several

Figure 10.2
Molecular/Bioelectronics: Key research areas

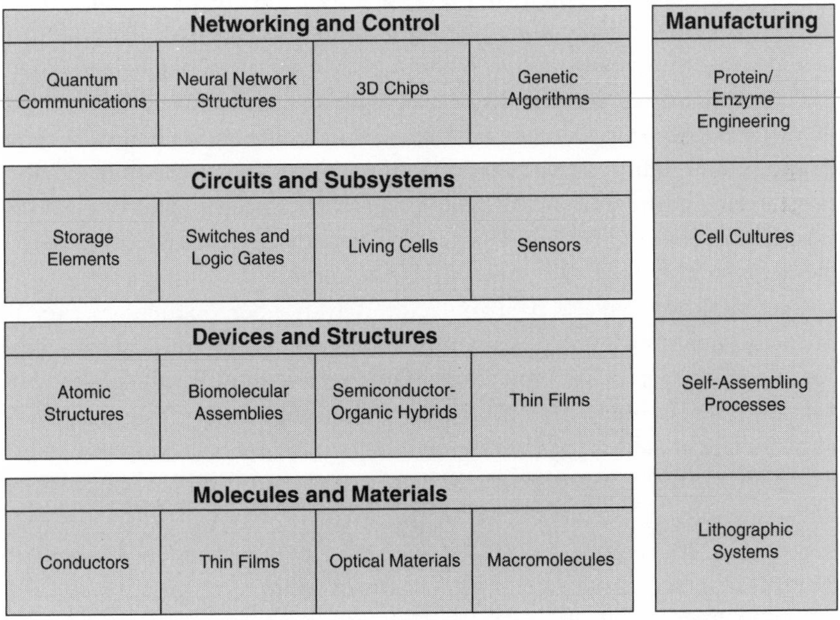

Networking and Control				Manufacturing
Quantum Communications	Neural Network Structures	3D Chips	Genetic Algorithms	Protein/ Enzyme Engineering
Circuits and Subsystems				
Storage Elements	Switches and Logic Gates	Living Cells	Sensors	Cell Cultures
Devices and Structures				
Atomic Structures	Biomolecular Assemblies	Semiconductor-Organic Hybrids	Thin Films	Self-Assembling Processes
Molecules and Materials				
Conductors	Thin Films	Optical Materials	Macromolecules	Lithographic Systems

hundred atoms wide and protruding from the surface of a substrate. Quantum dots are usually surrounded by an electrical insulator, and as a result, electrons can tunnel in and out of the quantum dot under the control of an electric field generated by a nearby metal gate. The electric field can be adjusted so that only one free electron is trapped in the quantum dot.[3] Switching from one state to another can be accomplished adiabatically, which means the process is reversible.

The manufacture of quantum dots, or for that matter anything on a molecular scale, usually requires different standard lithographic techniques. One of the attractions and of course monumental challenges of working with molecules is that almost anything is possible. For example, researchers have long known about self-assembling biomolecular processes (e.g., living cells), but now it is possible to find self-assembling inorganic materials as well. One example is self-assembled quantum dots (SAQDs) that utilize the properties of gallium (Ga), indium (In), zinc (Zn), germanium (Ge), and other compounds and Group IV semiconductors. Scientists have actually been able to grow Germanium or Indium quantum dot islands on top of a silicon substrate.

The excitement surrounding quantum dots stems from the promise of storing 1s and 0s by determining the presence or absence of an electron in the trapped wells. The potential storage density would be in the hundreds of gigabits or even terabits. A number of commercial labs have dedicated research budgets in quantum dots including IBM, Fujitsu, Hitachi, and NTT.

Researchers such as David Deutsche, Artur Ekert, and David DiVincenzo of IBM have even proposed various schemes in which quantum dots become quantum computing elements. IBM's scheme is to utilize the spins of electrons so that in the process of tunneling between dots the spins of electrons would be exchanged. It should be possible according to the IBM team to implement exclusive (XOR) gates with this scheme.

Quantum dots can also be manufactured from superconducting materials since the quantum effects in quantum dots needed for information processing only appear at very low temperatures—usually at liquid helium temperatures. The Japanese have continued to fund superconducting research in industry labs as well as in government labs and universities. Nippon Electric Corp. (NEC) recently reported achieving a single quantum state or qubit inside a quantum dot.

Single-electron transistors (SETs) are similar to quantum dots but tend to manipulate much larger numbers of electrons. SETs use controlled electron tunneling to amplify current. An SET is usually made from two tunnel junctions that share a common electrode. Tunnel junctions consist of two pieces of metal separated by a very thin (1 nm) insulator. The only way for electronics in one electrode to travel to another electrode is through quantum tunneling. Research in this area is still nascent, but more progress can be expected in the next couple of years.

10.5 ADVANCED ORGANIC MATERIALS

Synthetic organic materials have long found application in microelectronics. Organic photoconductors (OPCs), first used by IBM in electrophotographic devices, are used in various novel devices: photo-resists for semiconductor lithography, liquid crystal polymers (LCP) in thin film displays, and polyamide thin films as insulators in integrated circuits. The demand for enhanced materials is generating interest in organic materials that have active electrical or optical or chemical properties. Current research focuses on the fundamental relationship between molecular structure, architecture, and function. Some of the areas that have gained attention are nonlinear optical-organic films or crystals, electro-conductive polymers, OPCs, organic superconductors, ultra-thin films, storage devices and molecular-scaled diodes, transistors, and other nonlinear devices.

Another area that has attracted much attention is nonlinear optical-organic materials, usually in the form of polymeric structures. Materials which have nonlinear organic-optical (NOOP) properties have much potential in building waveguides, amplitude and phase modulators, gates and switches, second-order frequency mixing devices, and third-order (e.g., bistable) devices. The principle advantages of nonlinear organic-optical materials are that (1) they can be tuned during the manufacturing process, (2) they have high optical thresholds, and (3) they exhibit extremely fast response times on the order of 200 femtoseconds (fs).[4]

Electro-conductive polymers hold promise for integrated circuits, displays, mass storage media, batteries, protective coatings, chemical selective electrodes, sensors, and various input/output (I/O) devices for wearable computers. The research challenges are ambient stability, mechanical stability, ease of synthesis, and switching rates.

Ultra-thin (one molecule thick) organic films constitute another important area of molecular-engineered materials research. Such films, which are often referred to as monomolecular films, are being used by many molecular electronics researchers as building blocks in various devices. Hahns Kuhn of the Max Planck Institute in Germany describes the challenge and potential with these thin films.[5]

The design and construction of organized systems of molecules that interlock and interact like the parts of a machine is a great challenge. Materials thus obtained can have basically new properties depending on the exact localization of each component molecule. Tools to manipulate single molecules are of great interest. New fundamental physical and chemical processes can be studied and bio-processes can be simulated using man-made molecules as well as biomolecules as components. Molecular assemblies are of great potential interest in developing microelectronics, memories with much higher storage density than chips based on present day technology, microsensors of high-specificity, new catalysts for complex reactions as well as arrangement for solar energy conversion.

Some of the potential applications of monomolecular films would include:

- Sensors and transducers
- Biological membranes
- VLSI lithography tools
- Insulators and spacers
- Surface modification, lubricants, and coatings
- Interfaces to molecular-scaled devices

A number of companies have actually developed automated machines that can form monomolecular layers on substrates. The most popular technique used to form ultra-thin films is the Langmuir-Blodgett (LB) method, perfected in the 1930s by Irving Langmuir and Katherine Blodgett. The LB method is a wet technique that makes use of the oil-water phenomena to form floating organic monolayers on a water subphase and then transfers them onto a solid substrate such as glass or silicon. The interest in LB films was revived in the 1960s when Hahns Kuhn and coworkers in Germany investigated optical- and energy-transfer properties in multi-monolayer structures. The high uniformity of LB films, coupled with their optical- and energy-transfer properties make them a candidate for submicron lithographic resists. As with any wet process the LB method does have drawbacks, but they do not necessarily pose fundamental obstacles.

10.6 MOLECULAR-SCALE ELECTRONIC DEVICES

A number of research groups around the world are attempting to implement molecular-scaled devices using either organic or biomolecular materials. The original pioneers in this field were Ari Aviram of IBM and Mark Ratner,[6] who first envisioned active switching elements from organic materials in the early 1970s. In their landmark paper they proposed that unimolecular rectification or asymmetrical electrical conduction could occur in certain molecules through "bond-tunneling." In effect, what Aviram and Ratner proposed was bandgap engineering. From conversations with Ari Aviram while he was at IBM, Bill Rojas was astounded by the way that even in the mid-1980s molecular-electronics researchers found more support for their work outside the corporate environment. The computer industry just was not ready to accept that the almighty silicon transistor had a useful life of less than 50 years. Nevertheless, the U.S. government through DARPA, MITRE Corporation, and other far-sighted research organizations is funding a number of research programs in molecular electronics and bioelectronics. The Japanese, French, and Chinese governments have been quietly funding this research area for over 15 years, and at one time, one could count over 50 labs in Japan alone doing research in molecular-scale electronics and molecular-engineering materials for electronics. It is difficult to predict if and when commercialization might become possible, but if living organisms are any indication, we know that it should be possible to at least take advantage of nature's complex manufacturing, replication, and repair processes.

In the past three to five years a number of breakthrough experiments and demonstrations have been made with molecular-scale devices:

- James Tour of the University of South Carolina and Mark Reed of Yale University are collaborating on the chemical synthesis and testing of molecular wires.
- A research group at Purdue University has applied Tour and colleagues' ideas to a more complex heterogeneous extended structure that functions as a molecular electronic circuit array.
- In July of 2000 researchers at Hewlett Packard and UCLA announced that they had successfully built an electronic switch and an AND gate using a large structure consisting of about one million molecules of an organic molecule called rotaxane.
- Soon after, the Yale University team and researchers at Rice published results on a different class of molecules that acted as a reversible switch. The teams then modified the molecule so that it could retain electrons rather than trapping them briefly, with the result being a memory element that could retain its data for about 10 minutes, much longer than the 2 to 3 milliseconds of conventional silicon DRAMs.

The Holy Grail of molecular-scale electronics is the elusive three-terminal molecular-device that would operate analogously to the transistor. Such a device would have linear dimensions over 1,000 times smaller than the present 0.18-micron transistors. Thermal considerations are a major reason that scientists are looking for an alternative to the silicon transistor. For example, a 500 MHz microprocessor with 10 million transistors emits over 100 watts of radiant heat, more than a range-top cooking stove.[7] Mark Reed and James Tour estimate that the fundamental thermal limit of a molecule operating at room temperature and at today's speeds would be about 50 picowatts (50 × 10^{-9} watts), which suggests an upper limit on the number of molecular devices that can be closely packed—about 100,000 times more than today's chips (see Figure 10.3).

10.7 BIO-ELECTRONICS AND SELF-ASSEMBLY— LEARNING FROM NATURE

Living systems routinely do many things that no man-made computer can do efficiently such as olfactory and auditory sensing, three-dimensional vision processing, dexterous motor control, and associative memory search as well as many higher cognitive processes. Scientists have been studying biological processes and organisms for the past four decades in an attempt to better understand how architecture, function, and the lower molecular building blocks fit together. Numerous anatomical, clinical, neurobiological, and neuropsychological studies are eliciting some of the hidden secrets of biosystems and have provided us with a better understanding of the computational structure of living organisms and even the living neuron networks in insects, mammals, and humans. Insights learned from biological information processing could perhaps be applied to image processing, voice recognition, robotic control, and even machine intelligence.

In biology there are two main types of self-assembly: thermodynamic and coded. An example of thermodynamic self-assembly would be a raindrop forming on a leaf. The liquid drop has an extremely smooth, curved surface, just the kind of technology that could be used to make optical lenses.[8] Coded self-assembly refers to the kind used in cell replication. Complex molecules such as ATP help keep the cell balanced thermodynamically by energy dissipating structures. In effect, cell production is like an assembly line with instructions being read off the DNA/RNA molecules by a complex system of enzymes. The promise of using such processes in the production of future computer and storage chips is too compelling to ignore, and we believe that within the next 10 to 15 years practical systems will be created that utilize such bioassembling capabilities.

Figure 10.3
Example of molecular wires and switches

Molecular Electronic Wires and Nanometer–Scale, Quantum–Effect Switches

- Molecule can act as wire or as resonant tunneling diode
- Methylene groups create "barriers" along a molecular wire to control transmission of electrons through a quantum well

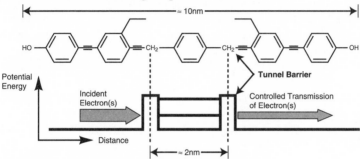

- Advantages:
  - Molecules much smaller and every one is exactly alike
  - Easily can be made in vast numbers (10^{23} at a time)

Note: Figure adapted from descriptive material provided by Prof. James Tour of the University of South Carolina.
Source: MITRE Corporation.

Thus, biotechnology and cell manufacturing have tremendous potential application to future manufacturing (and will hopefully be more environmentally friendly than current semiconductor manufacturing) of both semiconductor chips and future molecular-scaled devices. Perhaps one day it will be possible to "program" a microorganism to scan the surface of a computer chip for errors or defects and then repair them. Given that there are already more chips than humans, some of which are running critical systems like air traffic control, complex medical instruments, and guidance systems, but subject to problems beyond our ability to immediately detect and repair, self-healing capabilities will become increasingly important for deeply embedded systems that are expected to last for long periods of time.

NOTES

1. One angstrom = 1/10,000 of a micron or 1×10^{-10} meters. For comparison, the diameter of a hydrogen atom is one angstrom.

2. N. L. Mushkhelishvili and V. M. Sergeev, "Interaction of Biological Systems: Resonance Excitation Transfer," *Doklady Akademil Navk USSR*, 251, no. 1 (March 1980): 233–235.

3. Quantum dots are solids not vacuum, so many electrons are actually present. However, most are tightly bound to the neighboring atoms, and it is only the free electrons that are of interest here.

4. One femtosecond = 1/1000 of a picosecond or 1×10^{-12} seconds.

5. Hahns Kuhn, "Molecular Engineering—A Beginning and an Endeavor." International Symposium on Future Electron Devices—Bioelectronics and Molecular Electronics Devices (MITI Future Devices Project, 1985): 1–6.

6. A. Avarim and M. A. Ratner, "Molecular Rectifiers," *Chemical Physics Letters* 29 (1974): 277.

7. Mark Reed and James Tour, "The Birth of Molecular Electronics," *Scientific American* (June 2000): 86–93.

8. *Scientific American Key Technologies for the 21st Century* (New York: W. H. Freeman & Co., 1996).

CHAPTER 11

THE DIGITAL BIG BANG, QUANTUM MECHANICS, AND THE COSMOS

To see the world in a grain of sand,
  And Heaven in a wild flower,
To hold Infinity in the palm of your hand,
  And Eternity in an hour.

A poem by William Blake, Eighteenth Century

*Proclaim! in the name of thy Lord [Allah] and Cherisher [The Benefi-
cent, the Merciful], Who created-Created man, out of a (mere) clot of con-
gealed blood.*

Chapter 96, The Holy Quran

Things are in motion, hence there is a first mover
Things are caused, hence there is a first cause
Things exist, hence there is a creator
Perfect goodness exists, hence it has a source
Things are designed, hence they serve a purpose.

St. Thomas Aquinas[1]

11.1 INTRACTABLE COMPUTATIONAL PROBLEMS AND DETERMINISM

Quantum computing has become a very active area of research, and DARPA is now funding research at a number of U.S. universities including Caltech. On 29 December 1959 at the annual meeting of the American Physical Society, Richard Feynman of Caltech gave a famous talk that set the tone for what was to come in the next several decades and was subsequently published in February 1960 in Caltech's *Engineering and Science* magazine. In "There's Plenty of Room at the Bottom," Feynman discussed the problem of manipulating and controlling information on a small scale. Below is an excerpt from the talk that illustrates why molecular-scaled electronics is so appealing:

Why cannot we write the entire 24 volumes of the Encyclopedia Britannica on the head of a pin?

Let's see what would be involved. The head of a pin is a sixteenth of an inch across. If you magnify it by 25,000 diameters, the area of the head of the pin is then equal to the area of all the pages of the Encyclopedia Britannica. Therefore, all it is necessary to do is to reduce in size all the writing in the Encyclopedia by 25,000 times. Is that possible? The resolving power of the eye is about 1/120 of an inch—that is roughly the diameter of one of the little dots on the fine half-tone reproductions in the Encyclopedia. This, when you demagnify it by 25,000 times, is still 80 angstroms in diameter—32 atoms across, in an ordinary metal. In other words, one of those dots still would contain in its area 1,000 atoms. So, each dot can easily be adjusted in size as required by the photoengraving, and there is no question that there is enough room on the head of a pin to put all of the Encyclopedia Britannica.

Furthermore, it can be read if it is so written. Let's imagine that it is written in raised letters of metal; that is, where the black is in the Encyclopedia, we have raised letters of metal that are actually 1/25,000 of their ordinary size. How would we read it?

If we had something written in such a way, we could read it using techniques in common use today. (They will undoubtedly find a better way when we do actually have it written, but to make my point conservatively I shall just take techniques we know today.) We would press the metal into a plastic material and make a mold of it, then peel the plastic off very carefully, evaporate silica into the plastic to get a very thin film, then shadow it by evaporating gold at an angle against the silica so that all the little letters will appear clearly, dissolve the plastic away from the silica film, and then look through it with an electron microscope!

There is no question that if the thing were reduced by 25,000 times in the form of raised letters on the pin, it would be easy for us to read it today. Furthermore, there is no question that we would find it easy to make copies of the master; we would just need to press the same metal plate again into plastic and we would have another copy.

Feynman went on to show in his talk that, based on everything that physicists knew about atoms, particles, and molecules at the time, there was plenty of room for computer engineers to work within the realm of the microscopic world.

Some 23 years later, as recounted by David Deutsche, Feynman addressed the issue of simulating quantum-mechanical objects on a computer. Feynman pointed out something that many people were aware of but perhaps had not thought of the profound consequences: Simulating the quantum realm on a classical computer is an intractable task. No amount of time or processing power can do it. Feynman argued that reality is not classical but rather is governed by quantum mechanical principles only. The world of the human five senses operates in the classical realm basically oblivious to the quantum realm.

Deutsche draws an important distinction between intractable quantum systems and chaotic systems, the latter of which we believe could have broad and profound application to 4G wireless communications.

11.2 "INFORMATION" IS PHYSICAL

You might be thinking that 1s and 0s are quanta, but in the current electronic computer systems 1s and 0s are actually macroscopic whereby not one electron but thousands and millions of electrons are manipulated along silicon channels and on magnetic surfaces for the purpose of storing, moving, erasing, and retrieving information. You might argue that there is actually no such thing as a digital bit but rather an approximate representation of an analog signal, and you'd be right. However, information, whether in a man-made computer or a nature-made organism, is more than just 1s and 0s or analog signals. 1s and 0s are a representation or a language of something but that something is physical; it is part of the physical universe because information is intertwined with the physical universe(s)[2] comprising inanimate and intelligent creatures within its vast domain.

Over the last 75 years, scientists and engineers have wrestled with the fundamental physical laws and mathematical principles that determine bounded limits on the quality, the quantity, and the bandwidth associated with transmitting information between a sender and a receiver and for storing, erasing, and copying information on a storage surface or inside a logic or memory circuit. In a certain way, every particle-particle interaction that occurs is actually an exchange of information on the quantum state of the particles. It is difficult for humans to visualize the world of the quantum realm because it is rather contrary and counterintuitive to daily life. It is kind of like the antithesis of the ancient Chinese proverb that "a frog in a well does not know that there is an ocean out there." Theories such as Einstein's Special Relativity and General Relativity are also rather counterintuitive but yet they hold true, for our universe(s) holds many mysteries. Moreover, scientists are finding out that some of the deepest mysteries and complexities of the universe can be understood in terms of an information theoretic language.

Claude Shannon pioneered the field of information theory for communications in his famous monograph in a 1948 issue of the *Bell System Technical Journal*.[3] What got the attention of many from that publication was Shannon's introduction of a new concept that he called the entropy of information, which closely resembled mathematically conventional entropy S in the Second Law of Thermodynamics. Students of science probably recall that the Second Law implies that the entropy of the universe always increases. Entropy is thus a thermodynamic measure of the disorder of the universe. In the context of Shannon's formalism, entropy of information is a measure of "new" information. If you already know it then it is not information, it is a copy of "old" data.

In the ensuing 53 years since Shannon published his influential paper, the scientific community has come to realize that Shannon's information entropy and the thermodynamic entropy are two sides of the same coin. In fact, just as energy is quantified in quantum mechanics, information can to be thought of as quantified units because it ultimately has to be reduced to a representation of the physical world (transistors, electrons, something), which itself is quantum mechanical. Reality, as Feynman would remind us, is quantum mechanical, but none of this matters unless of course one wants to build a 1,000 gigabit memory chip or a ultra-low power CPU that can deliver thousands of MIPs of performance without taking all the city's power supply. In that case, one needs to understand how information can be represented, stored, and manipulated at the atomic and/or molecular level. Enter the quantum realm.

In the 1970s researchers at Oxford University, IBM, and Bell Labs gave birth to a new and exciting field known as quantum computing, where, in theory anyway, computers should eventually be able to carry out complex operations thousands or even millions of times faster than any present day man-made computing machine. The field of quantum information theory or quantum computing seeks to develop a theory for building theoretical and, eventually, physically real machines that operate on and capitalize on the principles of quantum mechanics. It was Richard Feynman who is often credited for emphasizing that a quantum mechanical computer is needed to genuinely simulate the physical world because computers that rely only on classical physics phenomena would never be able to grapple with the huge number of quantum states that exist in the quantum or nano-realm.

Device physicists have known for quite some time that semiconductor transistors have certain catastrophic physical limits once the minimum dimensions of the transistors began to approach the actual dimensions of the atoms. Thus, at somewhere around 5 to 10 billion silicon transistors per chip the transistors no longer function as macroscopic devices but rather are quantum entities, which means that if we want to construct computer chips with tens of billions of transistors we will need a new paradigm, a new type of switching device.

Researchers in both industry and academia are experimenting with atomic structures, synthetic organic molecules, and even biomolecular structures in hopes of someday creating a system where molecular-scale devices can be put on a chip, possibly in a self-assembling manner similar to the way that DNA guides the manufacturing of a living cell. And thus, the quest continues for smaller, lower-power, faster devices and circuits.

In a certain sense, information theory really is at the very heart of philosophy (cognitive research, behavioral studies, willpower, the soul, the mind, and so on). We can only speculate that if the great German eighteenth century philosopher Immanuel Kant had known what we know today about computational machines and brains, the universe, and quantum physics, how much more he would have been able to shed light on the essence of consciousness, morality, and reason. Sometimes the scientific community gets caught up in its mathematical formalisms and disregards the "softer" fields such as philosophy on the grounds that they are not rigorous enough. Yet, for all the pretensions of having figured almost everything out, present-day physics is loaded with inconsistencies and paradoxes, and we still seem far from putting it all together into a consistent theory.

As researchers delve into the potentialities of quantum computing, another seemingly unrelated field is also making discoveries that will affect future information theory. Quantum cosmology, one of a number of esoteric fields that physicists and mathematicians like Roger Penrose and Stephen Hawking spend their lives thinking about, is beginning to put information into a much larger framework—the universe itself. As Roger Penrose points out (see Figure 11.1), humans are actually quite large physically and human life span is actually quite long when one considers the entire universe and its space-time scales from the smallest vibrating superstring[4] (1×10^{-33} meters wavelength) to the atoms and molecules to the gigantic entities like comets, planets, stars, and galaxies (the Space Center of New York's American Museum of Natural History has an excellent walking spiral depicting this scale). Moreover, when one considers that the human brain is a structure more complex than anything else in the visible universe, having the ability to imag-

Figure 11.1
Sizes and time scales of the universe

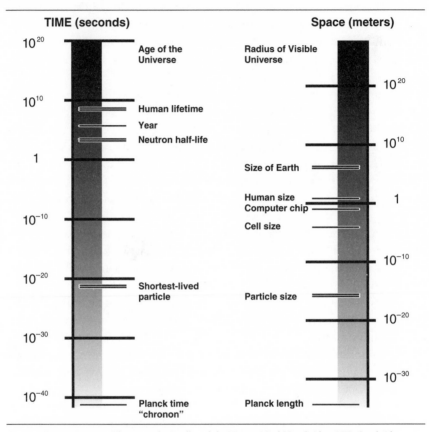

Source: Roger Penrose, *The Large, the Small, and the Human Mind* (Cambridge, UK: Cambridge University Press, 1995).

ine things that it cannot "see" (like God) and create a mathematics that does not exist and to abstractly reason about other universes that might exist, then we must humbly accept that we really are special. We are not an accident of the Universe. Our intelligence is not random. We are generators of information content in the universe. Entropy, as understood in the language information theory, is not necessarily increasing, because humans are creating orderly, complex structures, and enhancing them everyday. Out of the chaos a new information order is emerging, but a more intelligent order, a more sophisticated order. Thus, the universe is evolving, growing, and going somewhere. Although still a minority voice, some astrophysicists are taking the view that the Big Bang might never have occurred. We would like to conjecture, however, that there was a big bang of sorts, and we call it the Digital Big Bang because at some point in the space-time continuum of the universe highly intelligent creatures (that's us—notice we did not say "wise" though) came into existence.

We are advocating that we focus our collective efforts to develop and distribute, on a scale as massive as the human population, technologies for broadband wireless communications (4G), to populate the Earth with smart 4G sensors, to exchange our private messages with low-probability-of-interception 4G transport mechanisms, to fabricate molecular computers, to develop biochemical sensors that monitor our bodies and our surrounding environments for problems as well as intelligent nano-machines that can repair problems in the physical body. From and through all this, the Digital Big Bang evolves from its primitive roots toward a future path of enlightenment, a kind of entropic Darwinian evolution of the survival of the fittest information constructs.

11.3 QUANTUM INFORMATION THEORY

Thought Question: If a tree falls in the forest, does it make a sound? Can "information" exist without a "brain" to process it?

Quantum computing and communication (QCC) aims to apply specific aspects of quantum theory in the development of new systems and techniques for information processing and transmission. By employing the extraordinary properties of quantum mechanical operations, such as superposition, entanglement, complementarity and uncertainty, data can be encoded in the quantum states of matter or light and manipulated with unprecedented speed and efficiency.

Definition from the European Institute of Quantum Computing

NASA are now planning on the basis that Quantum Computing will be mainstream within five years.

Dennis Bushill, Chief Scientist, Langley Research Center, NASA

The [silicon] transistor will be superseded in 10 years . . . quantum solutions is the likely winner.

Joel Birnbaum, Chief Scientist, Hewlett Packard

Quantum computing, or more generally quantum information theory, has the potential to greatly alter the future of the high-performance computing and secure communications. One of the many fundamental yet unresolved questions of computer sciences is whether a computing machine could simulate quantum processes because in the quantum realm there are so many different states that atoms, electrons, and other particles can be in—rendering a comprehensive simulation virtually impossible with an ordinary computer (see Figure 11.2). As early as 1959, Richard Feynman of Caltech believed that such a computer would necessarily have to be constructed from quantum mechanical components and that such a machine might be able to simulate the macroscopic world in which humans interact through the five or more senses.

The very fact that such a prominent and brilliant scientist as Feynman said it was possible inspired other researchers to dig further. David Deutsch at Oxford University was probably the first person to actually propose something resembling quantum computers (QCs). Since the early 1970s, Deutsch had been working on a controversial theory known now as the many-worlds interpretation or multiverse, which invokes the concept of many universes existing in parallel. Deutsche developed the multiverse theory as a way to account for the many paradoxes of quantum mechanics such as the famous double-slit experiment where a photon actually appears to go through both slits at the same time or if two photons are fired through two slits they seem to be connected or entangled instantaneously, in seeming contradiction to the locality of Einstein's space in which nothing can travel faster than the speed of light.

Several years later in 1977, Deutsch extended his ideas to conjecture that it might be possible to build a QC that could simulate all of the parallel universes at once. The QC would operate by means of quantum-mechanical devices that exhibited the properties of quantum mechanics such as superposition. Although quantum computing was intriguing to theoretical physicists, nobody in the computer industry was taking it very seriously because, even if it were possible to build a QC, no one had proposed a computation problem that quantum computers could solve that would have any commercial value.[5]

A number of researchers further developed the mathematics for quantum computing, but it was Peter Shor of Bell Labs who found the first application for QC in a landmark paper entitled "Algorithms for Quantum Computing: Discrete Log and Factoring" in which he showed that if someone were to actually build a quantum computer then it would be possible to factor very large numbers with it; such prime number factorization could be used to crack encrypted signals. Suddenly, this esoteric field became mainstream, and the funding poured out of various government organizations including the NSA, NASA, and DARPA, all of which were extremely interested in the

Figure 11.2
Comparison of quantum and classical computation

Property	Classical	Quantum Computing
State representation	String of bits $\{0, 1\}^n$	String of qubits $\psi \Sigma_x c_x \mid x>$
Computation primitives	Deterministic or stochastic one- and two-bit operations	One- and two-bit Unitary transformations
Reliable computations from unreliable gates	Yes, by fault-tolerant gate arrays	Yes, by quantum fault-tolerant gate arrays
Computation speedups	Linear scaling	Quantum factoring—exponential speedup; Search—quadratic speedup
Source Entropy	$H = -\Sigma p(x) \log p(x)$	$S = -\text{Trace } \rho \log \rho$
Noisy Channel Capacity	Classical capacity C_1 equals maximum mutual information through a single channel	Classical capacity $C \geq C_1$; Unassisted quantum capacity $Q \leq C$; classically assisted quantum capacity $Q_2 \geq Q$
Entanglement-assisted communication	No	Superdense Coding Quantum Teleportation
Protection of secret cryptographic key	Insecure against unlimited computing power	Secure against general quantum attack and unlimited computing
Digital Signatures	Insecure against unlimited computing power	No known quantum realization

Source: Charles H. Bennett and Peter W. Shor, *Quantum Information Theory,* Sept, 1998.

implications for secure communication channels. Theoretical studies started to be churned out showing that QC could perhaps be used for other types of computationally challenging problems including pattern recognition, data bases searchers, and routing optimization.

Experimental Realizations[6]

Rolf Landaeur of IBM Thomas J. Watson Research Center, a world expert in the physics of computation and condensed matter physics, kept challenging the QC community to consider whether it was feasible to someday build a QC. It would take another five years before anyone would experimentally verify that a QC, albeit a simple one, could be realized in the laboratory. In April 1998,[7] two separate research teams, one lead by Isaac Chuang from IBM, with Neil Gershenfield from MIT and Mark G. Kubinec, a chemist at UC Berkeley, as well as a second team at Oxford University, reported that, for the first time, they had succeeded in demonstrating a two-qubit QC that worked on the basis of nuclear magnetic resonance (NMR) techniques. In the experiment of Chuang et al., isotopically labeled chloroform was used by manipulating, through NMR, the hydrogen and chlorine nuclei to create a two-qubit system. The Oxford team used NMR on cytosine to alter and read the states of hydrogen nuclei. Both teams demonstrated a simple quantum algorithm that had been first proposed by Deutsch in which the QC calculates the value of a function of two different inputs and allows the two values to be compared. The Chuang team also succeeded in demonstrating that their QC system could compute the Grover (of Bell Labs) search algorithm, which is considered to have much practical value.

The excitement created by this experimental breakthrough has prompted the research community to get into full swing with quantum computing. Already, the California Institute of Technology (Caltech), Oxford University, and Stanford University have established interdisciplinary QC research centers. The NSA is reportedly funding QC research at Los Alamos National Laboratory in New Mexico.

In the rest of this section, we briefly introduce some of the key principles of QC and refer the curious reader to the burgeoning literature and conferences covering this exciting field.

Landauer's Principle and Reversible Computing

Another question that Landauer wrestled with was whether information storage requires energy to be dissipated. What he discovered, and which is not intuitively obvious, is now known as Landauer's Principle. In a landmark 1961 paper published in the *IBM Research Journal* Landaeur showed that erasure of information and not the writing of it is where the energy must be used:

Landauer's Principle:
Computing itself does not require the use of energy because it is possible to exchange information between two systems without the loss of energy. However, there is no free lunch, and in fact it is the erasure of information that necessarily requires energy to be dissipated. Erasing one bit of information roughly requires an energy loss equal to the energy possessed by a bouncing molecule.

Shannon's Classical Channel Coding Theorem and Limits of Bandwidth

The theoretical limitation on the amount of information that can be transmitted on a classical (e.g., non–quantum-mechanical behaving) noisy wireline or wireless communications channel (see Figure 11.3) was worked out by Shannon in his original 1948 paper while he was a research scientist at Bell Laboratories. This law, now known as Shannon's Channel Coding Theorem, states that the maximum capacity C (bits per second) of a noisy channel is given by

$$C = \text{Bandwidth (MHz)} \times \text{Log}_2 (1 + S/N)$$

where S is the power level of the transmitted signal and N is the power level of the noise in the channel. In other words, in order to maintain a given rate of transmission C, a linear change in bandwidth must be accompanied by an exponential change in the signal to noise ratio, S/N. This is the reason that analog modems cannot go much higher than 56 kbps, prompting carriers to develop alternative methods of transmission such as digital subscriber line or ISDN.

Shannon's Law cannot be avoided when designing transmission systems, but fortunately there does not appear to be any theoretical limit on reuse of radio spectrum with spatial diversity. For example, communications infrastructure can be extended almost indefinitely just by adding more optical fiber, more switches, more routers, and more end-user terminals.

The concept of channel communication capacity can be extended to the quantum realm, but it gets a little complicated because of the strange

Figure 11.3
Schematic diagram of a general communication system

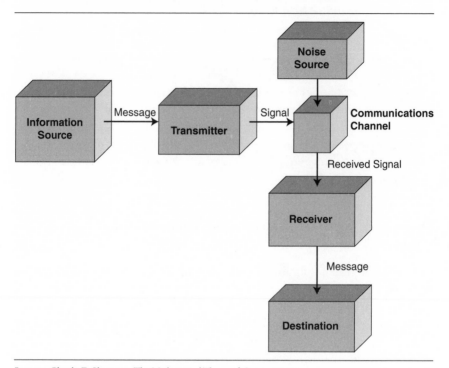

Source: Claude E. Shannon, *The Mathematical Theory of Communications.*

properties of a profound and deeply mysterious property known as quantum entanglement. Quantum entanglement is a concept and a property at the very heart of the mathematical and philosophical formalism of quantum mechanics. More specifically, it is tied to the principle of superposition of quantum states that generates a much larger space of possible states for a quantum system. In a classical digital computer, if you have two one-bit switching or logical elements you would get a total of four different combinations (00, 01, 10, 11). However, in a QC, you would get $2^2 \times 2^2 = 16$ different combinations, and a 32-bit system would generate 2^{32}.

Bell's Theorem and Quantum Entanglement

One of the fundamental precepts of Einstein's Special Relativity Theory is that the speed of light is constant in all frames of reference (moving or stationary) and that neither energy nor matter can travel faster than the speed of light. This principle is known as the locality of space-time continuum. Thus, if two physical bodies are to interact, such as a flashlight sending photons to a mirror or two planets coming in contact with each other through gravitational attraction, the interaction cannot happen faster than the speed of light. The principle of locality is the fundamental premise of relativistic space-time physics, but in the theoretical framework of quantum mechanics, a total different scenario is possible—the opposite of locality or nonlocality. Einstein was never much a fan of quantum mechanics, and one of the reasons was that quantum mechanics implies that it is possible to violate locality. In fact, in 1935 Einstein, Boris Podolsky, and Nathan Rosen published a paper, now known as the EPR-paradox in honor of them, in which they argued that particles (protons, electrons, photons, and so forth) under certain situations are actually entangled. The purpose of their paper was to show that quantum mechanics was incorrect because it predicted behavior that was impossible and violated locality. For example,[8] when an electron (spin $\alpha = \frac{1}{2}$) and an anti-electron (spin $\alpha = \frac{1}{2}$ also) (called a positron) are produced by the decay of single-spin zero particle, the two will move at opposite directions. By the law of conservation of momentum, the spins of the electron and the positron must add up to zero since that was the original spin of the original particle. The amazing result is that somehow the two particles know each other's states. The two particles could be miles apart and still they are entangled. If we measure the positron's spin to be up, the electron will be down; if we measure the electron to be up, the positron will be down. This implies that the two particles, no matter how far apart, are instantaneously in "communication" with each other. It was a great paradox back in 1935 to Einstein and his coworkers, and it still is a great paradox to the physics community. In fact, John Bell in 1964 gave a mathematical proof of what is known as Bell's Theorem that once and for all set the record straight.

Bell's Theorem and the Principle of NonLocality:
The Universe, according to quantum mechanics, is nonlocal everywhere. Distance does not seem to play a role in the behavior of entangled states.

You might be wondering what all of this has to do with computing. Well, not long after quantum computing came onto the scene, researchers realized entangled states was a powerful concept and potentially useful. Researchers have been able to show theoretically, and later in limited experimental scenarios, that quantum entanglement can be used for cryptography, teleportation, error-correcting, and search algorithms. Most of these algorithms can compute in exponential time, potentially thousands and millions of times faster than the thinly disguised sequential Turing-like computers that we call the state of the art today.

Cloning of Quantum States

In conventional transistor circuits, signals oftentimes need to be boosted using the amplification properties of transistors. Some bright minds have wondered whether a quantum amplifier could be built. The answer is no. Cloning of a quantum state is not possible. Those science fiction fans who are waiting for the *Star Trek* transporter to be invented might be disappointed to learn of this no-cloning theorem. Quantum mechanics postulates that no particle can be exactly cloned because in the process of "reading" the state, it would be affected, changing its original state. This is known as the Heisenberg principle and is a fundamental axiom of quantum mechanics. Thus, it appears that the transporter in *Star Trek* is impossible to build unless there is some way of imbuing the transported living body with the mental awareness or consciousness of the original person. (There are other obstacles though, which physicist Lawrence Krauss lists in *The Physics of Star Trek*, including the need for a hard drive the size of our solar system.)

Quantum Communication Channel and Capacity

The notion of a quantum channel capacity is much more complicated than the classical Shannon theorem. A quantum (communications) channel has three distinct capacities[9]:

1. An unassisted capacity Q for transmitting intact quantum states
2. A typically larger capacity C for transmitting classical information
3. A classically assisted quantum capacity Q_2 for transmitting intact quantum states with the help of a two-way classical side channel

The unassisted quantum capacity Q (N) of a noisy channel N is then the greatest rate (transmitted qubits per channel) at which for arbitrarily large n and arbitrarily small ε, every quantum state ψ of *n* qubits can be recovered with fidelity greater than $1 - \varepsilon$ after block encoding, transmission through the channel, and block decoding (see Figure 11.4).

Figure 11.4
The unassisted quantum communications channel

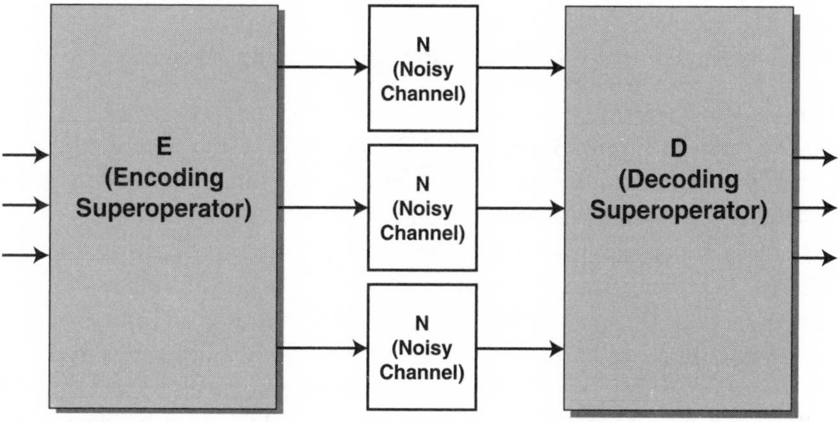

Source: Charles Bennett and Peter Shor.

Quantum Cryptography and Error-Correction Techniques

Quantum cryptography is a new and growing field within quantum computing that makes use of the unique properties of quantum superposition. The first idea proposed that used quantum cryptography by Stephen Wiesner, who in 1983 suggested "quantum money" that could not be forged. This would be particularly useful in stabilizing the money supply in countries like China where it is said that over 20% of the Remnibi bills in circulation are forged. Public shared key encryption such as the RSA algorithm relies on the extreme difficulty in computing the prime factors of very large numbers (100 to 1,024 bits). However, if you have a quantum computer, what would normally take exponential time could be done in something approaching polynomial time (P). Those at the leading edge of the signals intelligence and defense communities, as well as commercial banks and such funds-wire transfer networks as Swift, are probably having very serious concerns because quantum cryptography could potentially blow away all defenses.

If, however, the IT industry can build quantum key distribution (QKD) systems first, then the danger of hacking will be drastically reduced. It seems that QKD is the farthest along in terms of theoretical and experimental verification of the different QC applications. Optical prototypes working over tens of kilometers of fiber have been built and tested.[10]

The Turing–Church Thesis and Penrose's Turing Principle

God as the Ultimate Simulator.   If God exists and if He possesses a Universal Quantum Turing Machine then He should be able to simulate the universe(s), and if He can simulate the universe(s), why would He need to create a physical world? To test the simulation results?

Perhaps the physical world only exists as a simulation. Or, perhaps, the intelligent world of information processing entities (e.g., human brains) exists as a simulation? If humans have free will, should that not mean that we can change the outcome of the simulation at least in some of the universes?

If we do not have free will, we are carbon-based pinballs being bounced about in a cold universal quantum computer super high-tech arcade game, a Gameboy version of the ancient Greek's belief that the gods played with humankind! In some Eastern philosophies destiny and fate are sealed and cannot be altered, but we would conjecture that human free will, reason, consciousness, and intuition (a la Kant) might somehow be connected to certain unique and underlying quantum mechanical information processing properties, including the possibility of chaotic quantum behavior.

In 1936, within the space of three months, three mathematicians, Emil Post, Alonzo Church, and Alan Turing, independently provided the first abstract formalism for universal computers.[11] In what is now known as the Turing-Church Thesis or Conjecture, they postulated that it was possible to imagine a machine, now known as a Turing machine, consisting of a long paper tape with a finite number of distinguishable symbols written at even intervals and which could be read (and if needed written to) in a sequential order, backward or forward. He then showed that it would be possible to create a superset of all Turing machines, a Universal Turing Machine, which could compute "every function that would naturally be regarded as computable." But as David Deutsche and others have now shown, the Turing Thesis really only addresses what mathematicians can compute while theoretical quantum computers can perform tasks that a classical Universal Turing Machine or mathematicians could probably never be able to calculate. That led Roger Penrose to propose a stronger conjecture that Deutsche summarizes in his book *The Fabric of Reality:*

The Turing Principle: [For abstract computers simulating physical objects] There exists an abstract universal computer whose repertoire includes any computation that any physically possible object can perform.

The Black Hole Information Paradox—Quantum Info Vaporizers and Shredders

In *The Bit and the Pendulum*, Tom Siegfried recaps a fascinating story about a conversation between John Wheeler, a famous quantum cosmologist, and a graduate student, Jacob Bekenstein, in 1970[12] in which Wheeler and Bekenstein came to realize that black holes swallow information (or entropy) and that the size or, more precisely, the surface area of the black hole is related to how much information it had actually swallowed. The problem was that if a black hole had information or entropy then it must have a temperature, but if it has a temperature than it must emit radiation, meaning the black holes are not so black. They would be more accurately described as gray holes.

Stephen Hawking was able to explain this inconsistency. Black holes do emit radiation or evaporate but only on the black hole's edge or event horizon. Hawking showed that the radiation thus emitted was purely random and had no information content. This is where the paradox emerges—If no new information enters the black hole, the emitted radiation will eventually lead to the evaporation of the black hole, which begs the question: Where did the information go? A number of possibilities have been proposed, but the issue is far from being solved. Some physicists have suggested that quantum mechanics needs to be modified, but Hawking believes that the information is actually lost, perhaps to another universe. In other words, the possibility exists that information being generated in the universe is being lost. It is more than a little disconcerting for our human minds to fathom that the information describing our lives could be sucked up in a black hole, gone forever, or beamed off to another universe.

Bekenstein Bound—How Many Bits Can Be Packed in a Volume of Space-time?

The search for better cosmological models has led to some very mysterious, if not intriguing, properties of fantastic entities such as black holes.

One of the most relevant findings by cosmologists Jacob Bekenstein and Stephen Hawking was a formula that allowed them to calculate the entropy of a black hole. If this entropy is treated as information entropy, it becomes possible to provide an upper bound on the amount of information that can be represented in a volume of space. That limit is called the Bekenstein bound[13] and expresses the fundamental limitation on the number of possible quantum states in a bounded region or, alternatively, the number of bits that can be coded in a bounded region. As Frank Tippler notes in his bold book, *The Physics of Immortality,* the Bekenstein bound is a consequence of the basic postulates of quantum field theory. If we let I be the information related to the possible number of states (N) by the standard equation $I = Log_2\ N$, then the Bekenstein bound on the amount of information coded within a sphere of radius (R) containing total energy (E) is given by the following formula:

$$I \leq 2\pi ER / \bar{H}c\ log_2)$$

Where $\bar{H}$ is the Heisenberg constant, c is the speed of light, and log is the natural logarithm. Expressing the above equation in terms of the energy in mass units of kilograms we get

$$I \leq 2.57686 \times 10^{43}\ (M/1\ kilogram) \times (R/1\ meter)\ bits$$

For example, a typical human being has a mass of less than 100 kilograms and is less than 2 meters tall and such a volume could be enclosed in a sphere of radius 1 meter. The upper bound on the information content of a human being would thus be

$$I_{Human\ Being} \leq 2.57686 \times 10^{45}\ bits$$

Although the above number is obviously very large it is finite. In other words, human beings would not be able to store more than that amount of information in terms of bits. Of course, the architecture of the brain (i.e., neural networks and so forth) provides more constraints; nevertheless, it is intriguing to know that physicists have been able to estimate an upper limit on information that can be packed in a specific volume of space. This may become a metric by which we can start to compare the information packed into mobile devices or information accessible to them at various rates of uploading and downloading (see Figure 11.5).

Figure 11.5
Deterministic quantum mechanics vs. classical physics

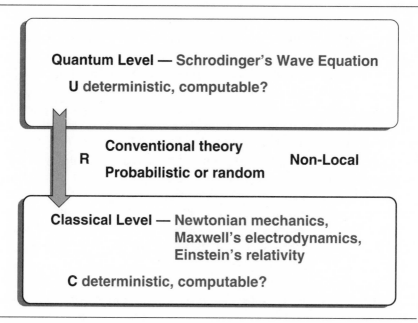

Source: Roger Penrose, *The Large, the Small, and the Human Mind* (Cambridge, UK: Cambridge University Press, 1995).

11.4 THINKING MACHINES AND CONSCIOUSNESS

Cogito ergo sum—I think therefore I am.

René Descartes

Moses said to God, "suppose, I go to the Israelites and say to them, 'The God of your father has sent me to you,' and they ask me, 'What is his name?' Then what shall I tell them?" God said to Moses, "I am who I am. I AM has sent me to you."

Exodus 3:13

One of the more speculative areas of cognitive science, neuroscience, and psychology is the classical problem in philosophy known as Cartesian duality, that is, the relationship between the mind and the body. Where is the mind? What is the subconscious? Are the conscious and subconscious connected to the physical brain? If so, how? Don't worry—we are not going to try to answer those questions here but . . .

Most people have the idea that the immense computational power of the human brain derives from the sheer volume of neuron connections. If that were simply the case, then it should be possible to build a machine with human-like thought and consciousness. Yet, all the great artificial intelligence research projects have consistently fallen short of their original targets. Sir Roger Penrose, known for his work in black holes and quantum cosmology, published two books, *The Emperor's New Mind* and *Shadows of the Mind,* in which he argues that the human brain and mind possess the ability to carry out certain noncomputable functions, which goes against the Turing-Church Thesis that it is always possible to create a machine that can compute anything. Penrose uses the famous mathematical theorem from Godel on logical incompleteness that says no logic system can be constructed that is entirely consistent—there will always be something that it can neither prove nor disprove.

Perhaps this is why it has not been possible to prove the existence of God. Not surprisingly, Penrose's ideas have received criticism as being unfounded and too speculative, but aren't scientists supposed to push the frontiers with new, novel, and more useful explanations?

Penrose has suggested that neurons may not be the only computational element in the human brain. He notes that in each eukaryotic cell, commonly found in most plants and animals, is a type of ubiquitous scaffolding called the cytoskeleton that is comprised of tiny microtubules. Microtubules are cylindrical structures made up of tubulin molecules measuring about 4nm in diameter. Microtubules are actually connected in a type of internetworked web inside the cell and undergo conformational state changes. Stuart Hameroff notes the multifunctional aspect of these mysterious ubiquitous structures:

> Microtubules (MTs) are cylindrical protein polymers interconnected by cross bridging proteins (MAPs), which structurally and dynamically organize functional activities in living cells, including synaptic regulation inside of the brain's neurons. They are the most prominent feature of the cytoskeleton which is at once (1) structural scaffolding of cells, (2) transport system, and (3) onboard computer.

The suggestion that microtubules may be involved in computation is an intriguing notion but not yet experimentally tested. In fact, Penrose and other speculative researchers are suggesting that the cytoskeleton acts as a computer, an idea that is supported by many observations including the complex behavior of the single-cell paramecia. Penrose has even gone out on a limb and put forth the fantastic idea that the microscopic cytoskeletal action may be mapped into larger-scale computation and awareness. Marie-Louise von Franz, in her book *Psyche and Matter,* wrote:

> If a tunnel breakthrough between psychology and atomic physics were to take place, confirming Jung's intuition of the archetype of the natural number as the joint ordering principle of the domains of psyche and matter, we would thus emerge at a place where lie the most ancient knowledge and traditions of the East, which in part have even long been forgotten there.[14]

It just might turn out someday that ancient philosophers from places including India and China may have been on the right track in terms of understanding the deep questions of philosophy whose answers have evaded solution since antiquity.

Thus, the question of duality gets deeper and deeper, and we are still far from solving this great question. We would like to impress upon the reader that the tools of philosophy, mathematics, physics, and chemistry all have to be used if we are ever to construct a model of intelligence and consciousness. After all, it was the Greeks who first proposed the concept of ether that was later verified experimentally in the early twentieth century to be totally unfounded and then was resurrected as very plausible, at least theoretically in superstring theory! In superstring theory, there is no vacuum space; instead the black empty space is an ether of tiny superstrings each vibrating with a wavelength on the order of 1×10^{-40} meters and thus not detectable with present instruments (see Figure 11.1).

NOTES

1. Quoted in Michio Kaku, *Hyperspace: A Scientific Odyssey through Parallel Universes, Time Warps, and the Tenth Dimension* (New York: Oxford University Press, 1994).

2. Or, multiverse for those that subscribe to the "many universe" theories.

3. 1948 was a pivotal year for communications and electronics with the publication by Shannon and the invention by the three-man Shockley team at Bell Labs who invented the

transistor that same year. Shockley et al. later received the Nobel Prize in Physics in 1956 for their revolutionary invention.

4. The theory of superstring attempts to unify the different laws of physics by postulating that matter consists of extremely tiny vibrating strings of the dimension known as Planck's length which is equal to 1×10^{-43} meters or 1 billionth the size of a proton. One of the fascinating results of the mathematical formulism of superstring theory is the necessity for a 10-dimensional space-time continuum, somewhat reminiscent of the higher dimensions in Eastern mysticism.

5. Tom Freigfried, in his book *The Bit and the Pendulum,* and Julian Brown, in *Minds, Machines and the Multiverse,* provide good background on how quantum computing came about and how it might be used.

6. Michael Brooks, *Quantum Computing and Communications* (London: Springer-Verlag, 1999).

7. Lisa Guernsey, "The Search Engine as Cyborg," *New York Times* (June 29, 2000).

8. Roger Penrose, *The Emperor's New Mind: Concerning Computers, Minds, and the Laws of Physics* (New York: Penguin Books, 1991).

9. Charles H. Bennett and Peter W. Shor, "Quantum Information Theory," *IEEE Trans. Info. Theory, 44* (1998), 2724–2742.

10. Charles A. Bennet and Peter W. Shor, *Quantum Information Processing,* September 1998.

11. David Deutsche, *The Fabric of Reality.*

12. John Wheeler, *A Journey into Gravity and Spacetime,* 221.

13. J D. Bekenstein, *Physical Review Letters* 46 (1981): 623.

14. Marie-Louise von Franz, *Psyche and Matter* (Boston: Shambhala), p. 5.

CHAPTER 12

WEARABLE COMPUTERS AND WIRELESS UBIQUITOUS COMPUTERS

12.1 INTRODUCTION

Wireless Ubiquitous Computers (WUCs), or wearable computers as they are sometimes known, are not clearly defined at this point in time in the industry. There is disagreement about whether wearable and ubiquitous computing is the same thing. The Gartner group, a leading world authority on information technology, considers wearable computing to be a subset of ubiquitous computing. Ubiquitous computing is the embedding of computers in the world around us. The human body is considered to be the natural medium relating to mobile, personal communications, and information management (e.g., messaging, calendaring, and contact information); whereas, environmental, ubiquitous computing is focused on situated activities (e.g., an office that senses when the occupant approaches and configures computer screens with the preferred configuration profile).[1]

Professor Steve Mann, a leading researcher in wearable computers, presents this definition: "A wearable computer is a computer that is subsumed into the personal space of the user, controlled by the user, and has both operational and inter-actional constancy, i.e., is always on and always accessible."[2] He identifies six attributes of wearable computers as follows:

1. Unmonopolizing of user's attention
2. Unrestrictive to the user

159

3. Observable by the user
4. Controllable by the user
5. Attentive to the environment
6. Communicative to others

Paradigm Shift—New Types of Human Interfaces Are Needed

For some time, graphical user interfaces (GUIs) have been the dominant platform for human to computer interaction. The GUI-based style of interaction has made computers simpler and easier to use, especially for office productivity applications. However, if mobile and wearable computing is to become ubiquitous, GUIs will not easily support the range of interactions necessary to meet users's needs.

A common focus shared by researchers in mobile, ubiquitous, and wearable computing is the attempt to break away from the traditional desktop computing paradigm (see Figure 12.1, Figure 12.2, and Figure 12.3). Computational services need to become as mobile as their users.

According to Edward Keyes of MIT in a Wearable UI White Paper published in January 2000, there are several reasons for the requirement for a new user interface (UI):

The command line interface (CLI) fails because it requires too much cognitive load to navigate. Imagine trying to compose a complicated recursive "find" command line while walking down the street: bringing up man pages and trying to memorize the options you need while simultaneously working out what the chord combination is for an ampersand. You'd get hit by a bus! The whole point of wearables is to augment your own capabilities. If you're using up 90% of your brainpower just to work the wearable, it's not an augmentation but a tremendous handicap.

Figure 12.1
Evolution of user interface paradigms

Era	Paradigm	Implementation
1950s	None	Switches, wires, punched cards
1970s	Typewriter	Command Line Interface
1980s	Desktop	GUI/WIMP
2000s	Natural Interaction	WAR—Wearable Augmented Reality

Likewise the WIMP interface fails because it is too inefficient. On a desktop, where you have a nice mouse and a big monitor, it makes sense to devote computing resources like screen space to interface elements. It's fast to mouse around, and friendly to have interface objects to directly manipulate. Unfortunately, on a wearable, pointing devices are much less efficient: moving a mouse cursor requires the attention of both the hand and the eye simultaneously, so it's nearly impossible to devote much attention to other tasks while navigating the interface. The situation isn't helped by the replacement of a mouse by a thumbpoint or tilt sensor. In a similar manner, screen space in a heads-up display is much more precious than on a 21" monitor: the wearable should use such space for relaying information, not interface.

Toward 4G Human Interfaces

The web-based information and services to which we have grown accustomed will expand only a little further, but the context in which we access

Figure 12.2
Paradigm shift

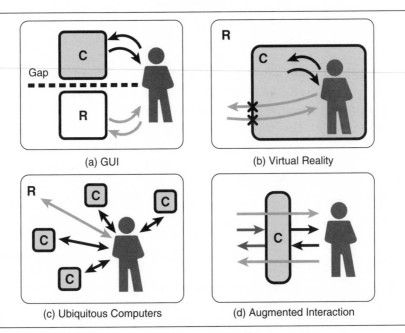

(a) GUI   (b) Virtual Reality

(c) Ubiquitous Computers   (d) Augmented Interaction

Source: Mark Billinghurst, University of Washington, HIT Lab.

Figure 12.3
Many different interfaces are possible

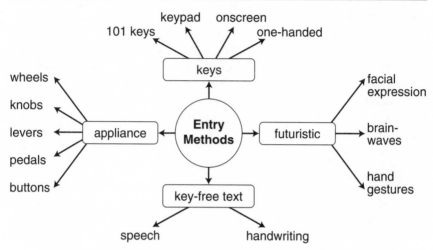

Combinations are important to consider: e.g., speech plus keyboard or keypad.

this information and utilize these services will change dramatically due to the pervasive mobility likely available with 4G networks. Given this, web content and information displays of the future must become more like the physical world with which they are to be integrated.

As 2-D windows-based interfaces are not ideal for 4G network users and in order to accommodate a wider range of scenarios, tasks, users, and preferences, we need to move toward interfaces that are natural, intuitive, adaptive, and unobtrusive. The most natural human interaction techniques are those that take advantage of our natural sensing and perceiving capabilities. Some of the obvious advantages to moving beyond the current typewriter/GUI mode (based on commands and responses) to a more natural model of interaction are as follows:

- Reducing the dependence on proximity that is required by keyboard and mouse systems
- Interfaces that are user-centered, not device-centered
- An emphasis on transparent and unobtrusive sensing
- User interfaces that take advantage of people's perceptual capabili-

ties in order to present information and context in meaningful and natural ways

Charmed Technology (Santa Monica, California) has proposed a new UI, called Wearable Augment Reality or WARface™ (see Figure 12.4).

Augmented reality (AR) systems in 4G networks are of interest not only because they provide a natural interface for mobile and wearable computers but also because we expect they will make possible new application areas.

For example, a user walking outdoors could see spatially located information directly displayed upon the view of the environment, helping to navigate and identify features of interest. To do this today, one would need to pull out a map, compass, and GPS receiver, convert the GPS and compass readings to one's location and orientation, and then mentally align the information from the 2-D map onto what one sees in the surrounding 3-D environment.

A WARface application could perform the same task automatically and display the landmark locations directly upon one's view of the surrounding area. A parallel example in the military sector would be that soldiers could

Figure 12.4
WAR portal interface

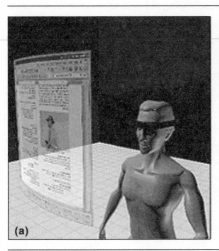

Source: Mark Billinghurst and Thad Starner, "Wearable Devices: New Ways to Manage Information," *IEEE Computer* (January 1999).
Note: WAR and WARface are trademarks of Charmed Technology.

see the locations of friends or foes and perhaps dangerous areas like mine-fields that may not be readily apparent to the naked eye.

Another WARface application area is the visualization of locations and events as they were in the past or as they will be after future changes are per-formed. Tourists that visit historical sites, such as a U.S. Civil War battlefield, do not see the location as it was in the past due to changes over time. It is often difficult for a modern visitor to imagine what historical sites really looked like in the past. A tourist equipped with an WARface application could see a computer-generated version of the site that would cover up modern buildings and monuments in the background and show, directly on the grounds at Gettysburg, where the Union and Confederate troops were at the moment of Pickett's charge.

Similarly, AR displays could show what proposed architectural changes would look like before they are carried out. An urban designer could show clients and politicians what a new building would look like as they walk around the neighborhood, to better understand how that building might af-fect nearby residents.

Implementation Issues[3]

While augmented reality applications offer some interesting possibilities, few have been able to build AR systems that work outside of a controlled envi-ronment. Steve Feiner's group at Columbia demonstrated the Touring Ma-chine, which allows a user to view information linked to specific buildings on the Columbia campus. Some wearable computers, such as the Carnegie Mel-lon University (CMU) VuMan systems, have been used for vehicle mainte-nance applications in outdoor settings. However, neither of these two projects were able to achieve accurate registration at a wide variety of outdoor loca-tions. At the International Symposium on Augmented Reality, held at Co-lumbia University on October 29–30, 2001 tracking and registration were core topics, with a number of near successes.

The biggest challenge lies in accurate tracking outdoors: determining the user's position and orientation with sufficient accuracy to avoid significant registration errors. Accurate tracking indoors is hard enough; accurate track-ing outdoors is even more daunting because of two main differences in the situation. First, we have less control over the environment. Second, there are fewer resources available—power, computation, sensors, etc. These differences mean that solutions for indoor AR may not directly apply to personal out-door AR systems. For example, several indoor AR systems have achieved accurate tracking and registration by carefully measuring the objects in a highly constrained environment, putting markers over those objects, and tracking the markers with a video camera.

This approach defies some of the constraints for an outdoor situation, as we rarely have control over the outdoor environment and cannot always rely on modifying it to fit the needs of the system. For example, in a military application it is not realistic to ask soldiers, friendly or enemy, to wear large markers to aid a tracking system.

Going Forward

While there has been significant progress on the registration problem, it is still far from a solved problem. AR systems, especially those that rely on closed-loop tracking, require carefully controlled environments. The user cannot walk and look anywhere she pleases; the system only works for specific objects, as seen from a limited range of viewpoints. By constraining the problem in this manner, the registration problem is more tractable, but it also greatly restricts the flexibility of the system and makes it difficult to build an effective AR system without expert knowledge.

From our research of the AR technologies capable of working outdoors (that is, in a pervasive 4G mobile environment), there is not as yet any single technology that provides a complete solution, nor is there any available technology that could provide the mass-market performance and scalability that we would require to meet our portal's goals.

Although the implementation of a Wearable Augmented Reality UI to the 4G Portal Portal interface is a difficult problem, it is a worthwhile challenge. There is a definite need to investigate and develop AR systems that can work in unstructured, real-world environments, both indoors and outdoors. Further research in this field by teams at Siemens, Columbia, Hughes Research, and Charmed Technology will help direct AR systems away from the highly specialized prototype systems of today to more flexible, portable systems that can be deployed anywhere.

12.2 PEER-2-PEER NETWORKING REQUIREMENTS

The P2P module of the 4G Portal Portal should allow users to interact with others in whatever way that is most convenient or makes the most sense: instant messaging, live voice, file sharing, discussions, transmitting video and pictures.

P2P computing at Charmed should facilitate entirely new ways of working within and among groups allowing spontaneous, secure communication between small groups that can be created instantly.

As part of our 4G vision, when a user launches the Charmed P2P module, he should be able to create a secure space or "federation" in which he and the people he invites will be able to federate or participate in. Each shared space (federation) would be stored locally on the computer of each of user. Then, when one member adds something new, like a video clip to the federation, that change would be reflected on everyone's machine. Suggested features and requirements for this P2P utility should include:

- Automatic configuration. Intelligently detects how the user is connected to the network and automatically adapts so that it works efficiently, whether using dial-up Internet access or broadband network access.

- Real-time interaction. Support communications to other users in real-time whether browsing the web, discussing and sharing videos or pictures, or creating outlines for new projects.

- Mobility. Provide support for off-line, disconnected use. Continue to interact and work with others in your federation, even if you're not actively connected to the Internet. The utility would then automatically synchronize the next time he connects to the Internet.

- Enabled from anywhere. Allow for federations to follow the user from one computer to another, so the user can have access from home, work, or on the road.

- Support open source tools. Provide users an extensive selection of tools and software, so they may create or add new functionality as needed.

- Allow multiple identities. Support the use of different personas (identities) so that the user can have a "business" persona, an "online" persona, and a "family" persona.

- Content creation. All content created should be owned by the user and stored securely on their computer (not a server), enabling the individual user to decide how and when to use it.

- Users have a private network. All shared spaces should be private: Only those members specifically invited by the user or other members of the federation should have access to content and activities.

- Encrypted security. The user's content and activities are completely confidential. Encrypts everything that goes across the network and into the user's hard drive.

- Support multiple accounts per computer. This will allow family members to use the same utility on a single computer, but each user's content is completely private to the other users.

- See who is online. Provide the user the capability to see not only which members are online in a space, but also where they are within a space (i.e., Joe is viewing your latest video; Ellen is reading your thesis).

- Enable access to content at all times (online and offline). Provide the ability to keep offline members synchronized with all other members. This will require the use of a relay server, which would act as follows: If one user is located in Los Angeles and another in Slovakia, it's unlikely they would be frequently online at the same time. The relay service allows the LA user to make some changes in a shared space and go offline. When the Slovakian user comes online, that user's device will fetch the shared space changes from the relay service.

- Invite new members. Provide (based on a users e-mail address) the capability to invite a friend or colleague into your federation.

12.3   A Closer Look at Augmented Reality

Augmented reality (AR) is the ability to superimpose computer generated text, graphics, and video in a person's view of the real world and is an important core technology component of the company's product strategy. The term *augmented reality* was first coined by Tom Caudell in 1992 in the context of a pilot project in which AR technology was used to simplify industrial manufacturing processes in a Boeing airplane factory. Research in AR draws on development from a number of other fields including virtual reality (VR), wearable and ubiquitous computing, and human computer interaction (HCI). In a certain sense, AR bridges the gap between virtual reality and the real world. Although AR is usually associated with head–mounted displays or heads–up displays (HUD) used by fighter pilots, it can also be provided in the aural domain.

It can be expected that over the next several years as heads–up displays improve it will be possible to implement AR on wearable computer systems. The first such project to be demonstrated to a large nontechnical audience was the AR effects that Charmed Technology developed for the Duran Duran show. The AR system will provide users with the ability to overlay a wide variety of data in the Communicator display's view of the real world including:

- Text
- Internet hyperlinks

- 3D graphics
- Video

Simulated examples of augmented reality are found in the following section. These images are from an article cowritten by one of Charmed's corporate founders, Dr. Thad Starner. They illustrate a person wearing a system similar to the Charmed Communicator. The top image represents an augmented reality video conference. The second set of images show Internet hyperlinks superimposed onto the real world.

Augmented reality technology has been in development for decades. Only now, with advances in visual displays, wireless Internet access, and mobile computing can these advances be made available to the consumer.

Augmented Reality–Based Services

Once the broadband wireless infrastructure, either through public base stations or through ad-hoc networks or some combination thereof, it will be possible, through a personal augmented reality viewer (which we call the 4G viewer) heads-up display, to receive a whole new array of value-added services. Some obvious examples would be:

1. Stock traders, in both the trading pits as well as trading floors of investment banks and brokerages, will find the 4G Viewer with integrated voice and data communications links to in-house trading systems and to customers directly so valuable they won't go to sleep without them at their fingertips.
2. Game players could provide a huge customer base for AR systems. Reuters (10 May 2000) reports that video games are a $20 billion industry worldwide. Furthermore, total game industry sales typically exceed revenues from the movie business. AR wearable systems will facilitate the creation of captivating immersive game experiences. Game players will be able to interact with computer-generated objects overlaid onto the real world environment.
3. Medical doctors who make rounds or work in the field for the Red Cross and other relief organizations could use AR systems for measuring vital signs, checking supply inventories, and consulting medical databases via advanced context-based database search engines such as Cobrain for information on rare diseases and treatments. Emergency medical technicians (EMTs) will also find this system highly useful.

Figure 12.5
Early example of augmented reality

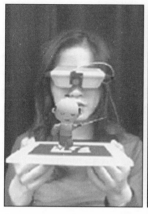 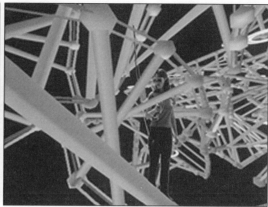

Source: University of Washington, MIT.

4. News professionals will be able to use the AR to view video, retrieve stories, and read live reports. Reporters will be able to access data search portals for research and fact verification while in the field.

5. Sports fans attending a live game will be able to view player stats superimposed onto their view of the actual game.

6. Fitness enthusiasts will be able to track their progress on many variables across time such as body fat, heart rate, blood pressure, and lung capacity.

7. Tourists could use their 4G Viewers for accessing maps and local information downloaded from a 4G portal. Free trials could be given for 15 minutes via department stores, malls, zoos, and museums. In Beijing, thousands of tourists each day rent an audio tape of the Forbidden City that takes approximately an hour. The system could also be rented, but it would allow the appearance of ghostly figures so that a sense of what it looked like prior to the present could be shown. Since tourists have spent thousands of dollars to get there, they are likely to be willing to spend an extra $20–$50 to get the premium service and then want to repeat this experience in other tourist locations.

8. Field personnel including salespersons, construction workers, office equipment technicians, and auto mechanics who need to access information while mobile will be ARPSS customers.

9. Soldiers, intelligence agents, police officers, firefighters, and other security and public safety professionals would find the AR wearable systems useful for accessing, viewing, and manipulating information superimposed onto their views of the real world.

The long history of AR is illustrated by the Aspen Project undertaken in the early 1980s by the Architecture Machine Group at MIT (precursor to the MIT Media Lab). It involved driving a car with six cameras mounted on the roof through the town and taking pictures every 10 feet. These photos were then organized on a Laserdisc so that they appeared to produce a movie. Viewers could stop at buildings, get a blueprint, and even get menus to overlay the doors of restaurants. Funding came from DARPA, which was rumored to want a system that could be used to completely map a town prior to an urban warfare scenario. All soldiers and their remote commanders would be able to know a town as well as its inhabitants by spending several hours with the AR simulation.

Similarly, with the 4G Personal Communicator envisioned in this book it will be possible to one day map the world and make annotations to it via "virtual post-it notes" so that future travelers will have the benefit of their comments. For instance, an augmented visitor to Times Square could be informed of all the restaurants that served sushi within two blocks. These locations could have arrows pointing to them. Upon seeing a restaurant, the video enhanced image could be highlighted or blink, and other users's comments could be viewed prior to ordering food.

Augmented Reality Rocks and Rolls at a Duran Duran Show

Chart-topping rock & roll band Duran Duran was probably the first performing group to deploy augmented reality in a live show. The rock band worked with Charmed Technology to create 2D and 3D visual effects that allow animated characters (in Figure 12.6 is an animated character of Nick from the band) to appear live on stage with the band as projected onto a large screen.

Figure 12.6 is an example of an AR model of one of the members of the band. The concept here is that these virtual people could walk around or stand on stage before the band arrives or after they leave.

12.4 WEARABLES MARKET SIZE AND VIABILITY

New International Data Corp. (IDC) research estimates the U.S. demand in the industrial, manufacturing, military, government, and medical sectors will

Figure 12.6
"Virtual Duran Duran" augmented reality object created for the Duran Duran show

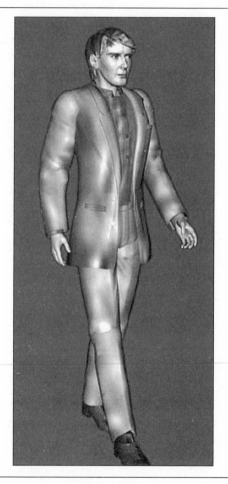

Source: www.duranduran.com. Courtesy of Charmed Technology and Duran Duran.

drive growth in the wearable PC market in the United States, pushing the potential market opportunity to $600 million by 2003. Because of the growing demand and the compelling applications in the manufacturing and military sectors, wearable computing rates 34 (on a scale of 1 to 100, with 100 being most viable) on the IDC emerging technology market's Commercial Viability Index. Baseline technologies or technology groups are used to calibrate the index; for example, baselines such as the World Wide Web score 75 on the grid rating system. IDC's new proprietary rating system to judge the commercial viability of new technologies indicates that, although wearable computing still has a lot of challenges to overcome, the device will be commercially viable (see Figure 12.7).

"Wearable computing will start to play a key role in cost cutting and increasing productivity for many industrial users in the next 5 to 10 years," said Christie Arrington, program manager for IDC's Emerging Technology Markets group and author of IDC's report, Alternative Computing Device Report Series: Wearable Computing. "The true mobility of wearable com-

Figure 12.7
Wearable computing

Wearable

Computing

Convenience

is the

name of the game.

Wearables can be anything

you want

Covers very large spectrum of taste!

– watches	– badges
– rings	– necklaces
– clothes mounted	– lead

Source: Charmed Technology.

puting will expand PC opportunities to markets and job functions PCs have not been able to penetrate up until now."

Each year the Gartner group identifies 10 technologies that are expected to attract the most attention due to marketing hype, rapid technology evolution, or growing application adoption. Wearable computers have been on that list for the past three years.

12.5 CHARACTERISTICS OF WIRELESS UBIQUITOUS COMPUTERS (WUCs)

Portable while operational. The most distinguishing feature of a WUC is that it can be used while walking or otherwise moving around or even at rest. This distinguishes WUCs from both desktop and laptop computers.

Sensors. In addition to user-inputs, a WUC should have sensors for the physical environment. Such sensors might include wireless communications, Global Positioning System (GPS), cameras, microphones, vital health signs, biochemical/electrical sensors, environmental biochemical/semiconductor sensors, and so on.

Multimedia outputs. A WUC should be able to convey information to its user in many different forms, even when not actively being used. For example, if your computer wants to let you know you have new e-mail and who it's from, it should be able to communicate this information to you immediately either using a display output or audio headphones.

Real-time operations. By default a WUC is always on and working, sensing, and acting. This is opposed to the normal use of pen-based personal digital assistants (PDAs), which normally sit in one pocket and are only woken up when a task needs to be done. However, it is possible that certain WUCs are put into standby mode to reduce power consumption.

Hands-free use. Military and industrial applications for WUCs especially emphasize their hands-free aspect and concentrate on speech input and heads-up display or voice output. Other WUCs might also use chording keyboards, dials, and joysticks to maximize hand availability for shooting, and so on.

Data and signal processing. In many cases, especially in the medical side, some sort of data recording device is needed so as to be able to record and examine data from sensors. For example, a pregnant mother can monitor her fetus's motions to be examined, which will improve chances of birth rate.

Lightweight power supply. A simple rechargeable battery or even one that has a very long life span can be used to power WUCs, but it has to be small and light in order for the WUC to be small and less uncomfortable.

Communications. WUCs may send information across a link for a real-time examination of a distant object. Medical monitors send their data back to a receiver in a medical facility and can then be studied. This improves the mobility of a patient who needs to be monitored constantly.

12.6 COMPETITIVE ANALYSIS OF WEARABLE COMPUTERS COMPONENTS MAKERS

Most of the major companies in the wearable computer space are still in the early stages of their development. These companies include:

1. *MicroOptical.* Makers of $2,500 IO displays that clip onto glasses and $5,000 eyeglasses with a tiny screen in one lens
2. *Xybernaut.* Makers of an industrial wearable computer system
3. *Charmed Technology.* Makers of wireless badges and user-friendly wearable computer systems
4. *Handykey.* Makers of the Twiddler one-handed portable keyboard

None of these component companies have sold many products, and they do not have a tie-in strategy to leverage the power of the Internet and connected communities. They are pieces of a nascent market in invisible wearable computing. Xybernaut, though "the leader in wearable computing," has invested over $100 million without making a profit in its decade-long existence.

At present, there is no consumer wearables industry, but it appears that Charmed Technology and IBM have done the most to create interest in that space. To date, IBM has not made the decision to get into the consumer wearable space. Philips, Sony, Nokia, and Toshiba are likely to enter in the near future as the wearables industry emerges. The list of wearable related components makers is growing and already surpasses 50 companies.

Product Profile: Wearable Computer from Charmed Technology

Current WUC technology is largely inaccessible to the everyday user. Many systems that exist today are expensive, highly proprietary, and not designed for all-day use. To remedy this, Charmed Technology has introduced the CharmIT Developer's Kit. The CharmIT was designed by Greg Priest-Dorman, with assistance from Dr. Thad Starner and is built on the PC/104 specification, which has been an industry standard for embedded computing for nearly 10 years. There are hundreds of companies that manufacture a wide variety of PC/104 hardware, and the majority of components are low power and ruggedized.

Available commercial wearable systems today can cost $5,000 or more, while offering little that would attract a nonindustrial user. The CharmIT Developer's Kit is lower cost (approximately $2,000), low power (approximately 7 watts with Jumptec 266), and offers enough computing power for most everyday wearable tasks.

A standard CharmIT kit consists of:

- Customizable, lightweight aluminum case
- Jumptec Pentium 166 or 266 MHz core board—includes on-board 10/100 Ethernet
- USB and SVGA
- PCMCIA board with two slots or SoundBlaster-compatible sound card
- Power conversion/distribution board
- Two Sony NP-F960 batteries (approx 5.5 hours run-time each)
- All necessary cables and connectors

Although this type of system is still in its infancy, we expect that numerous applications exist in the law enforcement, military, network operations, and emergency management areas, as well as health monitoring and educational systems.

12.7 APPLICATIONS OF WEARABLES TO HEALTH AND MEDICINE[4]

Wearables could become a core part of assistive technology, or technology used to help the disabled. There are a whole host of congenital, degenerative, and post-traumatic disorders and conditions that are responsible for a wide array of impairments that could benefit greatly from improvements in assistive technology (AT). Traumatic brain injury, spinal cord injury, stroke, Alzheimer's disease, multiple sclerosis, cerebral palsy, amyotrophic lateral sclerosis (ALS), and visual and acoustic impairments are merely a few of the many causes of disabilities, whose symptoms can be ameliorated by technological solutions. A very large number of illnesses and conditions exist for which there is treatment but no cure. Technological solutions already exist that provide greater independence and improvement in functioning for people with a wide array of disabling conditions.

Advances in technology will inevitably provide even greater freedom to those who are currently restricted in their activities due to disabilities. Many current solutions will merely be refined. Technologic innovations that have not yet achieved widespread use in the disability field, integrated with many of the currently available AT solutions, provide extraordinary potential for improving the quality of life for individuals with disabilities.

Many of the AT devices currently in use for individuals with visual impairments, speech and communication disorders, spinal cord injuries, learning disabilities, and so on have been developed as stand-alone devices that have evolved over time. Unfortunately, most of these devices don't yet capture the benefits that could be derived from the integration of advances in the different facets of information technology, telecommunication, and biotechnology.

Although wearable computer makers have not yet targeted the disability market, early products on the market can already accept input signals from speech, touch, keyboard, eye movement, Braille, and video devices while providing output in formats and modalities that are most suitable and provide the greatest accessibility to different users with various types of disabilities.

The wearable computer provides portability, versatility, and flexibility that is not currently possible with the various dedicated, stand-alone assistive technology devices that are widely used in the United States and around the world. Many other AT devices that currently require desktop or notebook computers do not permit the mobility that a well-designed wearable computer provides. There are other AT devices in use at present that enable a person with a disability to save data in a format that must be downloaded to a PC to permit manipulation of that data. When people use such devices away from their offices or homes, the delays in data transfer to their own computers reduce their productivity in work settings and reduce their capacity to fully participate in meetings and conferences and other comparable activities. Wearables already have the technology that can overcome the limitations of many such devices.

The applicability of wearable technology to improving the quality of life for persons with disabilities can be achieved almost immediately. Adding the wireless communication components to the wearability aspects of wearable computers and the potential for improving the independence and functional improvements for persons with disabilities become increased exponentially.

A whole host of AT devices exist for physically impaired but cognitively intact individuals. People with ALS, cerebral palsy, and other afflictions that interfere with verbal communication have access to speech synthesizers, but such devices do not easily accept data input except to produce synthesized speech. It is fairly straightforward to combine the output with input capacity, thus expanding the capability enormously. Currently there are many circumstances, particularly at meetings, when information that is presented in digital fashion, is translated by signers using American Sign Language (ASL). Capturing the digital data and converting it to an amplified audio signal via headphones or an earpiece, converting it to visual on screen signals, and/or saving the data on a hard drive in a wearable computer can enormously enhance the productivity of persons with hearing impairments.

Other people have what are characterized as invisible disabilities. Such individuals may have substantial cognitive impairments without external manifestations of physical impairments. Dyslexia and other learning disabilities fall on one end of a spectrum, and those with profound memory disturbances from stroke, Alzheimer's, or head injury are among those at the other end of the spectrum.

A wide array of software programs already exists to help students with learning disabilities. Wearable computers can permit context-awareness, user-awareness, and location-awareness, the ability to track exactly what is seen and (by measuring pauses and gaps) can guess what is understood and what needs further elaboration, and allows for group learning and interaction even if all parties are in different countries.

For those with substantial cognitive deficits, who may have poor impulse control, or become confused, disoriented, or lost, wearable computational devices can provide auditory cues that reinforce certain desired behaviors. For those with milder memory or cognitive impairments, a wearable could provide audible or onscreen messages, reminders, phone numbers, and so on. For those with more substantial cognitive impairments, the CharmIT input can be simplified so that the user can merely press a button to dial a phone number, send a pre-recorded telephone message, e-mail or other type of message to a predetermined set of individuals. Wearables could facilitate the communication that prevents the "in case of emergency notify" type situations. For those with even more profound cognitive impairments, wearable devices can be embedded in certain articles of clothing, like belts or bras, and if an Alzheimer sufferer, for example, wanders off, caregivers, police, or healthcare providers could receive signals from such devices that help them locate the lost individual.

For individuals who have incurred brain injuries from trauma, stroke, cancer, or other causes, the speech, occupational, and physical therapy treatments are very expensive and labor intensive. If it can be demonstrated that wearable computers as "wear alones" or with wireless connections can reinforce and replace some of the reminders, cuing, feedback, and other therapeutic functions currently provided by professionals and paraprofessionals, the reduction in healthcare costs would be monumental.

The U.S. federal government supports basic research in rehabilitation technology, much of which complements wearable technology. To date, the government has achieved very limited success in its efforts to foster commercialization of the scientific advances that it has supported. Wearables have the potential to combine research breakthroughs with highly profitable commercial applications of those breakthroughs.

In conversation with Alex Lightman, Dr. Robert Marks of San Diego notes that existing medical disorders such as traumatic brain injury, stroke, Alzheimer's disease, multiple sclerosis, cerebral palsy, cancer, and others have resulted in hundreds of thousands of individuals with cognitive and physical disabilities. Other victims with musculoskeletal disorders such as arthritis add greatly to those physically impaired. For many of the afflicted, there exist remedial or rehabilitation measures, but no cures. Recent advances in technology offer great promise in providing greater independence from disability and can be offered to the consumer at a moderate cost. The authors believe that the utilization of already existing wireless technology can be readily modified to provide therapeutic compensatory strategies. Although specific examples will be provided, it should be remembered that these do not exclude technological solutions for a variety of other medical problems.

Below is a simple list of potential medical uses of wearable computers:

1. *Distributed medical intelligence (DMI) for the Military.* Federal authorization allows for humanitarian intervention by America's Army, Navy, Air Force, and Marines at the discretion of their commanding officers. Soldiers and other nonmedically trained personnel can be equipped with a three-part medical assessment and emergency treatment system: wearable CPU with a medical database; sensor-studded glove that can detect and provide input (heart rate, blood pressure, blood oxidation) to the wearable; and goggles with a small camera mounted at eye level linked to both the computer and input, and, via a wireless radio link, to a local satellite uplink. From this, any doctor with an Internet connection can be accessed to give expert advice, with the same view as the attending soldier, the ability to speak and hear, and the ability to transfer files to and from the

wearable computer. Further information about this project can be found at www.strongangel.com, www.medibolt.com, www.mindtel.com, and www.quasar.org. Several companies including Xybernaut and Charmed Technology are selling wearable systems to the military for various applications, and the first 10 CharmIts sold were for a DMI-related application for the U.S. Navy.

2. *DMI for emergency medical personnel.* Firefighters and emergency medical technicians form a 230,000 person strong union, and firefighters alone provide over 70% of all preemergency room medical care. A wearable DMI similar to the military system could be used to dramatically improve the expertise of emergency responders, especially if citizens used their own 'personal black box.'

3. *Personal black box.* A wearable computer could be used to securely and privately store gigabytes of personal medical, health, and fitness data. Recent devices costing $99 or less can be worn on the belt and count steps, for instance, that are uploaded to a daily progress report. Some users, including Gordon Brown of Dana Point, California, report making sure to get 10,000 steps in a day because, for the first time, there is an easy way to keep score. However, there are many other things that can be recorded, such as blood pressure, heart rate, brain wave activity, and red and white blood cell count. It is even possible to put on a person's complete body scan, in 5 millimeter segments from head to toe, as well as all known allergies and medical history. An emergency medical provider, doctor, or caregiver who had this information could make a vastly more informed decision, and the personal black box could also warn against allergic reactions for prescription, based on its years of experience with the wearer.

4. *Memory glasses.* The MIT Media Lab has been working on memory glasses as "silver wear," or a mental appliance of particular use to the elderly, especially those ravaged by the scourge of Alzheimer's, a disease that affects over four million Americans. Though the MIT Media Lab has made substantial progress in hardware and software, the researchers have only written about the potential and have yet to actually provide their vest-related wearables and normal-sized eyeglasses with a tiny but expensive ($2,500) MicroOptical display to actual patients. Charmed can pick up where MIT stopped and make this technology affordable, widely available, and easy to use and maintain.

5. *Dyslexic digital assistants.* IBM estimates that there are between 7 and 42 million Americans with dyslexia, a condition that, while varying

greatly from person to person, generally makes it very difficult to read. By using wearable computers, written notes (such as e-mail and websites) can be read with synthesized speech to the wearers. An advanced application of AR would enable users to simply look at a sign or even a book through a small camera mounted in the heads-up display and have the system read signs or stories out loud whenever they looked at specific text.

NOTES

1. Carolyn Strano, "Wearable Computers: The Evolution of the Industry," available at http://users.erols.com/jsaunders/papers/wearable.htm. Gartner Group Research Note. (1997, October 30). Future Perspectives on Wearable Computing (Technology, T-ATT-539): Fenn, J.

2. Steve Mann, "Wearable Computing as Means for Personal Empowerment." Proceedings from the International Conference on Wearable Computing ICWC-98, Fairfax, Va., May 1998.

3. In this section, we reference the work of Ronald T. Azuma of HRL Laboratories in his paper "The Challenge of Making Augmented Reality Work Outdoors."

4. Source: Zeke Rabkin, unpublished correspondence with the authors.

CHAPTER 13

THE PLANETARY COMPUTER

The all-optical fibersphere in the center finds its complement in the wireless ethersphere on the edge of the network.

George Gilder

13.1 FROM ELECTRIC GRIDS TO INFORMATION GRIDS

Last December 2000, the state of California decided to provide $100 million to open a new research laboratory, California Institute for Telecommunications and Information Technology [Cal-(IT)²], to be operated jointly by the University of California at San Diego and the University of California at Irvine. Industry is contributing $140 million to the lab, and a number of companies including Sun Microsystems and Ericsson have already signed up as founding sponsors. Cal-(IT)² is also receiving $100 to $200 million from federal funds, $30 million from the two universities, and $30 million from private sources.

The total of $400 to $500 million in funding is being used to provide for a large staffing of 220 faculty and senior researchers. Cal-(IT)² is headed by Professor Larry Smarr who ran the Supercomputer Center at the University of Illinois at Urbana-Champaign. Smarr's list of research topics closely parallels our 4G vision (see also Figures 13.1 and 13.2):

- Advanced materials and devices
  - Biochemical sensors
  - Molecular electronics

- Quantum structures
- Bioinformatics

- Next-generation network infrastructure
  - Smart antennas
  - Broadband wireless is already here
  - Create wireless Internet "watering holes"
    - Ad Hoc IEEE 802.11 domains
    - Home, neighborhood, office
    - MobileStar—admiral clubs, major hotels, restaurants
    - UCSD—key campus buildings, dorms, coffee shops
  - Upsides
    - Ease of use
    - Unlicensed so anyone can be a wireless ISP
    - Will accelerate innovation—"living in the future"
  - Downsides
    - Not secure
    - Shared bandwidth
    - Short-range coverage
  - Planetary grid
    - Individual processors running at gigaflops
    - One million means a collective petaflops
    - One petaflops is roughly a human brain-second
    - Morovec-intelligent robots and mind transferal
    - Koza-genetic programming
    - Kurzweil—the age of spiritual machines
    - Self-organizing
    - Self-powered
    - Aware?

- Interfaces and software

- Applications
  - Digitally enable genomic medicine
  - Telemedicine

- Strategic applications

- Policy

Figure 13.1
The web will extend to become a planetary grid

- Wireless Access—Anywhere, Anytime
- Broadband to the Home and Small Businesses
- Vast Increase in Internet End Points
  - Embedded Processors
  - Sensors and Actuators
  - Information Appliances
- Highly Parallel Light Waves Through Fiber
- Emergence of a Planetary Computer
- The Web
  - The "Surface Web"
    - 2.5 Billion Pages
    - 7.5 Million Pages Added per Day
  - The "Deep Web"
    - 550 Billion Web-Connected Documents, Databases, etc.
    - 7.5 Petabytes of Storage
    - Much of This Is Large Scientific Documents
  - E-mail
    - One Trillion E-mails per Year
    - Roughly 500 Million Mailboxes
    - Up to 20 Petabytes of Storage
  - Globally Cached by:
    - Exodus, Akamai, WebEx, etc.

Source: Professor Larry Smarr, University of California, San Diego and UC Berkeley (see www.sims. berkeley.edu/how-much-info).

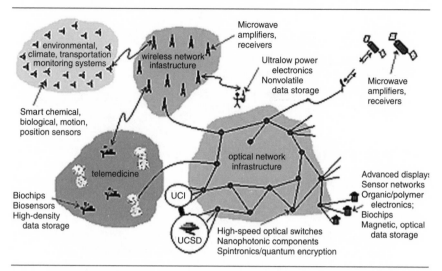

Source: NASA, UC Irvine, UC San Diego.

PART IV

A RECIPE FOR 4G SOLUTIONS

PART IV

ANALYSES AND
SOLUTIONS

CHAPTER 14

4G NETWORKS

The riders in race do not stop short when they reach the goal. There is a little finishing canter before coming to a standstill. There is time to hear the kind voice of friends and to say to one's self: "The work is done." But just as one says that, the answer comes: "The race is over, but the work is never done while the power to work remains."

Oliver Wendell Holmes
Radio address on his 90th birthday
(8 March 1931)

4G Technologies can evolve quickly, so we can skip 3G and go directly to 4G.

William C. Y. Lee, leading authority on wireless[1]

14.1 "CAPTAIN, A 4G ENEMY OBJECT HAS APPEARED ON OUR RADAR!"

Keith Woolcock, a telecom analyst at Nomura International in London, puts it this way: If the German government had used the billions of dollars extracted from telecom treasuries on 3G spectrum auctions on installing W-LAN base stations, they could have installed over 60 million, which would have been enough to cover all cities with broadband wireless base stations spaced 150 feet apart. There are a number of trends that good competitive analysts always watch for: interest by the defense and intelligence community, patents filed and issued, government research grants, number of technical conferences, number of PhDs, the flow of venture capital into a new area, and, finally, subtle changes in corporate press releases and public relations campaigns. On all of these fronts, 4G has in a matter of six to eight months in 2001 appeared on the radar!

Venture capital and second-round funding is beginning to flow into 4G technology companies. Examples would include Atheros (raised $60 million) which makes a single-chip 802.11a solution and Malibu Networks ($30 million) which is working on orthogonal frequency division multiplexing (OFDM), as is BeamReach ($35 million). The installation of 802.11 and HiperLAN cell sites all over the world is bringing massive bandwidth to thousands of hotels, Starbucks, and student dorms. Universities are rapidly deploying W-LAN on their campuses—and we know from wireline broadband what that means: The graduating classes are going to be hooked on this stuff and be unwilling to fall off a mobile version of what George Gilder called "a bandwidth cliff," and go back to puny telco-data driblets. Broadband is very addictive—if you don't have it you suffer withdrawal symptoms. Sonera's tests on what people did with wireless broadband revealed that people spent most of their time downloading music and playing games, which will obviously require a broadband connection. With 802.11b, it takes roughly a minute, or less, to download an MP3 encoded song, versus five hours on an I-mode or other 2G networks (see Figure 14.1). Even Microsoft is jumping on the 802.11 bandwagon. Amazingly, we really have not even begun to tap the potential of smart antennas, software radios, pulse-systems, and chaos systems, all of which could add a magnitude of improvements to the current system and even to 802.11b.

14.2 THE 4G ACCESS LAYERS

As shown in Figure 14.2, 4G will enable intelligent broadband informational and multimedia services to the Personal Area Pico-Network through broadband (greater than 1 Mbps) wireless links. The 4G communications architecture will comprise at least five access layers in a distributed environment and will need to accommodate a wide range of real-time devices such as video cameras, motion sensors, and so forth.

Broadcast layer: This is the world of the fixed and cellular-mobile base-station access points, which may themselves be connected into hierarchies of higher levels through fiber-optic channels, wireless microwave, or satellite links.

Public cellular/wireless layer: This is the world of the fixed and cellular-mobile base-station access points, which may themselves be connected into hierarchies of higher levels through fiber-optic channels, wireless microwave, or satellite links.

Ad-hoc/hot-spot layer: This is the world of the fixed and cellular-mobile base-station access points, which may themselves be connected into hierarchies of higher levels through fiber-optic channels or wireless microwave or satellite links.

Figure 14.1
Evolution to 4G systems

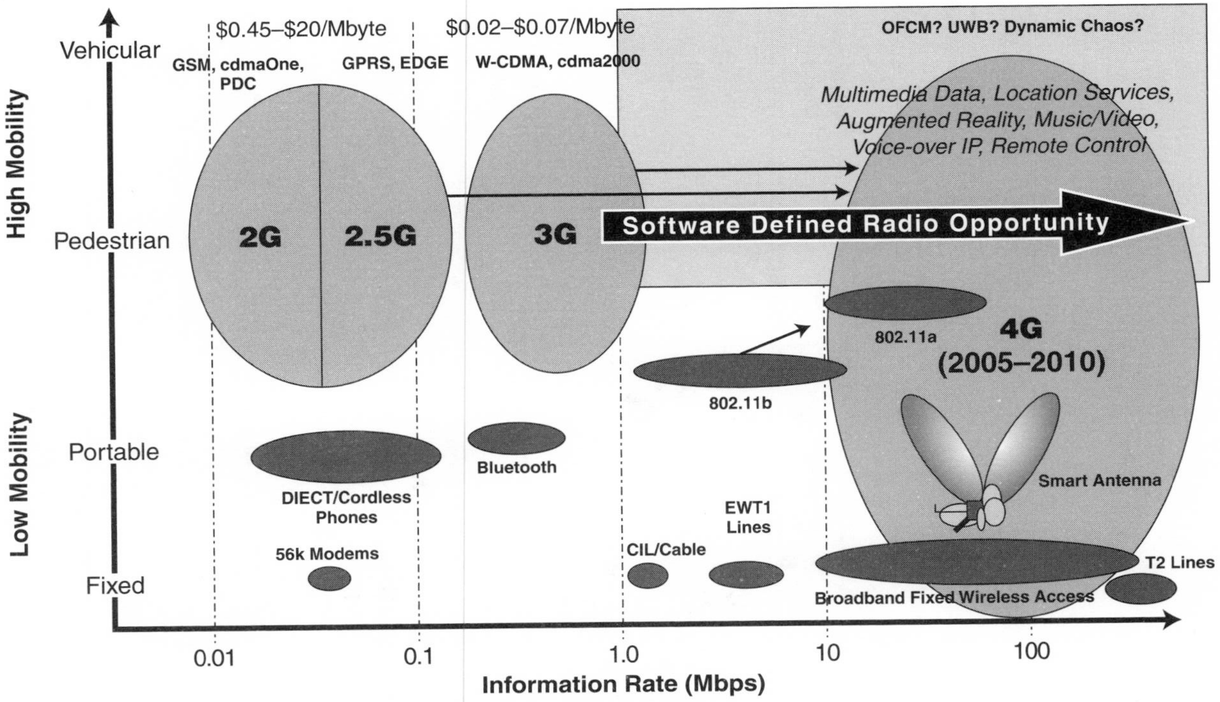

Source: Nortel Networks Qualcomm, Nokia, Siemens, Philips, NTT DoCoMo.

Figure 14.2
4G systems will connect to all access layers, directly or indirectly

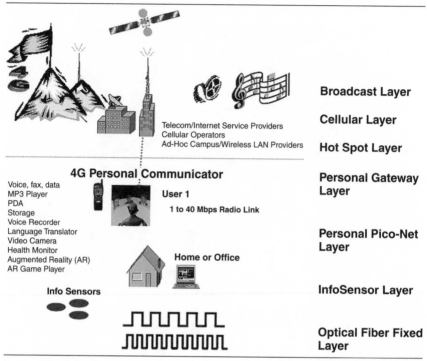

Source: Charmed Technology.

Personal gateway layer: This is populated by 4G Personal Communicators that are reminiscent of the Star Trek communicator and will be rich with function and intelligence. Specifically, these universal communicators will be able to receive across a wide frequency range. Their radio characteristics will be dynamically programmable through the use of *software-defined radio* techniques, and they will run the real-time operating systems (RTOS) tailored specifically for the stringent real-time signal processing requirements of software radios.

4G communications architecture extends the addressable Internet into a planetary grid with the 4G Personal Communicator as the *personal mobile control center* with the following basic functions:

1. Wireless IP router
2. Fax, voice, and data modem

3. Volatile DRAM storage
4. Non-volatile storage: flash, microdisks
5. Software radio universal transceiver
6. Encryption engine
7. PDA-type calendar and office functions
8. Augmented reality with video streaming
9. MP3 music player
10. Central command and control center for the user's personal pico-net (connecting through wireless links to home entertainment systems, home-security, automobile, family-member's wearable computer devices, temperature, and environmental sensors).

In other words, the 4G Personal Communicator is the all-in-one device that the electronics, computer, and mobile-phone makers have not gotten around to making yet.

We can envision would-be 4G technology companies implementing 4G Personal Communicators with embedded high-performance general-purpose microprocessors and custom-designed software radio chip sets allowing the Communicator to tune in to multiple types of modulation schemes simultaneously, such as AM/FM audio radio, IEEE 802.11x, GSM, TV broadcast, and walkie talkies. The 4G Personal Communicators can also be equipped with a radio chip set to communicate with InfoSensors in Layer1 such as one's home TV, automobile, or pet collars (see Figure 14.3).

Personal pico-net layer: This covers the personal environment around a 4G-PC user at any particular point in time. For example, while the 4G-PC user is driving a car, his personal pico-net is the automobile's computer system, and when the user drives into a 4G-enabled McDonalds drive-thru, the order will already be in process when the driver pulls up. And of course, the minute the 4G-PC user enters his home his personal pico-net becomes the home network that might include a robot, a 4G InfoSensor on his pet telling him what the pet did that day, and an entertainment system equipped with selected news articles and video news articles downloaded from the Internet.

Info-sensor layer: This is where the InfoSensors populate, but what are InfoSensors? They are intelligent object-based sensors (similar to localizers) that will be everywhere and nowhere at the same time. InfoSensors will become "inexpensive as jellybeans," as former *Wired* editor Kevin Kelly wrote about computer chips, and be used in the hundreds of millions to give us real-time reports on, literally, almost everything on earth. InfoSensors will run RTOSs that will need to have an object-based microkernel with an object-based application programming interface (API). Object-based technology facilitates changes, version upgrades, and software application proliferation, transforming Personal Area Pico-Networks into intelligent, thriving communities. Changes could be simple enough that entrepreneurial kids could have a "4G customization stand" instead of a lemonade stand. The limitations of an InfoSensors pico-community and the macrocommunity extended via the radio links to the Charmed Communicators are boundless as we add more and more dynamically programmable object-based primitives into the InfoSensor's core including personality, neural network-like features, and encryption capabilities.

Fiber-optic wireline layer: Although this subterranean labyrinth of fiber-optic cables and DWDM repeaters is rarely envisioned by the average driver originating a wireless call, without it broadband wireless wouldn't achieve even a fraction of its potential, especially in developed countries.

Figure 14.3
Potential 4G product evolution

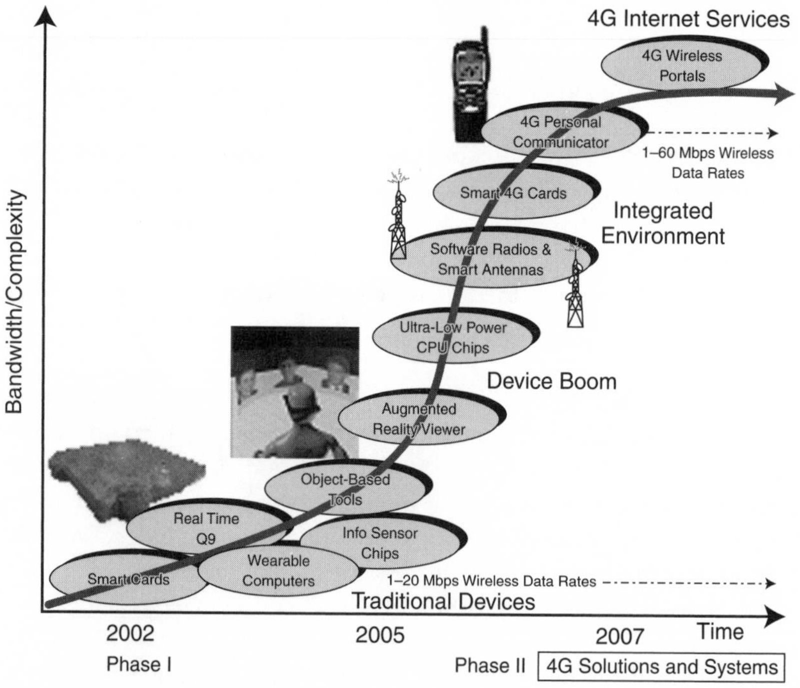

Source: Charmed Technology.

NOTES

1. Reported in Phone+ (March 2001), available at www.phoneplusmagcom/articles/131feat3.html.

CHAPTER 15

CHOOSING THE COMPUTER TECHNOLOGIES FOR 4G

15.1 THE 4G VIEWER—AUGMENTING OUR REALITY

In the near future, we may see augmented reality products for sale, perhaps even an infomercial offering the following pitch:

The augmented reality viewer (AR Viewer) is a head-worn display with a built-in digital camera that allows a wearer to capture and transmit real-time video while simultaneously displaying overlaying text, graphics, and video in a person's view of the real world. Its ultra-low power and small size make it ideal for portable computing applications. Its bidirectional interface is perfect for collaborative efforts such as mobile video conferencing—a meeting that can be held anytime, anywhere, and give some of the same powerful human communication cues as a face-to-face meeting. A wearer of an AR Viewer can have ubiquitous access to the entire world at any time and in any place. Wearers can see all—their immediate environment, the Internet, or any video stream. They are not isolated because at the same time others can see the world through their eyes and can communicate with them for a true global linking of minds.

By extracting and processing information from a user's perspective, filtered with eye-tracking or other means of measuring attention, interest, and arousal, portable computers can become aware and can see in context. For example, using face recognition software, a law enforcement officer could identify a person as being a potential threat. A tourist could immediately understand a sign in a foreign language. The heads-up-display (HUD) systems used by fighter pilots are early and expensive, yet very powerful, examples of AR through which computer-synthesized images are superimposed onto a pilot's view.

15.2   REAL-TIME OPERATING SYSTEMS FOR 4G

We need to design the 4G real-time operating system (RTOS) as an info-communications architecture with future-proofing, limiting obsolescence as much as possible by taking advantage of improvements in technology at many levels including:

1. Improvements in analog and digital-radio communications including coding, encryption, multiple-access schemes, and modulation methods
2. Enhancements to operating systems and programming languages and software development tools
3. Enhancements in digital-logic integration with the eventuality of migration to molecular/nano-technologies not just anticipated but expected
4. Dramatic improvements in storage systems (e.g., the IBM microdrive)
5. Evolutionary improvements in energy power systems (e.g., lithium polymer batteries)

Operating System Environments for 4G Wireless Systems

4G RTOS would be designed for three major uses:

1. In wearable computers and other WUCs that require sophisticated types of human interfaces such as in-display eyeglasses, speech recognition, and handwriting recognition where the user writes on a white board seeming to hover under the user's hand when it takes a writing position. The communications demands on 4G RTOS for such devices is rather high and includes support for MP3, music files, broadband streaming audio/video, publish/subscribe protocols (e.g., TIBCO/Reuters), and support for wireless standards such as GPS, IrDA, 802.11, 802.11a, 802.11b, and Bluetooth. Real time is not necessary, but it is highly desirable.

Figure 15.1
Prototype design of Charmed Viewer augmented reality viewer

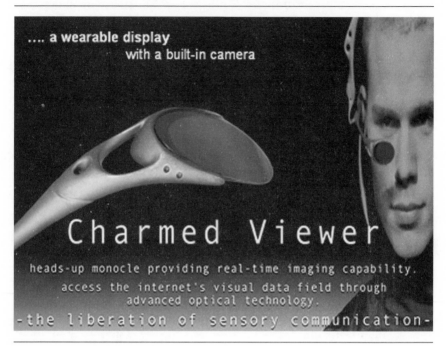

Source: Charmed Technology.

2. In InfoSensors, which means that it has to be real time, lightweight, fast, and support various artificial intelligence (AI) primitives and object-oriented functions. The communications requirements include interacting in real time with a wide range of electrical, mechanical, and biochemical sensors, encryption over the wireless link, and support for Bluetooth and IrDA.

3. In all WUCs, which need to implement a wideband, software radio system (the 4G Personal Communicators would be an example). These systems will have true RTOS kernel requirements because of the timing issues involved in processing on a general-purpose CPU digital communications filtering, wave-shaping, encryption, and so forth.

Each of the above application areas comes with slightly different demands on the architecture of the operating system, and as a result, we decided (see

Figures 15.2 and 15.3) to develop a single-core operating system initially based on Linux and later on a microkernel customized for InfoSensors.

15.3 LOCALIZERS AND INFOSENSORS

We estimate that in five years for every mobile-voice phone user there will be between two to fifteen InfoSensors-like devices in various applications such as toys, home appliances, automobiles, shopping malls, traffic lights, and so on. In our face-to-face discussions presenting the concept of InfoSensors, many industry watchers have jumped to the simplistic conclusion that InfoSensors are synonymous with Bluetooth. InfoSensors are designed to be *intelligent object-oriented wireless sensors,* which means that they have a potentially gigantic market. We believe that our 4G RTOS software architecture will have the flexibility to handle exciting advances in logic, radio, and storage technologies, including the eventuality of molecular and atomic-based systems.

InfoSensor chip sets are being designed to become the workhorse of the intelligent, wireless world and will be found in virtually every walk of life. For example, we can envision special InfoSensors for senior citizens that will warn drivers of a pedestrian's presence and can provide emergency medical communications services. We can also imagine the InfoSensors pet protector

Figure 15.2
Possible progression of operating systems for 4G systems

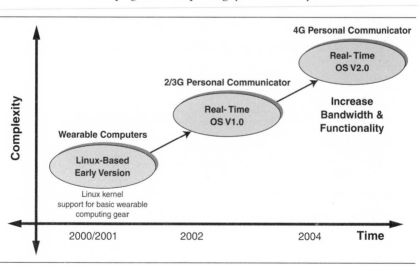

Source: Charmed Technology.

beaming the location of a pet's whereabouts and making a phone call warning the pet owner when the pet has strayed outside a boundary box made by simply clicking on a neighborhood map on the web.

The architecture outlined above is simple and elegant. We have borrowed this concept from biology, where a core set of cells can control most of the body's advanced, higher-level functions. By incorporating personality and context awareness at the chip level, future 4G networks (macro and pico) will have intelligence capability from the start.

Figure 15.3
Conceptual diagram of real-time Operating Systems for Wearables

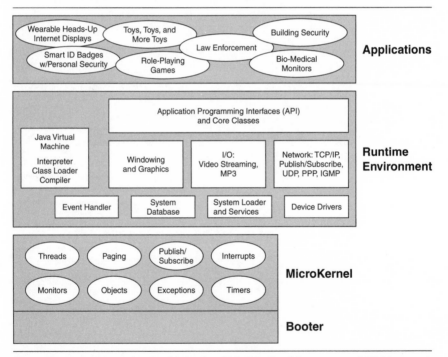

Note: Operating systems such as JavaOS, developed jointly by Sun Microsystems and IBM, have much of the functionality that will be needed for 4G Microsystems. However, true real time is not usually found in such operating systems and will have to be incorporated, probably at the kernel level.

Figure 15.4

Core technologies will be integrated into various 4G wireless user devices

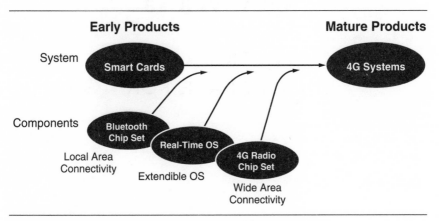

Source: Nortel Networks Qualcomm, Nokia, Siemens, Philips, NTT DoCoMo.

CHAPTER 16

SELECTION OF THE AIR-INTERFACE FOR 4G

16.1 COMMERCIALLY AVAILABLE UNLICENSED BAND SYSTEMS

In the last 30 years a number of advanced radio communications systems have been developed for defense and satellite communications applications. As integrated circuit technology performance and integration advances continue, it is becoming possible to implement these advanced (and sometimes declassified) technologies into commercial products. Currently, there are several commercial and experimental systems that are being used or evaluated by thousands of companies.

Bluetooth

Bluetooth is finding its way into many types of wireless systems including PCs, PDA, audio headsets, and cellular phones. The first generation of Bluetooth products that came to market in 2000–2001 had a range of about 30 feet (10 meters) and delivered data rates of 722 kbps at a transmission power of 100 milliwatts. In several years subsequent versions may be able to provide up to 2 to 12 Mbps, but most experts would wager on 802.11 as the dominant broadband W-LAN technology. A special interest group (SIG) was established by major technology firms including Ericsson, Nokia, IBM, and Microsoft to promote Bluetooth with a trademarked logo, tagline, and complimentary jingles. Over 2,000 companies have now joined the Bluetooth SIG. Cahners In-Stat Group estimates that the market for Bluetooth is huge, with sales of Bluetooth-enabled equipment and semiconductors reaching $5 billion in 2005. Applications include automotive, medical, industrial equipment, output equipment, digital-still cameras, computers, and communications systems. By mid-2001 over 140 qualified products had been listed on the SIG's website. More recent reports have expressed disappointment with the growth, cost, and utility of Bluetooth and are calling for greater progress in chips for Bluetooth.

A number of manufacturers including Toshiba and Motorola have developed Bluetooth chip sets. There are two different approaches being undertaken by the Bluetooth chip vendors: single chip or two-chip solutions. The drive toward a one-chip solution—baseband (BB) + radio frequency (RF) has been primarily cost and small-form factor. One chip Bluetooth requires that both the RF and BB circuits are implemented on the same chip using the same device geometry (CMOS) and fabrication process, a challenging feat because the digital circuitry causes considerable noise and interference to the RF circuits. A more practical approach for the short term is to implement a two-chip solution so that the baseband circuits are made with CMOS process or silicon germanium (SiGe) for low power consumption or Silicon on Insulator (SOI) for low leakage; the RF would be implemented with bipolar or Bi-CMOS process. For the case of the two-chip solution, it can be packaged on a multichip module that helps to reduce manufacturing when in volume production.

This highlights a future potential advantage of software defined radios—analog circuitry can be greatly reduced, allowing for more of the circuitry to be made in high-density, low-cost processes such as CMOS.

Wireless LAN Technologies: 802.11a, 802.11b, and HiperLAN

802.11x are W-LAN standards selected by the IEEE 802.11 committee and operate in the unlicensed industrial scientific medical (ISM) bands (see Figure 16.1). The 802.11 standards define a set of requirements for the physical layers (PHYs) and the medium-access control (MAC) layer. For high data rates, the standard provides two PHYs—IEEE 802.11b for 2.4 GHz operation and IEEE 802.11z for 5 GHz operation. The IEEE 802.11a standard is

Figure 16.1
High performance W-LAN technologies

System	Channel (MHz)	Modulation and Coding	Peak data rate (kbps)
IEEE 802.11a	20MHz@5.4GHz ISM Band	Coded Orthogonal Frequency Division Multiplexing (COFDM)	6,000–54,000
IEEE 802.11b[1] (up to 25 km range with high-power 4W transmitters)	70MHz@2.4GHz ISM Band	BPSK–1 MSps QPSK–1.375 MSps QPSK–1.375 MSps [MSps = MegaSymbols per second)	2,000 5,500 11,000
HiperLAN/2	150–200MHz @5.15–5.3GHz and 17.1–17.3 GHz ISM bands	BPSK, QPSK, 16QAM, 64QAM with Orthogonal Frequency Division Multiplexing (OFDM)	54,000
Wi-LAN's Wireless Local Loop[1]	33MHz@ 2.4MHz	Patented Multi-Code Direct Sequence Spread Spectrum	9,000

Source: ITU, ArrayComm Inc., Charmed Technology.

designed to serve applications that require data rates higher than 11 Mbps in the 5-GHz frequency band. A number of vendors make 802.11 cards for PCs and laptops including Lucent Technologies. Some 802.11b systems such as the one from Lucent are capable of transmitting up to 4 watts with a range of 25 km, but such high power would not be applicable to wearable systems, generally speaking. One of the drawbacks of 802.11b is that it is not compatible with Bluetooth systems because it uses the same frequency band (2.4 GHz) and thus causes interference. A special working group has been set up by Bluetooth supporters in an attempt to resolve the interference problems between Bluetooth and 802.11b. Start-ups also claim to have solutions ready.

We anticipate that 802.11a/b W-LAN systems will find their way into most U.S., Japanese, and Chinese university campuses. Nationwide franchise food and coffee chains are beginning to offer W-LAN services in their premises, including Starbucks. Even the airline industry has gotten into the act. Three major U.S. airlines—Delta, United, and American Airlines—in 2001 launched 802.11b W-LAN services in a number of airports including Chicago, Denver, Los Angeles, San Francisco, Dulles/Washington, New York, Newark, and Baltimore/Washington. At the same time a growing list of notebook and laptop computer manufacturers such as Dell Computer, Compaq, and IBM are selling computers with 802.11b PCMCIA. IBM and Dell also offer notebook computers with built-in antennas and 802.11b modems.

Bluetooth versus 802.11b and 802.11a

One of the issues that many people ask about is Bluetooth versus 802.11. Although Bluetooth chip set prices are falling below $15 to $20, with some $10 volume orders in 2001, this is not so low-cost that 802.11 cannot catch up. In fact, one company, Atheros, a Silicon Valley startup that raised $60 million in venture capital, has developed an 802.11a single-chip solution that the company believes can sell for only $5 in volume quantities. The Atheros chip can reach speeds of up to 72 Mbps, beyond the proposed IEEE 802.11a spec of 54 Mbps. Thus, the proponents of W-LAN technology such as Wi-LAN's CEO, Hatin Zaghloul, believe that Bluetooth will be dead in three years.[1] Bluetooth and 802.11b operate in the same ISM band that is already getting very congested in buildings, campuses, and even cities, so in the long-term the 5 GHz 802.11a systems might have more breathing room. Also, despite many qualified Bluetooth products, volume manufacturing will not ramp up until mid- or late 2002. By that time, 802.11b and 802.11a single chip sets could also be ramped up (though opponents argue that 802.11a standards are still changing), so it was difficult to call a clear winner as this book went to press. By mid-June 2001 several large chipmakers including Siemens, Intersil, and Philips announced single-chip 802.11b baseband processor and medium-access controller products. Most Bluetooth solutions are still implemented in two chips while 802.11b is usually three to four chips for the complete system. Finally, we should keep in mind that 802.11b and 802.11a are broadband and Bluetooth is not.

As a rule of thumb it has been our experience that the success of a product or service is usually inversely proportional to the amount of hype. Why is that? Because if something is so good then manufacturers and service providers can avoid spending "hype" dollars and instead spend target-marketing dollars. If we apply that rule, then 3G, WAP, and Bluetooth are definitely all in the hype.com bucket.

Of course, as we explain in more detail below, software radios have the potential to render all of these issues moot so that whatever spectrum is available at that location at that time will be used. We call this "wireless system hopping" noting that it is not just frequency hopping that could be done but the entire modulation scheme as well, limited only by the onboard processing power.

16.2   SMART ANTENNAS—UTILIZING THE SPATIAL DIMENSION

The increasing popularity of wireless-communications services coupled with the scarcity and expense of available spectrum means that infrastructure providers need to develop highly efficient usage of traffic channels in the wireless system. One class of techniques that has been developed is beam forming at the receiver so that two or more transmitters can share the same traffic channel to communicate with the base station's transceiver (BTS) at the same time. An adaptive antenna array is an advanced antenna system used in the BTS to form several antenna beams simultaneously. Each beam captures one transmitter by automatically pointing its pattern toward the transmitter while nulling other cochannel transmitters and multipath signals.

In a number of 2G and 2.5 systems, a simpler technique called sectorization is used, which is an alternative to smart, adaptive antennas. The sectorized cell sites employ hardware beam-forming array elements in which each beam is assigned a distinct RF channel set. The direction and gain of sectorized antennas is fixed in the hardware. It cannot place nulls on interference like smart antennas. Smart, adaptive antennas, on the other hand, generate beams that are not fixed and, instead, are dynamic per user and will place nulls that cancel interference.

Company Profile: ArrayComm

A number of companies are developing smart antennas, but it is worth focusing on one mentioned earlier, ArrayComm Inc.

Martin Cooper, the original developer of the analog mobile phone for Motorola, leads ArrayComm, which in 2001 was still privately held and developing advanced smart antennas for deployment in 2G, 3G, and beyond. The company has developed a proprietary transmission system that it calls I-Burst designed to deliver between 1 and 2 Mbps per mobile user, a marked improvement over the actual throughputs being demonstrated by W-CDMA 3G systems. ArrayComm's smart-antenna technology is currently licensed to base-station manufacturers, generating ongoing royalty income per unit of the installed base. I-Burst technology will be licensed, and chip sets, to be housed in both base stations and handsets, will be marketed by the company. As an intellectual property company, ArrayComm relies on its exceptional research talent—20% of the employees have PhDs (40% with master's degrees), and the departments are headed by some of the world's recognized experts, including the former Head of Wireless at Lucent. Operated by KDDI and manufactured by Kyocera, ArrayComm's IntelliCell is already commercially deployed in over 90,000 base stations in Japan and China, offering PHS and WLL services at up to 128 kbps.

Sony Corp. executives, seeing a growing importance of an new networked environment for the distribution of consumer applications at extremely low cost, have invested in ArrayComm to propel the development of a technology that will enable the delivery of new, media-rich wireless services built around Sony's core content and technologies. By forming a consortium with Redback Networks and several global operators and manufacturing partners, ArrayComm and Sony intend to promote I-Burst as a global standard.

Based on spatial division multiple access (SDMA) technology, Array-Comm's patented IntelliCell platform blends a digital processing system with multiple-element antenna arrays, giving wireless network operators a significant increase in signal quality, capacity, and coverage, all at reduced cost per subscriber. ArrayComm's I-Burst broadband Internet application, being developed with Sony's support, can out-perform 2G data solutions by up to 400 times, and 3G by more than 40 times. The FCC authorized ArrayComm in early 2000 to conduct experimental market tests with paying customers in the 2300 to 2305 MHz band. The FCC later authorized ArrayComm to conduct full commercial trial in 2001 in San Diego, where ArrayComm is expected to offer up to 1.0 megabit per second wireless access—with the freedom to move virtually everywhere—to the mass-market consumers, aiming for prices comparable to the low-speed dial-up prices. ArrayComm is also exploring several key strategic alliances with major carriers and global equipment manufacturers in the United States later this year for its IntelliCell application in the 3G networks.

SDMA and Smart Antennas

SDMA is advanced technology for achieving broadband capacity in a mobile cell by utilizing antenna arrays in the cellular base station together with adaptive signal-processing techniques (resource allocation, estimation, and detection algorithms) with origins in satellite military communications. ArrayComm Inc. has developed SDMA base stations for Japanese PHS and North American cdmaOne systems as well as I-Burst, designed to deliver up to 256 kbps uplink and 1 Mbps downlink services to each cellular user. I-Burst might end up competing with Richochet, an ISM 2.4 GHz unlicensed ISM band service from Metricom (USA).

ArrayComm's system employs very high performance signal processors that, when attached to an antenna array, can beam radio signals precisely at individual users. As each user moves around, the smart antennas track them. The result is a cloud of radio signals that follows each user around. The system can reuse the same radio frequencies for different users in the same vicinity, without worrying that the transmissions will interfere with one another. The result is a very efficient use of the carrier's spectrum, which affords the high data rates necessary for true wireless Internet communications services.

The antennas are already in place, and most cellular base stations have signal processors with the necessary computational power. So in most cases a software upgrade is all that is required to turn them into smart antennas. The drawback is that high data rates come at the expense of movement. Although the system is able to track a walking subject, it currently can't keep pace with a fast-moving vehicle. ArrayComm planned to begin a San Diego trial in the fall of 2001 and has teamed up with Sony to deliver video, music, and games.

16.3 ULTRA-WIDEBAND (UWB)

Ultra-wideband (UWB)—or Time-Modulated UWB from Multispectral Systems Inc. (Gaithersburg, Maryland) and Time-Domain (Huntsville, Alabama)—is a way of transmitting information on the radio interface very differently from the main line of wireless development. UWB uses pulse-position modulation technology in which extremely short (0.5 picoseconds), very low-power super-fast pulses are transmitted across a wide range of frequencies. Signals are transmitted as pulses at quasi-random speeds and modulations and are organized and decoded through the use of special codes programmed into the receivers that translate the pulses into binary 1s and 0s. The result is that UWB opens up virtually the entire electromagnetic spectrum and can deliver 10s and 100s and 1,000s of megabits per second of data throughput.

UWB technology has its origins in time-domain electromagnetic research dating back to the early 1960s in the United States and the Soviet Union. In the case of the United States, UWB was developed to characterize certain classes of microwave networks through their characteristic impulse responses. A number of subsequent advances included the sampling oscilloscope by Hewlett Packard (c. 1962), the development of techniques for subnanosecond (baseband) pulse generation, wideband and radiating antenna elements (c. 1968), and the invention of the short-pulse receiver. These led to the first U.S. patents in the field, which were issued to Sperry Research Center (then a division of Sperry Rand Corporation). In the later 1970s the principle use of UWB was in radar and communications applications, but 30 years later it is beginning to receive attention again as a short-range, ultra-low power (50 microwatts), ultra-wideband (e.g., 1 gigabit per second) transmission capability. Let's emphasize "gigabit per second." That's almost 100 times the throughput of 802.11b and greater than the average wireless Internet capacity offered by the entire American cellular industry as of 2001.

Time Domain is one of the pioneers of UWB and was founded in 1987 by Larry Fullerton, who is the inventor of the technology and the company's chief technology officer (CTO). Time Domain has demonstrated a UWB device that transmits 1.25 Mbps up to 230 feet at only 50 microwatts or 0.05 milliwatts—only one-two thousandths the power consumption of Bluetooth! Several big communications companies have taken equity stakes in Time Domain including Siemens Venture Capital and Quest. The company has teamed up with IBM to develop its PulsON 200 chip set, which will utilize IBM's SiGe fabrication process to realize a chip capable of transmitting 40 Mbps, exact location positioning, and indoor radar all at 50 microwatts.

The FCC is taking UWB quite seriously and in May 2001 the U.S. regulatory authority opened a public consultation with a view to allow the technology for unlicensed operation. Time Domain asserts that the pulses should be classified within the FCC's "Part 15" classification, which allows digital devices to emit low levels of electromagnetic (EM) radiation without interfering "harmfully" with devices licensed to use the radio spectrum.

Because this is a highly advanced technology, there are still only a few industry analysts who follow UWB technology, but one such person is Simon Forge of OSI, an IT consultancy, who believes that UWB could become a viable candidate for 4G systems: "UWB, as spread spectrum, could compete with all existing technologies in that it embraces them all, functionally, be they PHS, DECT, Tetra, Bluetooth, CT2, GSM, IMT2000, or AMPS."[2] The major downside of Bluetooth is that it is restricted to the ISM band while UWB can operate across a wide range of frequencies.

16.4 Wideband Orthogonal Frequency Division Multiplexing (W-OFDM)

W-OFDM from Wi-Lan (Calgary, Alberta, Canada) is a patented[3] variation of OFDM, which is now being deployed in 802.11a systems and improves on OFDM by correcting for distortions, allowing greater transmission speeds and maximizing the signal range. OFDM is a multicarrier modulation technique and is suited for short-wavelength (e.g., microwave) RF transmission because channel distortion, which is caused by frequency selective fading, can be all but avoided with OFDM. The discrete multitone (DMT) used in xDSL systems is a type of multicarrier transmission system that utilizes digital passband transmission in which the incoming data stream is modulated onto a carrier (usually sinusoidal) with fixed frequency limits imposed by a band-pass channel of interest.

While OFDM has long been acknowledged as a very efficient technology, it has proven difficult to implement on a chip set until now. The digital audio and terrestrial DVB (digital video broadcasting) standards are based on OFDM. In 1998, the IEEE 802.11a task group elected to use OFDM in its high-speed (6–54 Mbps) extension to the 802.11 W-LAN standard. 802.11a will operate in the new 5 GHz ISM frequency band.

In June 1999, Wi-LAN, after six years of R&D, released its I.WiLL wireless local loop system utilizing its W-OFDM technology. I.WiLL achieves a peak data rate of 30 Mbps in 20 MHz of bandwidth. Currently, this system represents one of the industry's most spectral efficient systems along with ArrayComm's i-Burst. Wi-LAN licensed its patented W-OFDM technology to Philips Semiconductors in September 1999 and is currently working with them to develop proprietary W-OFDM integrated circuits (ICs) based on I.WiLL.

16.5 Dynamic Chaos Technology

All of the above-mentioned air-interface technologies can be treated as evolutionary technologies, with the possible exception of UWB for piconets, but there is another system on the technology horizon that could revolutionize the entire wireless industry. This technology is called dynamic chaos and is based on the same theories as chaos theory and fractals that became hot research topics in mathematics and physics in the 1980s. Dynamic chaos, which has its roots in military research carried out in the former Soviet Union, has the potential to completely alter the landscape of military communications, just as Hedy Lamar's 1947 spread-spectrum patent (focused on allowing torpedoes to avoid being jammed) did in the 1950s and 1960s.[4] Until recently, chaotic nonlinear behavior in electronic and optical-digital transceivers had been considered a form of unwanted noise and efforts focused on reducing or eliminating its effects altogether. However, nonlinear behavior is not noise and, instead, follows a set of complex and much richer rules; thus, chaotic systems are deterministic. The key feature of chaotic systems is that an arbitrarily small change in input can result in an exponential change in the output. That feature could be exploited in wireline and wireless communication systems.

The first commercially available nonlinear transmission systems were fiber-optic systems based on soliton transport. The nonlinearity built into the optical fiber is actually the mechanism that ensures a digital pulse in the form of a soliton retains a constant shape over large distances, without diffusing or dispersing and arriving in a shape that can be recognized by the receiver. In this case, nonlinearity is employed to prevent complicated or distorted signal patterns from occurring.

Until very recently it was possible to control chaos in communication systems, but a number of breakthroughs in the area are convincing people that chaos holds almost incaluculable potential for 4G networks. Early experiments at Siemens Roke House laboratory in England have confirmed that up to 60 Mbps can be achieved using the same parameters of conventional wireless systems that eke out 1 to 20 Mbps transfer rates. Theoretical studies are now suggesting that 100 Mbps to 3 Gbps (fiber speed, but wireless means) is feasible within the next 5 years. The potential advantages of chaos-based wireless communications systems include:

- Much greater efficiency
- Lightweight and compact
- Significant improvements (several orders of magnitude) in capacity
- Greater number of channels
- Low-cost manufacturing
- Much lower probabilities of interception (LPI) and detection (LPD), crucial to military field ops

Though the press has missed this trend, virtually all of large telecom makers started quietly slipping "3G and beyond" circles in their 3G PowerPoint presentation slides with labels such as "100 Mbps moving, and 1 Gbps stationary." Ladies and gentlemen the word is out: Chaos is where the action is. Already, DARPA and the NSF are funding a number of chaos communications research projects around the country at universities such as Stanford and UCLA. Given that the USSR exhausted itself through military spend-

Figure 16.2
Mobile SDR architecture

- Modular hardware and software
- Open H/W and S/W interfaces defined by SDRF APIs
- Hardware reconfigurability and software programmability

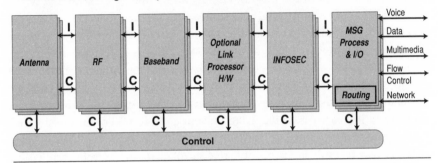

Source: SDR Forum Technical Report 2.1, November 1999.

ing targeting the United States and NATO members while failing to successfully market a single leading product to the world, the commercialization of dynamic chaos technology will open a new historical era for Russia while improving communication by a greater margin, in absolute terms, than any other single technology.

16.6 SOFTWARE RADIOS— TOWARD THE UNIVERSAL TRANSCEIVER

Software-Defined Radios (SDR) and Software Radios

Software-defined radios (SDR) are being promoted by the communications R&D community as an efficient solution to help address many of the migration and standards impediments that exist in the wireless industry today. SDR research is being promoted with high expectations to help future carriers better manage the technology standards maze and to provide users with increased access through multimode and multiband service capabilities.

We believe that SDRs will become a critical ingredient of the future wireless Internet, data, multimedia, and voice markets in the next three to five years. It is worth providing a more rigorous definition of SDR and another concept, software radios:

Definition of SDR: A software-defined radio is a radio in which the receive digitization is performed at some stage downstream from the antenna, typically after wideband filtering, low-noise amplification, and down conversion to a lower frequency in subsequent stages, with a reverse process occurring for the transmit digitization.[5]

Definition of Software Radio: As technology progresses, a software-defined radio can migrate to an almost total software radio where the digitization is at the antenna and all of the processing is performed by software residing in high-speed digital signal processors.

To understand the vast potential for SDRs, consider the complex situation that many mobile service providers have found themselves in: Although the mobile cellular, mobile trunked radio, and mobile satellite services have experienced tremendous growth in the past five years, it has been done at the price of complexity and too many communications standards (see Figure 16.4). Bell South Cellular is a case in point. Today the company operates seven different cellular networks:

- IS136 TDMA   @850 MHz
- IS136 TDMA   @1900 MHz
- PCS1900   @1900 MHz
- GSM   @900 MHz
- DCS1800   @1800 MHz
- IS95 CDMA   @850 MHz
- AMPS   @850 MHz

The cellular carrier is also having to evaluate 3G systems from the list of UWC136, WB-CDMA, WP-CDMA, and cdma2000 as well as various satellite systems. There are at least four major trends that are driving the cellular carriers to either a common set of standards or, if that is not realistic, a common radio transceiver system that can receive multiband and multimode (e.g., multiple modulation schemes):

- Convergence of information, computing, and communications technologies
- Need for mass customization of products to meet niche markets and individual needs
- The demand by the user for increased functionality in communications services
- The strong need by the user to manage the substance, form, and presence of their communications

Cellular carriers understand that in the future there will be a number of demands expected of them by users:

- Universal coverage
  Other networks (e.g., roaming)
  In-building coverage
  Single subscriber terminal
  Mobile, pedestrian, stationary, and fixed local loop
- Wide range of services
  Variable bandwidth
  Differing modes, connectivity
  User controlled features, network selections
- Highly flexible network infrastructure
  Flexible service creation and billing environment
  Access to services across and within other networks
  Future proofing

Thus, in the near term we will have SDR, and in the longer term we will have software radios (see Figures 16.3 and 16.4).

Figure 16.3
The concept: Software-defined radios (SDR) can be reconfigured via network downloads

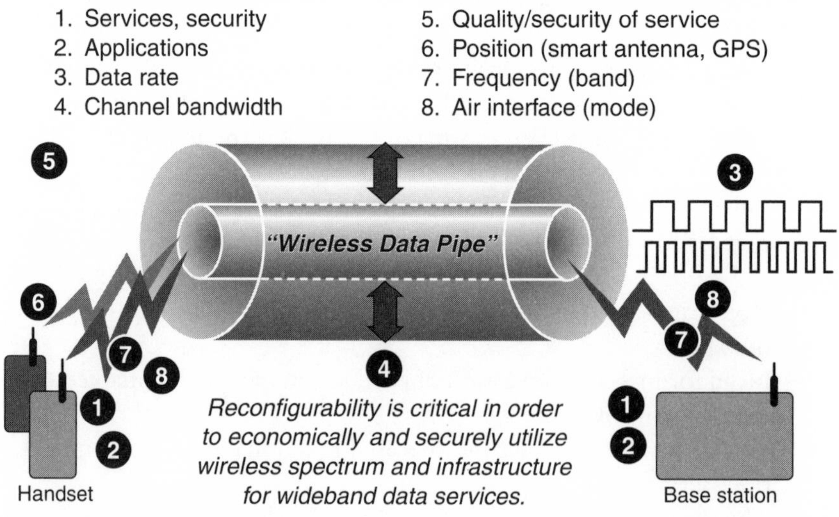

1. Services, security
2. Applications
3. Data rate
4. Channel bandwidth
5. Quality/security of service
6. Position (smart antenna, GPS)
7. Frequency (band)
8. Air interface (mode)

"Wireless Data Pipe"

Reconfigurability is critical in order to economically and securely utilize wireless spectrum and infrastructure for wideband data services.

Handset   Base station

Source: Software Defined Radio Forum.

The key benefits envisioned for SDRs are as follows:

- Reduce development, upgrading, and deployment costs.
- Reduce the number of product platforms to develop and support.
- Introduce product and service architectures that can be systematically scaled to higher data rates and user densities.
- Enable over-the-air product upgrades, service upgrades, and bug fixes.
- Differentiate and customize value-added products and services.
- Revenue enhancements by offering access to advanced digital services and seamless roaming on any wireless technology.

Software-Defined Radio Forum (SDRF)

The SDRF was established by a group of equipment vendors, research organizations, and government institutions for the expressed purpose of

Figure 16.4
Software-defined radios will accelerate 4G development

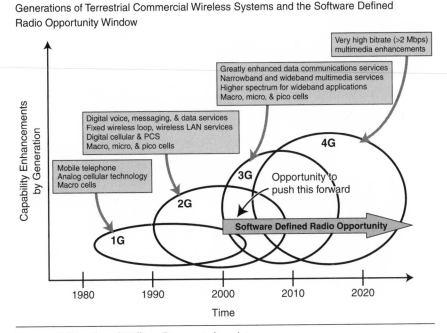

Source: BellSouth and William Benton & Associates.

accelerating the deployment of software-defined radios and then software radios. Currently, membership includes among others the companies listed in Figure 16.5.

The SDRF Technical Committee is organized into the following working groups:

- Basestation and Antenna Working Group
- Mobile Working Group
- Handheld Working Group
- Software-download Working Group

The SDRF is also cooperating with other wireless standards groups including the WAP (Wireless Access Protocol) Forum and the MexE (Mobile Station Application Execution Environment) Forum. The MexE Forum is group of about 20 companies including equipment makers and service operators that are working together to define specifications for software (S/W) transfer to/from mobile terminals for upgrade of services, applications, applets, and contents. The idea that MexE is pushing is to have a full application execution environment on the mobile terminal that operates as a Java Virtual Machine. If the goals of MexE can be achieved users will be able to enjoy:

- Sophisticated intelligent customer menus
- A wide range of man-machine interfaces such as voice recognition, icons, and softkeys
- A strict security framework to prevent unauthorized remote access to a user's data

Electronic encryption techniques already being assessed by the MexE Forum for mobile e-commerce transactions and other secure mobile services are expected to be robust enough to provide the necessary security for SDR software download.

The Federal Communication Commission (FCC) on 17 March 2000 announced that it is taking up the issue of software-defined radio as it has now realized that SDR holds potential for greatly altering the landscape of the cellular market. As a consequence, the FCC is opening a formal channel seeking comments from industry participants on various issues relating to the current state of technology, specific functions, and impact on regulatory environment.

16.7   4G SOFTWARE RADIO CHIP SETS

We believe that within the next two to four years it should be possible to offer a commercial SDR chip set that will serve as the workhorse of future 4G Personal Communicators. Figure 16.6 provides a block diagram of a conceptual 4G chip set, and as can be seen, the architecture is quite different from most other vendors's products that have been announced as being

Figure 16.5
SDRF corporate members

Telecom Equipment Maker, Other		Semiconductor/Electronics Maker	
Motorola	Qualcomm	Sony CSL	Radio Design AB
General Dynamics	Nokia	Agilent Technologies	Raytheon Systems
Kokusai Electric	Omron	Conexant	Rockwell
Metawave	Mnemonics	LG Electronics	Samsung
Mitsubishi Electric	Ericsson	Logic Devices	Sharp
NEC	Lucent Technologies	Morphis Technology	Harris Corp.
ITT Industries	Exigent International	enVia	Toshiba
Altera	Boeing	STM Microelectronics	Triscend
		Titan/Linkabit	

Telecom Service Provider		Research & Policy Entities	
NTT DoCoMo	Kyocera DDI Institute	Department of National Defense, Canada	Yokohama National University
Vodaphone	NTT	The MITRE Corp.	University of Oulu
Bell South Cellular	SK Telecom	ETRI, Korea	
COMSAT	Sonera	US Army–PMTRCS	
Southwestern Bell Technology Resources	Telefonica	US Air Force Research Laboratory	
Orange PCS			

Source: SDRF.

under development.[6] The design philosophy behind the proposed chip set is as follows:

1. Utilize a general purpose CPU to carry out waveform synthesis and to replace the traditional digital signal processors (DSPs). A number of novel techniques will be used including the use of precomputed tables of samples for different modulation schemes such as frequency modulation (FM), phase shift keying (PSK), and quadarture amplitude modulation (QAM). By using a generic CPU, it will be much easier to port an open source operating system (e.g., 4G RTOSOS RadioLink) to the SDR chip set.
2. Utilize an object-based software radio communications protocol layering architecture similar to the OSI layers. In this way, changes to a particular attribute can be handled efficiently.

Figure 16.6
Overview of a conceptual 4G software-defined radio chip set

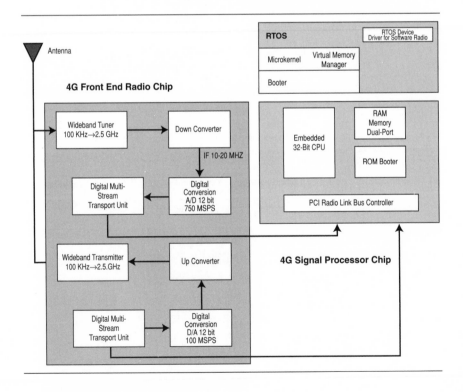

3. Develop a digital front-end chip that converts that wide RF signal into an intermediate frequency (IF) (10 to 20 MHz) signal that is then down-converted and sent to a high-speed, high-resolution analog digital converter (ADC).

4. Eventually, multiband digital front ends will become available, which will allow the SDR software to select the center frequency and width of an RF band in the range from 2 MHz to 2 GHz. This is consistent with the U.S. Department of Defense's Joint Tactical Radio System (JTRS) design goals.

5. Choose a virtual-memory and direct-memory access architecture that will enable the digital front end to transport bit streams on the order of 500 Mbps or higher.

NOTES

1. Reported in *Wow! Wireless* newsletter (11 October 2000).

2. Paolo Di Mia, "Escape from the Bandwidth Cul-de-sac: Wideband Technology," *Financial Times* (September 20, 2000).

3. U.S. Patent 5,282,222.

4. Strategic Assessment Report, U.S. Army Research Office.

5. Source: S. Blust, Bell South Cellular, available at www.sdrforum.org.

6. See Vanu Bose research (including his online thesis) while at MIT Computer Science Lab for an example of a working prototype demonstrating FM and several other modulation schemes.

CHAPTER 17

THE 4G PERSONAL COMMUNICATOR

Star Trek *Technology 400 Years Early*

17.1 THE 4G COMMUNICATOR— "BEAM ME UP, SCOTTIE"

The 4G component technologies (software radios, low-power CPU chips, ultra-dense flash memories) will enable the construction of true convergence consumer products in the form of a single device, which we will refer to as the 4G Personal Communicator (4GPC). The 4GPC will be used to access voice (via wired/unwired phones, radio, and Internet), TV signals, data, video, and text, and to seamlessly track across any available frequency and network. In other words, 4G puts the power of the air waves at your fingertips.

The 4GPC will be able to connect to public networks through cell sites and to wireless LAN cell sites when they are available. We can expect for quite some time that public networks will have as much as 10x slower data rates than wireless LAN clusters. The 4GPC will also be able to interact through very high-speed links to surrounding picocells in the home and in the environment such as a smart thermometer placed outside one's home window, on-board computers, for cars, or smart collars with GPS receivers for pets.

We envision a 4GPC with different software/hardware modules that provide GPS, MP3, digital photography, and videos capture capabilities. These modules can be made available in a variety of shapes, colors, and sizes, giving consumers a variety of fashion and image options. Numerous display and

Figure 17.1

The 4GPC can be built from several chips

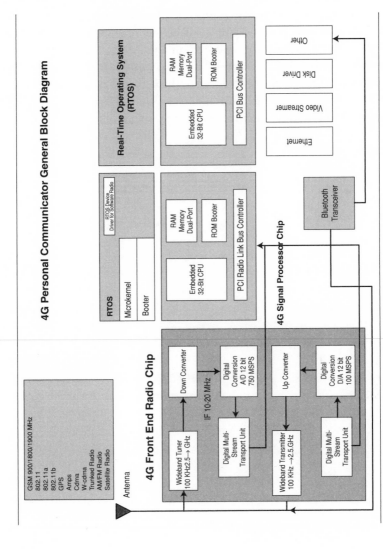

Source: Charmed Technology.

input options will be available including a head-mounted display and a wrist microphone. The 4GPC's key feature will be upgraded via these add-ons to suit the user's needs. Through the addition of peripherals, the Communicator may function as a mobile, wireless web-browser, e-mail terminal, video game system, or fully functional desktop-computer replacement (see Figure 17.1).

The 4GPC will have to run a totally new operating system optimized for real-time control and sensory environments. Multiple conceptual configurations of Charmed Technology's Charmed Communicator running Nanix™, Charmed's OS specifically tailored to the demands of mobile, on-body computing devices were demonstrated in the Brave New Unwired World technology fashion show, in cities around the world in 2000 and 2001.

CHAPTER 18

4G PORTALS

Wireless AOLs

18.1 INTRODUCTION

We are going to say the dreaded "P" word here. *Portal* is a word more associated with the failed dot.com stock disasters than with real business. If you can accept that later versions of wearable computers will have integrated wideband/broadband communications capabilities, you quickly realize that there is an exciting opportunity: the 4G Multimedia Portal that will make the wearable/wireless computer user community effectively the "last 100 feet" or "first 100 feet," depending on one's point of view.[1] If you put AR services on top of that you can envision a renewed demand for rich multimedia content.

4G portals will become distributed communications and informational gateways for users of wearable and wireless ubiquitous computers (WUCs). In this section we describe the key features and functions to be designed into future 4G portals.

18.2 LOCATION/CONTEXT-AWARE CAPABILITIES

Location- and context-aware applications are those that can determine and react to the current physical and computing context of mobile users and devices by altering the information presented to users. A context-aware system adapts according to location of use, neighboring entities, accessible devices, and changes to all of these.

Location-aware applications are becoming increasingly attractive due to the widespread dissemination of wireless networks and the emergence of small and cheap(er) locating technologies. We envision subsequent releases of the 4G Portal through which wearable or mobile users are continuously presented with new information and interfaces that are associated with the user's physical locations. Then, through collaboration with positioning technology services, the 4G Portal will be able to integrate location-based information services with any wireless gateway. A good source of research information for location- and context-aware applications may be found at two Georgia Tech sites: www.cc.gatech.edu/fce/ and www.cc.gatech.edu/research.htm.

To enable an effective development of location-aware applications, we must develop a sophisticated location information server based on directory data models and services. The approach should integrate location-awareness into a generalized framework for 4G mobile multimedia communication services. Consequently, the location information server will have to be an integrated part of our portal platform for mobile multimedia applications, and it must interact with the other platform support functions and mobility management services. For example, the platform will have to filter the 4G Portal applications from the underlying communication networks and locating infrastructures and offer a set of support functions and high-level APIs to third-party application programmers.

Reference Figure 18.1, which presents a diagram of the architecture and platform for mobile and location-aware multimedia applications at 4G Portal.

Typically, the location-information server (LIS) and the location-aware applications will run on different machines. The applications may, for example, run on mobile laptops, mobile phones, wearable devices, and PDAs, whereas the LIS will usually run on a network server with an interface to the physical locating infrastructure. The support functions of this platform offer three different location levels:

- Location-transparent. This level completely hides the effects of mobility to applications and users. Network services and resources will be transparently accessed by means of a resource- and service-broker function that maps the application's service-type requests.
- Location-tolerant. This level is necessary in the wireless broadband environment to allow applications and users to tolerate those effects of mobility that cannot be hidden by the platform. Such reasons can be

Figure 18.1

Platform for mobile and location-aware multimedia applications

Applications	Applications	Mobile and location-aware multimedia applications
APIs	APIs	
Mobile Application Platform		Mobility management services
Mobility Manager		Platform access protocols
APIs		
		Generic support functions
QOS Manager	Location-information server (LIS)	profile handler	Infrastructure and network interfaces
wireless and wired networks	locating infrastructures	**Mobile Management Domain**

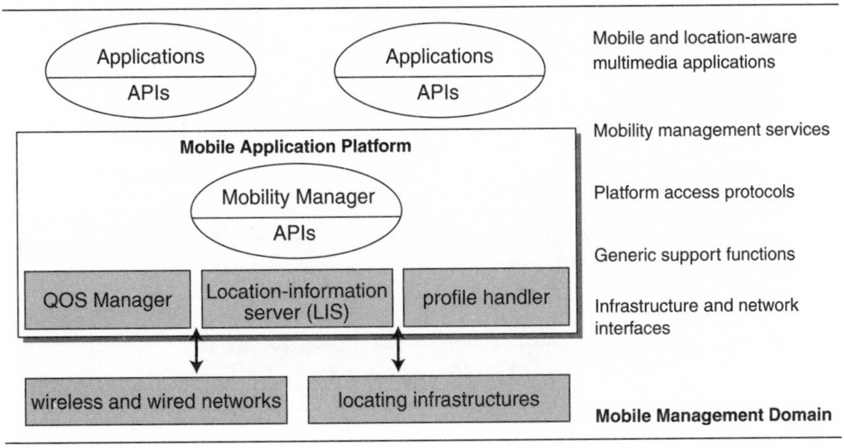

Source: Charmed Technology.

congestion of radio cells, degradation of radio link qualities, or change of terminals in case of user mobility. A function will be required to allow the application to perform a service and service-type renegotiation (i.e., a profile to retrieve user and device characteristics so an application can adapt according to the type of device currently being used).

- Location-aware. This level allows applications and users to be aware of their mobility and the absolute and relative physical positions of real-world objects. Applications can exploit this information for customizing their functionality, and users can benefit from this information for navigation purposes. This level is realized by the LIS function assisting applications to query location information and to be notified about the occurrence of location-related events.

The APIs will communicate with the platform through a suite of mobile application access protocols based on the widely accepted lightweight directory access protocol (LDAP). The advantage of LDAP is that it allows application programmers to employ off-the-shelf LDAP APIs that are widely available on numerous platforms. This way, no proprietary communication

Figure 18.2
LIS in 4G application platform

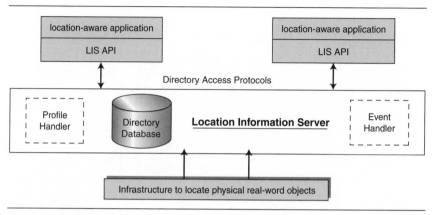

Source: Charmed Technology.

protocol stacks have to be developed, neither for the application, nor for the location information server. Additionally,because many networked applications need the directory access protocols anyway, the additional effort for the location-aware features of the application is minimized and a smooth migration path from conventional to location-aware applications is provided.

As shown in Figure 18.2, the LIS acquires information about the absolute or relative physical location of real-world objects in which an application is interested.

Approach

Location Aware. Providing services to mobile devices is more than just converting Web information to match the capabilities of the device (small screen, low bandwidth, etc.). A typical Web portal like Yahoo! or MSN is jammed with as much information as possible, usually in the form of links to other information repositories. However, what makes the whole wireless portal concept interesting is that once the capability is provided for the Web server to recognize the geographical location of a user, the server can then adapt and provide services or information that are relevant to the current location.

It is easy to envision a large number of location services built with content that is specific to one's location. For example, a location service can monitor local buses and trains, as well as airline traffic. Another location service tracks local restaurants, advertising their menus; hotels with room availability; theaters that have last-minute tickets for sale; and so on. Along the same lines of thinking, we can provide location services that are only physical devices that just advertise their availability: public printers on a campus, ATMs, vending machines, etc. Obviously, the number of services potentially relevant for a given location can grow rapidly and be dynamic, with new services appearing and disappearing constantly based upon usage, which, of course, can also be tracked and evaluated.

The suggested 4G Portal implementation approach is to associated services with geographical areas or regions. A region can be defined as a member of a hierarchical structure (country, state or province, county, city or municipality, district, street, etc.), by metropolitan areas, or the path of a predefined route, which follows multiple roads.

The 4G Portal-defined hierarchy would go something like this:

World > Continent > Country > State > County > Zip Code > Latitude/Longitude

---

In addition to the company's own 4G Portal-defined regions, designers should also allow the end-user to define his or her own user-defined regions (UDR), which would intersect with 4G Portal-defined regions. Additionally, in such a model it is essential for the mobile user to be provided with means to filter the relevant services, as well as means to classify and prioritize services.

Crucial to the implementation is the need to store the metadata associated with the different objects and their location (location ↔ metadata mapping). Then, given the location information (a point or a region) and the metadata criteria, we could get all the different businesses and services in that location/region satisfying the metadata category.

Context Aware. Context-aware applications gather knowledge about their users and operating environment. Contextual knowledge is typically obtained from sensory data in real time and, perhaps, after making inferences. Equipped with knowledge about the current situation of usage, context-

Figure 18.3
Location-aware profiles

Service Influence	Uniqueness	Example
Physical location	Specific	Record shop nearby has recent shipment of CD you've been looking for.
Physical location	Generic	What will the weather be here, tomorrow?
Device	Specific	Print this article when I am connected back to my corporate LAN printer.
Device	Generic	Send this message when connected to a network.
People	Specific	Remind me (or notify me) when I see (or am near) this particular person.
People	Generic	Send the next meeting's agenda to everyone in this room.

Source: Charmed Technology.

aware applications are able to automatically perform appropriate actions without the user's needing to request them explicitly. Almost any information available at the time of an interaction can be seen as context information. Some examples are as follows:

- Identity—what is the background of this person I am talking with?
- Spatial information—e.g., location, orientation, speed, and acceleration.
- Temporal information—e.g., time of the day, date, and season of the year.
- Environmental information—e.g., temperature, air quality, and light or noise level.
- Social situation—e.g., who you are with, and people who are nearby.
- Resources that are nearby—e.g., accessible devices and hosts.
- Availability of resources—e.g., battery, display, network, and bandwidth.
- Physiological measurements—e.g., blood pressure, heart rate, respiration rate, muscle activity, and tone of voice.
- Activity—e.g., talking, reading, walking, and running.
- Schedules and agendas.

Possible Applications

There are a multitude of applications and services that are possible with lo-cation- and context-aware services (see Figures 18.3 and 18.4). First, let us consider the service classes as presented in Figure 18.3. From this example,

Figure 18.4
Overview of requirements for a sample context-aware application

Possible Applet for a Context-Aware Calendar

When the user records a new calendar entry, the active calendar service sets out to find the pertinent information and downloads it to the client to display in the calendar application. For example, the user might record an entry for a meeting with "John D" at company "XYZ-Soft" about "Project X"; the user prefers to fly into "LAX" airport. The applet would collect information for the meeting, which is then downloaded through the network and over the wireless link, to be displayed in the user's mobile or wearable computer's calendar application. The calendar applet automatically collects the following information:

- Contact information, such as telephone number, e-mail address, office location, and job responsibilities, for each person attending the meeting
- Home pages and a brief project description, obtained by querying a project database for the subject(s) of the meeting
- A timetable listing all flights from the user's home city to the destination on the particular dates of the event
- Driving directions from the airport to the destination
- Hotels and restaurants in the neighborhood of the destination
- Any events in the destination city occurring during the visit
- A weather forecast for the destination, updated daily and starting five days before the actual event

Because the attributes of elements can be interpreted in a "location-aware context," both the style and the content of the calendar interface can vary in real time. Thus, views should be tailored to the user's present needs ("Load driving directions when I am driving") and to the user's preferences ("Show full company news on company I am visiting now"). The interface must also be tailored to the hardware device's capabilities. For example, on a mobile phone display only thumbnail images, snippets of local restaurant information, and text reminders appear, but the mobile PC or the wearable computer could display a full map and play reminders as speech.

Source: Charmed Technology.

we can see how the 4G Portal may be able to navigate the 4G world by providing a display of interesting objects, both nearby and far away:

- To keep a record of objects and persons one has encountered, for use by applications such as activity-based information retrieval, which uses the context at the time the data was stored to assist in retrieval.
- To detect location-specific information; for example, electronic messages left for the user or for public perusal at a specific meeting place.
- To keep a lookout for nearby devices that can be used opportunistically

Figure 18.5
Architecture of a future sensor portal

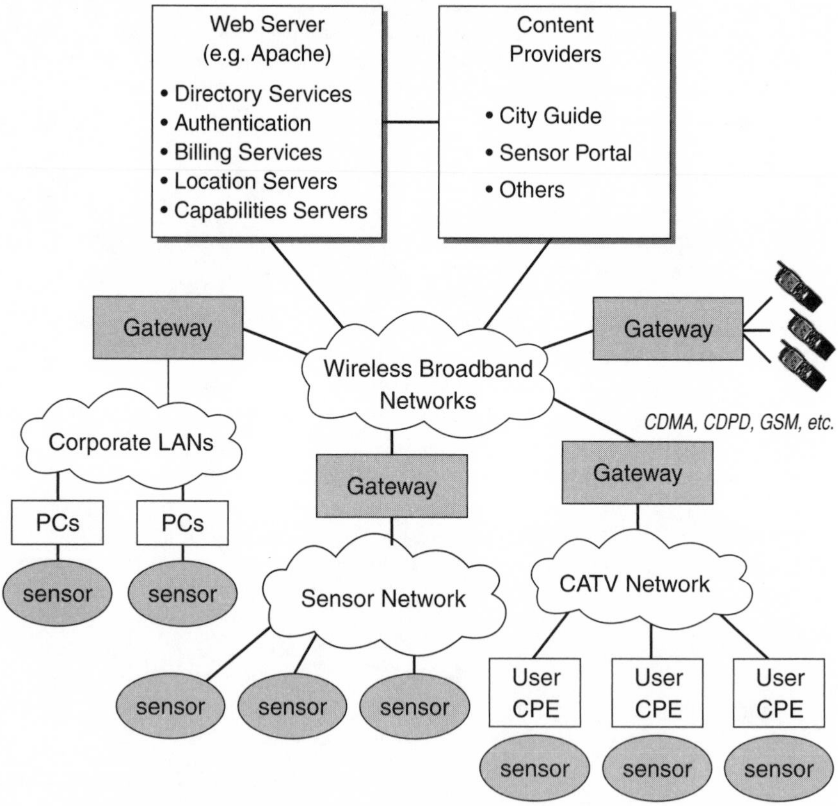

Source: Charmed Technology.

by applications, such as additional PCs with idle capacity that could be used for inclusion on a distributed computing project.

- To detect nearby people, located-objects, or services that are relevant to reminders or actions set to be triggered by their presence.

- Tracking a particular located-object as it moves around a region. Examples include tracking a coworker you wish to talk to or notifying (or warning you) when your spouse is nearby.

- Tracking located-objects with a specified set of attributes in a particular region. An example is tracking all members of a workgroup at a conference.

18.3 4G InfoSensor Portal

Closely related to the location-aware and context-aware capabilities is the notion of a sensor portal, which will be a strategic part of some 4G Portals. The following diagram represents a high-level schematic of a sensor portal architecture (see Figure 18.5). It can consist of both business-oriented and consumer-oriented services with a collection of different access networks and gateways.

In the architecture, location sensors can be attached to fixed devices (computers, displays), mobile devices (wearable and palm-top computers, mobile telephones), and other things (e.g., people and equipment). The location server keeps track of the current location and orientation of each tagged device in the system. This information is augmented with the device's address and type. This information will allow us to locate the device, determine its orientation, and then answer questions like, "Am I anywhere near my car in the parking lot?"

The architecture allows location information about each device to be collected and queried, and the type of each device can be determined and the access methods for the device can be activated.

Note that much of the location information could be represented as adjacency relationships. For example, two sensors are adjacent if they can see each other. If the exact location of one of the sensors is known, the location of the other can be inferred. Attributes of the connected devices would need to describe what the device can do and how to communicate with it. The basic queries that the sensor portal must respond to are as follows:

- Where am I?
- What is near me?
- Where is X; what can X tell me?

Notes

1. Telecom service providers and equipment makers like to use the term "last mile" to refer to the copper wire or fiber-optic wiring that connects the phone company's network to the end user's house or building.

PART V

CASE STUDIES: FIXED WIRELESS, JAPAN, AND CHINA

CHAPTER 19

BROADBAND FIXED WIRELESS ACCESS

19.1 INTRODUCTION TO LMDS

In the United States, broadband fixed wireless access (BFWA) is usually referred to as LMDS, which stands for local multipoint distribution service. This technology shows considerable promise for both broadband fixed access users and as a technology to construct backhauls for future 4G W-LAN networks. LMDS is a broadband point-to-multipoint microwave technology that is capable of offering wireless phone, data, Internet access, and video services. LMDS services are beginning to catch on in a number of locations including the United States, Japan, and Hong Kong. The main attraction of LMDS and the problem that it solves is relieving the local access bottleneck for many residences and offices. The main advantages of LMDS are presented in the following list[1]:

1. Can be deployed quickly, relatively inexpensively, and has a variable cost-driven structure. Fiber networks typically cost around $250,000 per mile to install.
2. Attractive for new entrants (such as xDSL providers) who do not have existing copper or fiber networks.
3. Attractive to incumbent operators who want to complement their existing wireline infrastructures.

4. Provides high-bandwidths up to 155 Mbps, and when combined with transport technology such as ATM switches, can efficiently carry multimedia data.
5. The spectral efficiency is quite good, on the order of 4.57 megabits/Hz.
6. Highly scalable and can be adjusted to changing customer needs.
7. Can be used for video-on-demand and other types of bandwidth-on-demand services.
8. In some countries, such as the United States, extremely large blocks of LMDS spectrum are available.

LMDS bands are usually in the 2 to 42 GHz range with specific allocations varying from country to country. The higher frequencies (as compared to cellular systems) require high-performance DSPs, advanced modulation systems, and very high RF chips, which are usually built out of gallium arsenide (GaAs) and in the future may be built out of silicon germanium (SiGe).

The LMDS spectrum in the United States has been allocated mainly in the 28 GHz and 31 GHz bands. When added together, the FCC has allocated a whopping 1150 MHz of "A" Block LMDS spectrum and 150 MHz of "B" block LMDS spectrum. It is interesting to note that the 31.2 to 31.8 GHz band is one of many restricted bands in which FCC Part 15 rules permit unlicensed devices to emit only very low-level emissions.[2] As will be described in more detail below, Japan has allocated the 22 GHz, 26 GHz, and 38 GHz bands for LMDS and is mulling over the 60 GHz submillimeter band as well. To date, the FCC has auctioned about 1.3 GHz of LMDS spectrum in the 28 GHz millimeter band. Canada has set aside 3 GHz of spectrum for its LMDS equivalent called local multipoint communication systems.

Figure 19.1 provides a diagram of a typical LMDS network. As can be seen in the figure, there are two major configurations, Point-to-Point (P-P) and Point-to-Multipoint (PMP). LMDS cells typically are 2 to 5 km in radius. LMDS cell sites are designed for stationary use only, in contrast to cellular base stations that have to track mobile users who may be moving at speeds as high as 100 km/hour. LMDS is a line-of-sight technology and requires that the antennas are placed in such a way that buildings or other objects do not obstruct the transmission path. The LMDS cells are usually connected into the wireline network through an ATM switch because ATM switches are able to handle mixed data such as voice, Internet, and video conferencing streams.

Figure 19.1
Conceptual diagram of LMDS

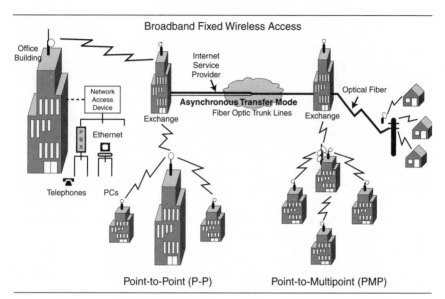

19.2 BROADBAND FIXED WIRELESS SPECTRUM ALLOCATION IN JAPAN

In Japan, LMDS is referred to as broadband fixed wireless access (BFWA) (including LMDS, MWS/MVDS,[3] and WLL). In line with international trends, the Japanese government has recognized the need for new measures and policies to promote the continued development of the telecommunications industry.[4] A number of policies have been adopted in support of this recognition including the Advancement and Diversification of Networks, which encompasses Wireless Access Systems for Subscribers, and the Promotion of Mobile Telecommunications, which encompasses the Next Generation Mobile Communications System (IMT-2000).

Japan is the largest broadband market in the Pacific region by far. Japan sees wireless broadband as a technology that can help stimulate competition in the newly deregulated local-access market and address the growing demand for broadband. In 1998, Japan allocated spectrum for fixed wireless broadband access in the 22 GHz, 26 GHz, and 38 GHz bands and defined its policy for granting spectrum licenses.

The fixed wireless access (FWA) system includes both point-to-point and point-to-multipoint types. Both incumbent and new operators are eligible to become service providers using fixed wireless access. To stimulate competition in the local-access market, however, Type I carriers that already have market power in the local networks are only eligible for frequency within bands shared with existing fixed wireless access systems, where sharing is possible, until April 2001. The policy will be revisited in April 2001 and revised based on the functioning of the FWA system after it is implemented.

In the MPT's policy report "Vision 21 for Info-Communications," it is stated that fiber optics will be the first choice for subscriber access. Wireless will, however, be incorporated both as a transitional technology in the process of developing fiber networks and in areas where it is difficult to lay fiber. According to the policy document, a high-speed wireless local loop system is being developed for seamless connection with hybrid fiber coaxial (HFC) cable networks. The policy objective is to establish a system for business users with speeds up to 156 Mbps by the year 2000 and a maximum transmission speed of 600 Mbps by 2010. For individual subscribers, Japan hopes to provide a high-speed network with a maximum speed of 6 Mbps by 2000 and 156 Mbps by 2010.

Frequencies Currently Set Aside for Broadband Fixed Wireless Service

In March 1998, Japan's Telecommunications Technology Council (TTC) submitted a report to the MPT on technical conditions for fixed wireless broadband access systems at 22 GHz, 26 GHz, and 38Ghz. The MPT requested the Radio Regulatory Council (RRC) report to it on technical standards. It also solicited opinions on its guidelines for the introduction of the new broadband wireless access system; written views were due by the end of October 1998.

Two systems are now licensed, point-to-point (with a maximum transmission speed of approximately 156 Mbps) and point-to-multipoint (with a maximum transmission speed of approximately 10 Mbps). The frequency bands assigned for LMDS services are identified in Annex A.

Operators who install equipment for the operation of fixed wireless access systems must make sure that the equipment conforms to E49.19 of the Ordinance for Regulating Radio Equipment and C2-15-15.3 articles in the Ordinance for the Certification of the Conformity of Specified Radio Equipment with the Technical Standards.

Frequency will be allocated in blocks with separate bands for transmission and reception. The bands will be 60 MHz each, for a total of 120 MHz per block. There are currently some stations using parts of the frequency bands allocated for the FWA system. Because these stations will need time to relocate, additional frequency blocks will become available over time, as shown in the following table (Figure 19.2). The table presents the number of assignable frequency blocks given the time required for existing stations to transfer to the new frequencies.

For both point-to-point and point-to-multipoint (PMP) systems, companies that want to deploy more than a certain number of stations will be assigned a single frequency block per region (see Figure 19.3). One additional block will be granted to a company using a P-P system if it has plans to build more than a certain number of stations, has already established stations, and cannot procure additional frequency in its original block. For companies deploying PMP, up to three additional blocks will be assigned. Companies deploying fewer than the designated number of stations will be assigned frequency blocks on a shared basis. Japan will consider allocating an additional frequency band if demand for frequency is greater than the current allocation.

The regional blocks for frequency are Hokkaido, Tohoku, Kanto, Shinetsu, Tokai, Hokuriku, Kinki, Chugoku, Shikoku, Kyushu, and Okinawa.

Introduction of the system on an additional frequency band will be considered, if demand for frequencies exceeds current expectations and provisioning.

The 60 GHz band in Japan

On 21 June 1999 the MPT made an inquiry to the TTC concerning the technical requirements of radio equipment using 60 GHz (submillimeter) band. The millimeter band has been used for vehicular radar for collision

Figure 19.2
Frequency blocks for fixed wireless access

	Initial adoption	After April 1999	After April 2001
22-GHz band	3	4	4
26-GHz band	7	7	13
38-GHz band	7	7	7

Note: A block is 60 MHz, and two blocks are needed, one for uplink and one for downlink.

Figure 19.3
Summary of frequency allocations and assignments (in tabular form)

Band	Range	Total Spectrum	Type
22 GHz	22.0–22.4 GHz, 22.6–23.0 GHz	800 MHz	P-P
26 GHz	25.25–27.0 GHz	1750 MHz	P-P, PMP
38 GHz	38.05–38.5 GHz, 39.05–39.5 GHz	900 MHz	P-P, PMP

prevention since 1995, but most recently, interest has arisen in using the 60 GHz band for large-capacity, short-distance communications systems, W-LAN, home links, and other indoor applications.

The Japanese government has told the WRC-2000 that it is considering the frequency band 31.8 to 33.4 GHz, which was distributed for high density fixed service (HDFS) in WRC-97. Japan has already allocated the frequency bands 38.05 to 38.5 GHz and 39.05 to 39.5 GHz for HDFS (broadband fixed wireless access). Japan is still considering how to use the 40.5 to 42.5 GHz band, which in some countries is used for video distribution and fixed satellite service (FSS).

19.3 FWA LICENSEES IN JAPAN

British Telecom/Japan Telecom

In March 1999 British Telecom, through a 70%-owned joint venture with Marubeni Corporation called BT Communications Services (BTCS), was awarded broadband fixed wireless licenses (in the 26 GHz band) in three Japanese cities: Tokyo, Osaka, and Nagoya. BTCS had received a Type I carrier licence in July 1998.

Japan Telecom, as part of its strategy to implement the last mile, has applied for and been awarded broadband fixed wireless licenses in the 22 and 38 GHz bands. Japan Telecom has formed a joint venture with Air Touch and Nissan Motors Corp. and plans to use W-CDMA as the air-interface for the broadband fixed wireless service.

TTNET

TTNet, a subsidiary of Tokyo Electric Power and a local access competitive provider, has won broadband fixed wireless licenses in the 22 and 38 GHz bands. It is currently conducting broadband wireless trials. At present, 75% of TTNet's local call revenues go directly to NTT in the form of interconnection fees.

KDDI/Winstar

At the end of February 1999, it was announced that KDD Winstar Corporation was awarded a spectrum grant in the 38 GHz band as well as a Type I carrier license (which permits a company to build its own facilities), allowing it to offer high-speed data services to businesses. KDD, which thus far has been left out of the three designated consortia that have received ITM-2000 3G Mobile licenses, set up in spring 1999 a joint venture, KDD Winstar Corp. (55% KDD) along with New York-based Winstar Communications Inc.[5] (35%) and Sumitomo Corp. (10%). The initial capital of the JV is $5.3 million (600 million yen). KDD has stated publicly that it hopes to be able to offer tariffs up to 20% cheaper than NTT's fixed-line service. KDD is introducing broadband fixed wireless services in Tokyo, Osaka, and Nagoya from May 1999 and hopes to offer services in Sappora, Fukuoka, and other major cities. Its annual revenue target within three years is $8.79 million.

Sony Corporation

Sony Corporation applied in 1999 for a Type I carrier license. Sony is applying for FWA spectrum to offer wireless Internet access and other wireless data communications services, starting no later than July 2000. Initially, Sony will target individuals and small businesses that are heavy users of telecoms services. Sony aims to start commercial services in the Kanto, Tokai, and Kinki regions.

Osaka Media Port (OMP)

Osaka Media Port (OMP), an affiliate of Kansai Electric Power Co., has tentative plans to start testing wireless broadband system in May 1999 after it gains authorization from MPT. OMP hopes to launch commercial service by the spring of 2000. Testing will include Internet and high-speed data transmission using ATM at frequencies of 22 GHz, 26 GHz, and 38 GHz. OMP is collaborating with Kansai Electric, Matsushita Electric Industrial Co. (who will make the wireless, antennae, and other equipment), and three additional regional telecom operators.

OMP sees the technology as a way to compete with NTT's near monopoly on local service in urban markets by building a wireless system at low cost.

19.4 THE OPPORTUNITY EXISTS FOR NEW ENTRANTS IN JAPAN'S FIXED WIRELESS MARKET

Frequency allocation and assignment, examinations, and granting of licenses is handled by the Frequency Planning Division of the Telecommunications Bureau, MPT. The Trunk Communications Division, another division inside the Telecommunications Bureau, is responsible for authorization and supervision of radio stations for communications between fixed stations.

All major policy issues are reviewed by a five-person team, the Radio Regulatory Council. The general procedure for assignment and granting of licenses is that the Frequency Planning Division will submit to the Minister of the MPT a prepermit request for a radio-station license and then the Minister will usually ask the Radio Regulatory for its review to ensure that no conflicts may arise.

Presently, frequencies are allocated by the Radio Frequency Council, which considers frequency requests in light of equipment to be used and services to be provided. Frequency allocation is dealt with together with radio station license applications.

Procedures Used to Award Frequencies to Individual Licensees

Experimental Licenses.   Although not well known, a framework for experimental licenses actually exists in Japan. Such trials are conventionally carried out to demonstrate technology. In relation to wireless trials, applications would need to be made to the Radio Frequency Council. The application procedure is not dissimilar to that followed for licensing of service provision.

Operational Licenses.   The MPT currently has sole responsibility for telecommunications regulatory issues in Japan. The Japanese government is proposing to merge the MPT with the Management and Coordination Agency and the Ministry of Home Affairs in 2002, to create a new Ministry of General Affairs. Under the Japanese Telecommunications Business Law (TBL), all telecommunications business is divided into Type I and Type II telecommunications business. Type I telecommunications business is defined in Article 6 of the TBL as any business that provides telecommunications service by establishing its own telecommunications circuits and facilities. Type I companies must obtain MPT permission to begin and cease operations, as well as change their tariffs. A Type II telecommunications business encompasses all telecommunications business other than those licensed under Type I. Type II carriers need only register their operations with the MPT: No authorization is required.

In addition to a Type I license, a potential operator of wireless services will also need to obtain a radio station license.[6] Both applications are conventionally submitted at the same time and will involve consultations with the Telecommunications Council (in the case of the Type I license) and the Radio Regulatory Council (in the case of radio station license), unless a blanket license of specified radio is applicable. Where (in the case of radio station licenses) a blanket license is not available, a provisional license may be issued until inspections prove satisfactory.

Additionally, rates, terms, and conditions must be set before commencement of commercial operations. There appears to be no requirement to obtain authorization for rates prior to commencing provision of mobile communication services (as for other Type I services), only an obligation to give prior notification.

The market for Type I carriers was opened to foreign competition on 5 February 1998. The standard examination period for processing applications is reported to be between one and two months. A summary of carrier statistics comprises Annex B.

Alternatives to "Traditional" Licensing. One feasible alternative may be the acquisition of the shares in a license holder. Another is the reaching of commercial arrangements with licensed entities.

Exclusive or Shared Use of Spectrum. Eligible service providers will include incumbents and newcomers. In order to foster competition in the local telecommunications market, until the end of March 2001, system frequencies will be allocated to operators, other than Type I carriers, currently operating local telecommunications networks. These carriers will be permitted to introduce new services using such frequencies, provided that sharing is feasible. After April 2001, this policy will be revised in line with the prevailing circumstances.

Rights of Licensees to Assigned Spectrum. Although our inquiries in this regard have not proved entirely satisfactory, it would appear that a licensee is entitled to exclusively use spectrum allocated to it for the duration of its license. As we understand it, there are essentially three types of Type I license: voice, data, and leased circuits. Assuming a licensee holds a Type I leased circuit license, it appears that the licensee can sublease capacity (regardless of whether it is wireline or wireless). We have written to the MPT seeking clarification in this regard. As clarification was not received by the deadline for submission, we will inform you as soon as it is received via the Web site for this book.

Rights-of-Way, Wayleaves, Tower Site Location, Colocation. Type I carriers do have access to private and public land. In relation to private land, the carrier must make a request of the owner and negotiate the required right-of-way on a commercial basis. Any agreement in this regard must be sanctioned by the prefectural governor for the relevant area. If no agreement can be reached, it is the prefectural governor who will arbitrate a resolution.

In the case of public land, an application must be made to the authority that administers that public land, and the parties will invariably negotiate a solution.

Rights of Incumbents to Additional Spectrum. We understand that appropriately licensed carriers may apply for additional spectrum on an as needs basis. The discretion, however, rests with the MPT. We have made a formal request to the MPT for clarification in this regard. We are awaiting a response.

Limits on Amount of Spectrum Held by Individual Licensees. In general, Japan does not impose maximum limits on the amount of spectrum that a licensee could receive or acquire through an acquisition.

NOTES

1. John R. Vacca, *Wireless Broadband Networks Handbook: 3G, LMDS, and Wireless Internet* (New York: McGraw-Hill, 2001).

2. Bennett Z. Kobb, *Wireless Spectrum Finder: Telecommunications, Government, and Scientific Radio Frequency Allocations in the U.S., 30MHz–300 GHz* (New York: McGraw-Hill, 2001).

3. MVDS stands for multipoint video distribution service and is a system that has been field tested already in Europe.

4. Vision 21 InfoCommunications published in June 1997 by the Telecommunications Council.

5. Winstar Communications Inc., based in New York, has already won some 15 LMDS licenses in the United States for which it bid a total of $43.4 million.

6. As specified by the Radio Law (see Articles 6, 27-3) and the Regulations for Procedure for Obtaining a Radio Station License (see Articles 3, 4, 8, and 20).

CHAPTER 20

NTT DoCoMo—
Crouching 4G Tiger;
Sony—Hidden Dragon

20.1 Sony Is Preparing for the 4G Market

NTT DoCoMo and Sony Corporation are two companies that are taking 4G very, very seriously and have been investing heavily in hopes that they will be prepared to ride the future 4G tsunami wave and stand among the technology and service leaders of the future brave new unwired world. Each company is approaching the 4G market from different legacies. Sony is the leading household name in consumer electronics, the leading global market share in game platforms and one of the leading brands in music labels and movie studios through its acquisition of CBS Records and the creation of Sony Studio, but Sony,[1] founded in 1946 by the late Akio Morita whose team of engineers invented the silicon transistor radio in the early 1950s, wants to reinvent itself and become the *leading broadband network entertainment company.*

To understand Sony's strategy for broadband wireless we need to look closer at its business and R&D activity:

- In 1999 Sony received a broadband fixed wireless access LMDS license in Japan and began installing microwave transmitters in the major metropolitan cities in Japan.
- Sony Communications Network Corp. (SCNC) operates So-Net, the fourth largest ISP in Japan with over 650,000 subscribers. SCNC is

244

jointly owned by Sony Corp., Sony Music Entertainment, and Sony Finance, an insurance underwriter and financial services concern. SCNC and So-Net have become the focal point for Sony's effort to get into e-commerce, on-line banking, and electronic distribution of music. So-Net is backed by Sony with its large music and video library; thus, So-Net is well positioned to meet the future expected demand of multimedia services. Sony is exploring spinning off SCNC for a public listing in order to attract Internet talent.

- Sony has launched a game portal, Playstation.com on the back of its success with Playstation 1 and, now, Playstation 2. It appears that games have shown the highest margins for Sony, to the point that the company does not seem to mind selling the Playstation at a loss or near loss.
- Sony is not a major wireless-telecom infrastructure-equipment maker (in contrast to Matsushita), but it does make PDC and GSM cellular phones.
- In 2000, Sony took up a private placement in ArrayComm (San Jose, California), which, as we've seen, specializes in making adaptive array antennas.
- Sony was an early investor in Transmeta, the maker of low-power CPU chips based on long word instruction sets.
- Sony has been an early member of the Software-Defined Radio Forum and has published a number of articles on its software radio chip set work (See Figure 20.1).
- The company has also hedged its bets on wireless narrowband and has teamed up with NTT DoCoMo to supply content to i-Mode users.
- Sony has been making various wearable computer accessories and has received a lot of positive feedback for its Glasstron Heads-Up Display, which it recently discontinued.

With all of the resources that Sony has at its disposal it is just a matter of time before we see the company combining its various assets into a full-blown Sony broadband wireless network, first in Japan and then in the United States. We would not be surprised if Sony considers purchasing spectrum at future auctions in the United States. Although software radios would cannibalize many of Sony's consumer products, it is inevitable that the company will build something like the 4G Personal Communicator system that we have proposed in this book and will own and operate its own Sony Wireless Entertainment Network.

As we will show in the rest of this chapter, NTT DoCoMo is not taking any chances and is expanding rapidly its R&D capability in 4G.

Figure 20.1
Sony's software radio chip research is taking shape

- SOPRANO (version 1): Software Programmable and hardware Reconfigurable Architecture for NetwOrk

"A hardware and software platform set up to demonstrate and investigate technologies and algorithms needed to implement a software radio transceiver."

- Direct conversion RF front end based on six-port technology
- Single-carrier multimode non data aided receiver
- Demodulation of B/Q/8-PSK and 16/64-QAM signals up to BW = 15 MHz
- 2.4 GHz and 5.25 GHz
- Design of the Multimode receiver
  - Top-down design methodology: From C to HDL.
  - FPGA-based implementation of a digital receiver.
  - Features:
    - Direct-conversion using six-port technology (with a 5-port device).
    - Multiband operation (2.4 GHz and 5.25 GHz).
    - Demodulation without prior knowledge of the incoming
    - signal format (BPSK, QPSK, 8-PSK, 16-QAM, 64-QAM).

Ongoing . . .

Source: Haruyama et al., Advanced Telecommunications Laboratory, Sony CSL.

20.2 NTT DoCoMo[2]

NTT DoCoMo (or NTT Mobile Communications Network) is Japan's largest company in terms of market capitalization at $279 billion in September 2000. Even at 2001-depressed market prices and rapid depreciation of the Japanese yen, the company's market cap was still some $171 billion as of 10 June 2001. DoCoMo (which signifies "everywhere" in Japanese) also ranks in the top 10 of the world's largest market caps. In our view, among the global wireless operators it stands heads and shoulders above most because not only has the company found a way to make money from narrowband wireless data services through its phenomenally successful i-Mode service, it also conducts its own world-class research—operating four research laboratories with the newest lab focusing exclusively on 4G wireless technologies. In fact many analysts such as Goldman Sachs[3] are valuing the i-Mode service as high as 30% of the company's total stock price, an extraordinary valuation.

NTT DoCoMo, formerly the mobile communications division of NTT, was incorporated as a provisional company in August 1991 with a capitalization of 1 billion yen (about $80 million). Provisional subsidiaries were established in eight regions in November 1991, and by July 1992, the company took over all of NTT's mobile operations and sales activities. The following July, DoCoMo transferred sales activities to each of the eight regional subsidiaries. In March 1996 the company set up DCM Investments Inc. in the United States, and in August 1998 it set up its first European subsidiary. In late 1999 it established two subsidiaries in the United States: NTT DoCoMo USA Inc. and NTT DoCoMo Laboratories USA, the former of which absorbs the DCM Investments Inc. previously established in 1996.

Before its spin-off from NTT, DoCoMo had been owned 94.68% by the NTT parent behemoth, but in October 1998 the company was finally publicly listed on the First Section of the Tokyo Stock Exchange. In just 12 months from the listing, DoCoMo's market cap reached approximately 65% of the NTT parent company's market cap, which seems to be a growing trend with some of the more successful mobile arms of incumbents; on 4 October 1999 the company's market cap surpassed NTT's and was over 21.15 trillion yen ($192 billion). IT has never fallen below its parent's market cap since then. Even though NTT owns 67% of NTT DoCoMo, its share price did not move that much as DoCoMo's share price skyrocketed leaving analysts and industry watchers to try to figure out if NTT DoCoMo was behaving as an Internet stock or not. As we shall see it was not an Internet stock in the negative sense because it developed a unique and viable business model for wireless data in the shape of its i-Mode service (see Figure 20.2).

20.3 FINANCIAL OVERVIEW

NTT DoCoMo has exhibited a fair amount of resilience to competition, and although it actually lost market share in fiscal year (FY) 1998, it was able to rebound in 1999 and secure the market share it had lost in 1998. As any equity analyst would tell you, the key benchmark to watch in valuing telecom service providers is the average revenue per user (ARPU). In most cases, ARPUs in the wireless cellular industry fall as regulators allow more competitors into the market, which means that cellular providers have to find a way to keep the ARPU from falling and if they are really lucky even increase the ARPUs. NTT DoCoMo seems to have found a way to offset the decline in voice-based ARPU by maintaining robust subscriber growth and by introducing a new service, i-Mode, which was launched in the first quarter of 1999 and achieved over three million subscribers in just nine

Figure 20.2
NTT group structure

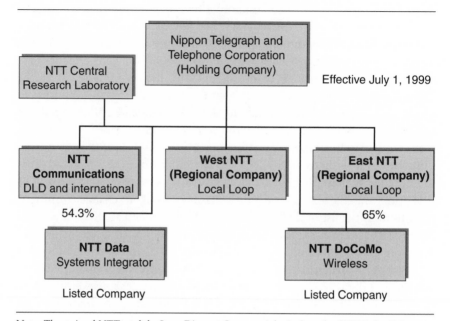

Note: The regional NTTs and the Long Distance Company inherited much of NTT's R&D, but research that is common to all entities is cost-shared.
Source: NTT, William Benton & Associates.

months. ARPUs have been steadily declining since FY 1996 but have been offset largely by robust subscriber growth.

In FY 1997 the company reported Net Income of $268 million, but by its net income for FY 2000 grew to an astounding $2.38 billion, making it one of the most profitable telecom service companies in the world, and that is in spite of annual R&D expenses on the order of $700 million. Do you know of any other service provider that spends that much money on R&D?

On the expense side, although the company has a Type-I license, it still has to pay NTT (its parent company) interconnection charges for calls involving fixed line phones.

20.4 DoCoMo's 2G Voice and Pager Networks and Services

NTT DoCoMo actually operates a number of service networks:

Digital 800 MHz and 1,500 MHz PDC Mobile Cellular Networks

This is DoCoMo's main money maker, comprising over 6,000 base stations and about 300 mobile switches. The company has made considerable investments in enhancing its network through the introduction of smaller, lighter handsets, use of half-rate transmission (5.62 kbps), increasing the sectors in cells located in busy areas, and migrating analog phone users to digital PDC. The company offers voice, Internet, and packet data services on its mobile networks. In April 2000, the company began testing a new system for downloading music from the Internet via PHS mobile phones. NTT DoCoMo carried out the tests jointly with Sony, IBM, and Matsushita Communications Industrial as part of the Mobile Media Distribution Project. We expect the service to be extended to its 3G W-CDMA network. The music system enables music to be downloaded onto flash memory cards, like Sony's Memory Stick and Matsushita's Secure Digital (SD) memory card.

International Gateway

Taking advantage of its special Japanese Type II license, DoCoMo launched its World Call service to its mobile users enabling them to contact six foreign destinations as of January 1999 and over 201 foreign countries and territories by March 1999. The company has signed international telephony service agreements with AT&T/AT&T Wireless and IDC. In fact in 2001 DoCoMo liked AT&T Wireless so much that it spent $9.9 billion for a 16% stake in the company.

Pocket Bell (Pager) National Network

This network supports NTT DoCoMo's FLEX-TD paging service, which is a high-speed, high-capacity paging standard that allows pagers to receive not only teletext messages but also news updates, weather reports, emergency information, and e-mail messages via the Internet.

Mobile Satellite Network

DoCoMo uses the N-STAR communications satellite whose footprint extends to all regions of Japan and the surrounding ocean up to 200 nautical miles offshore. As of December 1999 the company had 24,000 mobile satellite users. The company has announced plans to offer data-packet transmission on its mobile satellite service in April 2000. The service will enable users to download Internet web pages at ISDN basic rates (i.e., 64 kbps). The company currently operates two satellites that were launched originally by NTT. However, the potential for subscriber growth is limited due to the high costs of handsets at around 400,000 yen ($3,636), which is even more expensive than the Iridium handsets.

Maritime Mobile Network

The company also uses the N-STAR communications satellite. By the end of 1999, there were over 16,000 subscribers.

In-Flight Telephone System

This service is similar to GTE's service in the United States to allow users to make unrestricted phone calls from the aircraft and the ground. By year end 1999, 277 systems were in operation.

Wireless Private Branch Exchange (PBX)

Although technically not a network service per se, the company does sell a wireless private branch exchange (PBX) system which it calls "Passage" and offers 32 kbps data transmission rates for e-mail, database searches, and so on.

20.5 I-MODE SERVICE—JAPAN'S PREEMINENT MOBILE INTERNET SERVICE

NTT DoCoMo launched its i-Mode mobile Internet service in February 1999 as a predecessor to its planned 2000/2001 launch of full 3G services. i-Mode uses no rocket science, for it is actually a narrowband service combining 9,600 kbps PDC technology, packet-based communications, and text-based HTML browsers on specially equipped mobile handsets to connect users to a wide range of online services including stock updates, telephone directory service, restaurant guide, ticket reservations, and e-mail service. i-Mode can be used to send and receive e-mail messages from PCs, PDAs, and other i-Mode cellular phones. The user simply sends an e-mail to the cellular phone number followed by @docomo.ne.jp, and the e-mails are automatically forwarded to the i-Mode handset similarly to the way that SMS messages are delivered on GSM phones.

As shown in Figure 20.3, i-Mode uses a separate packet-based network called PDC-P to support data transmission over the Japanese personal digital communications (PDC) air interface at a basic rate of 9.6 kbps per channel.

The PDC network is a time division multiple access (TDMA) system which means that multiple time slots or channels can be aggregated to increase bandwidth. DoCoMo i-Mode phones and software upgrades to the PDC base station allow up to three channels to be combined, similar in principle to GSM's GPRS, providing for a maximum of 28.8 kbps, but of course this occurs at the expense of the total number of users that can be handled simultaneously by a PDC base station.

When DoCoMo launched its i-Mode service in 1999, it thought of it more as an experiment and did a very non-Japanese thing—it hired an outsider, Mr. Natsuno, to run its business partner program. What happened in the ensuing six months has become a business legend of sorts: NTT's parent spent three years and lots of money to acquire half a million *wireline Internet* subscribers, but DoCoMo got one million *wireless Internet* subscribers in only six months.

Apparently someone forgot to tell Mr. Natsuno that NTT doesn't do things this way, and he proceeded to implement a very savvy business partner

Figure 20.3
DoCoMo's i-Mode network infrastructure

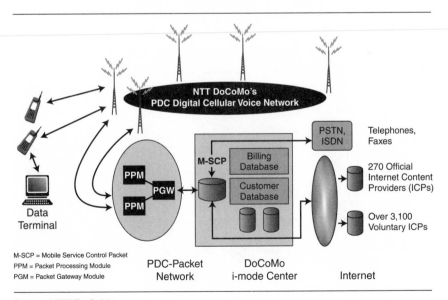

Source: NTT DoCoMo.

promotional program recruiting over 250 "application alliance partners" and some 2,700 voluntary web sites in just six months. At the end of 2000, Do-CoMo had 270 official web sites and over 3,100 voluntary web sites. Subscriber growth was absolutely spectacular (see Figure 20.4): In March 1999, one month after starting the service, there were 18,249 subscribers; by the end of June 1999, there were over 310,000 subscribers; by the end of December 1999, over 2.8 million users had the service; by March 2000, the subscriber base had grown to 5 million users and the growth just kept coming. As of 10 June 2001 the i-Mode subscriber base stood at 24.35 million users.

In December 2000 i-Mode users accounted for over 40% of all Internet users in Japan—in other words, Japanese Internet users are almost split between mobile and fixed users. This is even more impressive when you consider the fact that i-Mode is still a narrowband service with a maximum transmission rate of 9.6 kbps!

Business Model for i-Mode

DoCoMo derives i-Mode revenue from five main streams:

- Monthly subscription fees
- Monthly subscriber airtime usage charges

Figure 20.4
DoCoMo's i-Mode subscriber growth, April 1999–June 2001

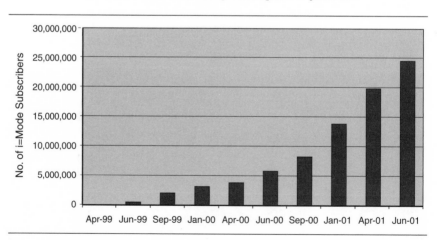

Source: NTT DoCoMo.

- Monthly subscriber packet usage fees
- 9% commission on premium e-commerce transactions
- 9% maintenance charges for Internet content provider (ICP) tenants

The key to understanding the i-Mode business model is that ICPs use the DoCoMo i-Mode data center as a type of e-commerce transaction clearing house. That is to say that DoCoMo collects the monthly bill payments and distributes them to the ICPs according to actual usage. ICP tenants are also charged a monthly maintenance fee to offset the costs of operating the data center, customer billing, and information databases (see Figure 20.5).

Subscribers have to sign up for i-Mode as a separate cellular service in addition to the regular PDC voice service. i-Mode customers are then billed for three types of items:

- Monthly i-Mode subscription of 300 yen ($2.50)
- Air time usage
- Packet usage fees regardless of usage time

Subscribers pay typically between 100 and 300 yen per month to access premium content web sites such as fortune telling services, character photo

Figure 20.5
Wireless data services can boost ARPUs

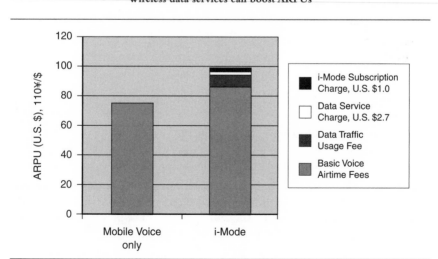

Source: NTT DoCoMo.

pages, ring tones, news, and games. Packets are fixed-length at 128 bytes and are priced at around 0.3 yen (0.25 U.S. cents) per packet. For example, an e-mail of 50 words with an average of 7 letters per word would come to 700 bytes (in Japan characters are represented in double bytes because of the Kanji system), which would translate into six packets or 6 x 0.3 yen = 1.8 yen (1.5 cents). At the end of 2000, i-Mode users were averaging 100 packets per day, or 3,000 packets per month. Including the monthly subscription fee of 300 yen, this averages to a monthly ARPU for i-Mode users of 1,200 yen or $10 to $12 depending on the exchange rate. Goldman Sachs[4] forecasts that i-Mode ARPUs will remain stable and grow gradually at a rate of 11% per annum to 170 packets per day in 2005. Of course, that estimate is not taking into account 4G and the potential when i-Mode goes broadband!

Early 1999 data suggested that the ARPUs for i-Mode users were 25–30% higher than voice only service, which is providing support for high expectations for 3G systems. Increase in ARPUs has tremendous impact on profit and revenue growth potential for the DoCoMo because, as shown in Figure 20.6, in the last several years ARPUs have declined at a rate of 7–10% per year and minutes of use has been somewhat sporadic with the last year showing an increase of 5.8% against drops of 1.9% and 7.1% in FY 1997 and 1996, respectively.

Wireless Internet Is Reversing All the Bad Financial Benchmark Trends in Cellular

There are four negative trends that all cellular operators, and their shareholders, loath to see:

1. Decreasing number of subscribers
2. High churn rate (number of users canceling or changing their service plans)
3. Decreasing ARPUs (average revenue per user)
4. Decreasing voice usage (minutes of use per month)

Any of the above are unsettling, but if an operator is showing all of the above, they are in trouble and must find a way to increase revenues. A lot of people who touted 3G claimed that WAP and then 3G bandwidth was needed to reverse the above negative trends. However, DoCoMo has demonstrated in Japan that a narrowband service could do it; hence, bandwidth was not absolutely necessary to make a profit in wireless Internet. Early 1999 data from DoCoMo

Figure 20.6
NTT DoCoMo PDC cellular ARPU trends in Japan, 1994–1998

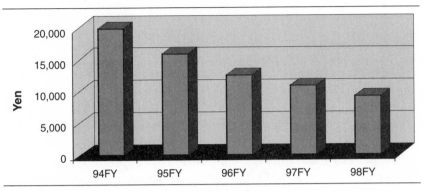

Source: NTT DoCoMo Annual Reports, Pyramid Research.

suggested that the ARPUs for i–Mode users were 25–30% higher than voice-only service. Data available at the end of March 2000 confirmed that the increase in APRU was not going away with DoCoMo reporting that the average i–Mode user generates an additional $14.00 per month more in revenue than do conventional voice-only users. Data in the first half of 2001 seems to confirm the same trend. Increase in ARPUs has tremendous impact on profit and revenue growth potential for DoCoMo because in the last several years ARPUs had declined at a rate of 7–10% per year and minutes of use has been somewhat sporadic with FY 1998 showing an increase of 5.8% against drops of 1.9% and 7.1% in FY 1997 and 1996, respectively. Moreover, the average total daily packet transmission in August 1999 (one packet = 128 bytes) was on the order of 5 to 15 million packets per hour, depending on the time of the day. That is one of the reasons that the market has looked so favorably on DoCoMo's 2G network. 3G is another story, though, as we shall discuss below.

The challenge for the 3G carriers will be to find the magic mix of revenue streams from voice and different types of data services and content application support services to stem the decrease of ARPUs. As music and video content increases its share of 3G traffic, ARPU growth will become dependent on data transmission services and voice air time will become less and less significant, perhaps even to the extreme situation where voice-only transmission will be essentially free.

Another interesting trend is that voice usage is increasing for DoCoMo because as people receive e-mails over their i–Mode phones, they call back.

Dot-com companies liked to talk about "stickiness," meaning that if the service is really compelling users will want to stay with that portal. i-Mode has proven to be quite sticky as churn rate has actually decreased.

Content Providers

One of the key marketing strategies that DoCoMo adopted was to introduce core support systems for its Internet content providers (ICPs) including a common billing system and Java-libraries (see Figure 20.7). The willingness of the company to provide such a support structure clearly has been one of the behind-the-scenes reasons for the phenomenal success of i-Mode.

The list of i-Mode business and information or application content partners reached 258 by mid-November 1999, including over 30 banks such as Sakura Bank, Sanwa Bank, Daiwa Bank, Fuji Bank, 22 regional banks; brokerages such as Daiwa Securities, Nikko Securities; credit card companies such as Sumitomo VISA, JCB, Million Card; life insurance companies such as Nippon Life and Meiji Life; airline ticketing such as Japan Airlines, ANA, Japan Air system; travel agencies such as JTB; news and information providers such as Asahi Newspaper, NHK, Nikkei Business Post, JIJI Press; data base applications such as Ajinomoto for recipes, Sanseido for language dictionary; and entertainment companies such as Bandai for network games. As one can see, the potential applications are limitless, as long as the bandwidth is there to support the network.

Handsets, Java Phones, and the Rejection of WAP

Handsets are being manufactured by Fujitsu, NEC, Mitsubishi Electric, and Nokia. For the time being, NTT DoCoMo has abandoned the European standard wireless application protocol (WAP) because it felt that there was no content available based on wireless markup language (WML) at the time. The next major development for the i-Mode service was the introduction of Java-based services where Java applets are downloaded dynamically into the user's handsets creating a virtually limitless number of enhanced and new applications. NTT DoCoMo has, however, spurned the WAP consortium though it attends WAP forum meetings and adopted instead HTML for its i-Mode cellular phones. NTT DoCoMo then formed an alliance with Sun Microsystems to codevelop Java-based applications in order to introduce Java-enabled i-Mode phones.

DDI and IDO are offering Internet access for their cdmaOne networks

Figure 20.7
NTT DoCoMo i-Mode market development strategy

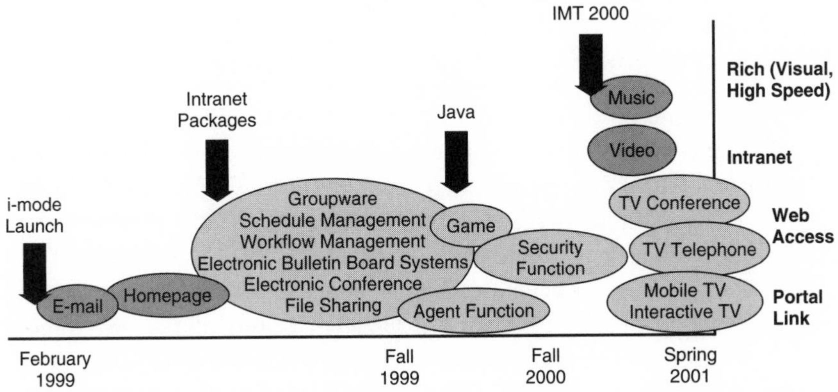

Source: NTT DoCoMo, Pyramid Research.

via a packet delivery service call "PacketOne," which was developed in partnership with Phone.com (formerly Unwired Planet).

Groupware Offerings

In October 1999, NEC started shipping a version of its StarOffice group-
ware product called "PocketWev" that supports i-Mode. Other makers followed suit by announcing similar plans including Fujitsu (Teamware), Hitachi (Groupmax), Lotus Development Japan (Notes/Domino for i-Mode),
and Microsoft Japan (using technology licensed from Puma Technology
called Intellisync Anywhere).

Bluetooth

DoCoMo has decided to incorporate Bluetooth technology into all of its future 3G handsets, a move that has the potential of creating an entire submar-
ket for Bluetooth services and devices. The number of Bluetooth members
in Japan is almost as long as the list of electronics companies! It is no surprise,
therefore, that many of the Japanese electronics and consumer-electronics
makers have announced plans to ship Bluetooth-enabled products ranging
from laptop PCs to various PDA-type devices—the number of products that

could benefit from Bluetooth is almost limitless, and it will be limited to the boundless imagination of product designers in Japan, such as toy makers and entertainment system makers.

Teething Problems Highlight the Issue of Backhaul Bandwidth

One of the biggest problems for NTT DoCoMo, in addition to the 3G base station's ability to handle the maximum of 3.9 Mbps of total cell traffic, is that it has to deal with NTT for the upgrading of the PDC-P network because it leases it from one of NTT's subsidiaries. Naturally, NTT would want to control the backhaul infrastructure and not allow DoCoMo to own it.

The situation is reminiscent of what happened in Thailand where the two major cellular operators, AIS and TAC, realized that after building an advanced backhaul national infrastructure they had extra capacity. They then decided to sell excess capacity to other telecom and Internet service providers, thereby competing ultimately with the incumbent fixed and long-distance operators. It has even gotten to the point in Thailand that it is cheaper to call domestic long-distance on the mobile phone than it is on the fixed lines!

If 3G or 4G services are really to take off in Japan, DoCoMo will need to operate its own truly broadband wireline fiber backhaul network to connect its nationwide web of 3G (or 4G in the future) cellular base stations. The tough technical challenge will be to have a flexible asynchronous transfer mode (ATM) switched architecture that can be enhanced on a regular basis to respond to customer demand for bandwidth. The average total daily-packet transmission in August 1999 when there were fewer than 3 million users (one packet = 128 bytes) on the i-Mode service was on the order of 5 to 15 million packets per hour, depending on the time of the day; this should have been taken by DoCoMo network planners as an ominous sign because by mid-2000, the PDC-P network was experiencing serious teething problems. Sure enough, when the network surpassed 8 million users, after having forecast that it would have 10 million i-Mode users by year end 2000, it suddenly pulled all i-Mode advertisements off the air because it simply could not cope with the traffic. It did not stop people from signing up for i-Mode, and the subscriber growth continued well into the spring of 2001. The moral to the story? Even at narrowband data rates the backhaul IP network becomes absolutely critical, and the costs of the backhaul, which in conventional 2G systems was about 9% of the total network build-out, increases significantly and will continue to be expanded as usage goes up. Put another way, usage begets bandwidth begets more usage begets more bandwidth, until something gives and the bridge collapses under pressure!

We cannot overstate how critical the backbone IP network connecting the base stations to the mobile switching center and content servers is. If the backbone does not have all the necessary functionality, scalability, and bandwidth, the entire network is at risk along with its billion dollar investments! DoCoMo is also addressing the issue through its participation in the 3G.IP alliance with Cisco Systems and Motorola.

Impact of i-Mode on Other Markets Outside of Japan

In Europe the success of i-Mode has prompted a number of operators to consider scrapping WAP technology and opting for DoCoMo's i-Mode approach. The main reason for this is that the enormous amount spent on 3G spectrum is forcing European operators to reduce all forms of risk including WAP because i-Mode has been proven to work and to make a profit, even when you take into account the different cultural factors between Japan and Europe. Some analysts such as Tarifica, a group member of the consultancy pbi Media, have taken the view, which we do not disagree with, that operators in the U.K., Germany, Netherlands, Italy, and France are likely to adopt i-Mode in their delayed run-ups to full 3G launches in 2003 and 2004. Tarifica estimates that by the end of 2002 adoption of i-Mode could increase the ARPUs of European operators by as much as 3.5 euros per subscriber per month as opposed to WAP-based services that were designed primarily for GSM based circuit-switched networks.

i-Mode and 4G

The key thing to remember about i-Mode is that it uses a packet network and hence is *always connected,* similar to digital subscriber lines (DSL). Thus, if the backhaul network is high-speed IP (such as GPRS and planned 3G) networks, the traffic from base stations can be handled. In the 4G network, the handset or 4G Personal Communicator will be packet-based so that the base stations support only one protocol and do not have to reroute the packets as they must do with DoCoMo's current i-Mode service. We can expect a lot of heated regulatory debates in Japan because 4G networks based completely on IP will present lethal competition to the long-distance fixed operators such as KDDI, NTT East, and NTT West who are already under severe pressure as long-distance tariffs fall. Why sign up for long-distance service if you 4G Personal Communicator does it for free or nearly free?

20.6 DoCoMo's Acquisition Binge

Most of NTT DoCoMo's business partnerships had concentrated on technology transfer relationships, but through a series of domestic and international bond placements, the company embarked in 2000 and 2001 on an acquisition binge, buying stakes in a number of large Asian and European cellular operators:

- In early December 1999, NTT DoCoMo announced that it had agreed to purchase 19% of Hutchison Telecom's mobile division in Hong Kong for $410 million cash, valuing the mobile unit at $2.7 billion or roughly $2,600 per subscriber. Part of the rationale in taking a stake in Hutchison was that Hutchison operates two networks—a dual-band GSM network and a cdmaOne network, and DoCoMo hoped to leverage on Hutchison's experience with cdmaOne in Hong Kong and China. At this stage though, it was not clear if Hutchison Telecom would be prepared to migrate its cdmaOne network to NTT DoCoMo's W-CDMA system since Motorola was still a 23% stakeholder in Hutchison and the principle supplier of cdmaOne infrastructure equipment to Hutchison. Interesting supplier-operator relationship, don't you think?
- On November 30, 2000 DoCoMo purchased a 20% equity stake in KG Telecommunicatios (KG Telecom) of Taiwan. KG Telecom operates a national GSM 1800 MHz network and is owned by the powerful Koo family who operates satellite, CATV, and fixed and wireless services in Taiwan.
- On January 22, 2001 DoCoMo completed its purchase of a 16% stake in AT&T Wireless for a paltry $9.8 billion. In our view, this was quite a risky investment because of AT&T Wireless' dependence on TDMA technology. In order for AT&T Wireless to do anything interesting with its nationwide TDMA network, it would have to upgrade its 10,000+ base stations across the country!
- DoCoMo announced a memorandum of understanding (MOU) with Koninklijke KPN Mobile N.V. of the Netherlands and Telecom Italia Mobile (TIM), Italy's largest mobile operator, to jointly develop mobile Internet services based on DoCoMo's i-Mode to target over 30 million

subscribers of KPN Mobile and TIM in Belgium, Germany, Italy, and the Netherlands. DoCoMo and KPN Mobile have also agreed to establish a joint venture with E-Plus of Germany and KPN Orange of Belgium (see Figure 20.8).

- DoCoMo shelled out $100 million for a 42.3% stake in AOL Japan, which was originally formed between AOL (United States), Mitsui & Co., and *Nihon Keizai Shinbun* (Japan's premier economic journal). One of the outcomes of the deal is that DoCoMo will feature AOL Instant Messenger on its i-Mode phones.

Ultimately, DoCoMo is hoping to make its W-CDMA system a standard across Asia—with the possible exception of Korea, which has such a large cdmaOne subscriber base already and many manufacturers that have licensed cdmaOne and cdma2000 technology from Qualcomm. However, in Europe the most that DoCoMo can hope for is that its i-Mode system will replace WAP for 2.5G deployments.

Figure 20.8
Companies that have signed W-CDMA MOUs with NTT DoCoMo

Date	Country	Company Name
April 96	Korea	SK Telecom
July 97	Indonesia	PT Telecom
Sep 97	Japan	Japan Telecom
Oct 97	Italy	Telecom Italia
Nov 97	Singapore	SingTel Mobile
Nov 97	Finland	Telecom Finland
Jan 98	Philippines	Smart Communications
Mar 98	Thailand	Telephone Organization of Thailand and NEC
Apr 98	Malaysia	MEAST Broadcast Network Systems
Jul 98	New Zealand	Telecom New Zealand
Nov 98	Hong Kong	SmarTone
Feb 00	Hong Kong	Hutchison Telecom

Source: NTT DoCoMo.

20.7 TECHNOLOGY PARTNERSHIPS

On the technology front, in 1999 NTT DoCoMo and Sun Microsystems entered into a joint alliance whereby DoCoMo will incorporate Sun's Java on the i-Mode phones. DoCoMo has also paired up with Symbian of the U.K., which is a joint venture between Psion, Nokia, Motorola, and Ericsson. Symbian has developed an operating system for mobile phones called Epoc.

In October 1999, DoCoMo formed a $1.9 million 50-50 joint venture called Mobimagic with Microsoft that will let DoCoMo's mobile customers retrieve files from office or home PCs over the mobile phone, read e-mails, and view calendars and schedulers using Microsoft's Windows CE operating software. The logic behind the joint venture is very simple: According to Microsoft, over 80% of a corporation's data files that workers need to access lies in workers's PCs. DoCoMo has also setup a joint venture with Matsushita called AirMedia that will deliver music over the mobile phones, presumably to compete with Sony's announced plans to operate its own wireless data/content network.

Figure 20.9 provides the diagrammatical view of some of the major technology alliances that have been formed in the last couple of years between Japanese carriers and domestic and foreign vendors. Although foreign vendor market share is still less than 15% of the total telecom equipment market in Japan, foreign vendors are making inroads in selected areas where they have very competitive products such as DWDM, fiber-optic access systems, giga/terabit routers, wireless infrastructure equipment, intelligent network management software, and so on.

Research & Development—The Path to 4G

For the fiscal year ending 31 March 2000 NTT DoCoMo reported 850.1 billion yen ($700 million) in R&D expenditures—a 29% increase over the previous year. To put things in proper perspective, NTT DoCoMo's annual R&D expenditures are more than its two major competitors's, Japan Telecom or KDDI, annual capital network expenditures. DoCoMo is unlike most other global cellular operators and, for that matter, wireline operators in that it maintains a world-class research and development program.

Currently the company employs over 850 R&D staff members, who are housed in three research centers, but following the announcement of the 4G Research Center, it will have four labs. The Yokosuka Research Park (YRP),

Figure 20.9
Next generation Internet and wireless technology alliances in Japan

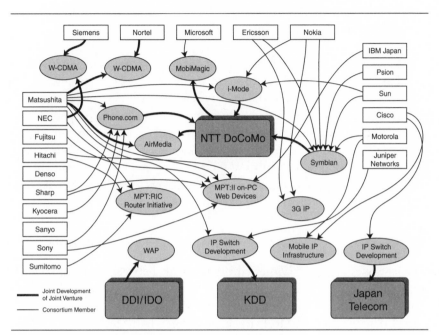

Note: DDI, IDO, and KDD merged in the fall of 2000 to form KDDI.
Source: William Benton & Associates, Pyramid Research.

completed in March 1998, is where the company cooperated with R&D labs of over 30 Japanese and foreign mobile cellular companies to conduct 3G research. DoCoMo has four laboratories, six development departments, and one planning department.

The company's R&D spans the full spectrum of the mobile communications sector:

- Aircraft radio telephones
- Maritime mobile telephones
- Satellite telephones
- Pocket bell (pager) systems
- Portable and automobile telephone systems
- Mobile computing

- Mobile cellular (PHS, Digital PDC, and W-CDMA)
- IMT-2000
- Wideband CDMA
- Packet mobile data communications

IMT-2000 and W-CDMA are two areas in which the company concentrated its 1997–2000 R&D resources on, partly because the company has carried out a lot of research in W-CDMA systems over the past four to five years and has consequently developed a fair amount of intellectual property in the field. The strong intellectual property position of NTT DoCoMo with respect to W-CDMA played a crucial role in winning over European makers such as Nokia and Ericsson to support its W-CDMA strategy. DoCoMo thus entered into cross-licensing arrangements with those makers to prevent a repeat of the contentions between Qualcomm and other foreign manufacturers.

W-CDMA and the IMT-2000 Standards and DoCoMo's Role

The past two years have witnessed a fierce battle between two major camps for the standardization of the IMT-2000 mobile cellular systems: the North American camp led by Qualcomm and Motorola and the Japan/Europe camp led by NTT DoCoMo, Ericsson, and Nokia. In the first quarter of 1999, the basic dispute ended with Ericsson's acquisition of Qualcomm's cellular infrastructure division; although for the cdmaOne operators, there were still a number of practical issues to be resolved including migration from cdmaOne to W-CDMA and various back-end issues such as roaming and billing and accounting.

The company proposed its W-CDMA system to the ITU for consideration for incorporation in the IMT-2000 system. The main features of NTT DoCoMo's W-CDMA system are as shown in Figure 20.10.

DoCoMo's 3G Network—False Expectations and on to 4G

DoCoMo branded its 3G network in Japan, the world's first commercial 3G network, as "FOMA" which stands for "Freedom of Mobile Multimedia Access." The FOMA network is designed to utilize high-speed ATM switches interconnected to form a nationwide backhaul network. One of the key challenges for the company's network designers is *capacity planning* (this concept is very familiar to mainframe makers such as IBM, and their mastery of the art determines their bottom line with an exclamation mark) especially in view of the projected explosive demand for multimedia and packet-data services that will become possible due to the transmission speeds of up to 384 kbps per user. Or so the theory went . . .

3G is where the rubber meets the road for DoCoMo. The company had committed some $4 billion for its 3G network, hyped up the media leading to the commercial launch in Spring 2001, and then lo and behold, suddenly in the second half of 2000, NTT executives began talking about the need for 4G networks and how 3G could not deliver the necessary bandwidth. In the spring of 2001 DoCoMo stunned the industry by announcing that it would only do a soft-launch in May 2001 and that the full launch might be delayed one to two years. What is going on here???

To put things in perspective, in December 2000 Hewlett Packard and DoCoMo announced that they would be cooperating to develop 4G multimedia architecture and applications. In January 2001 the industry learned that DoCoMo was investing $250 million for a new R&D center to develop 4G wireless. The company's R&D website now contains a section devoted to

Figure 20.10
NTT DoCoMo's W-CDMA system features in Japan

Feature	Description
Chip rate	4,096 chips per second
Multi-band	
Dual-spread codes and inter-cell asynchronous timing	Contrasts with the Ericsson/Qualcomm wideband cdma2000 system which utilizes Global Positioning System (GPS) synchronization of each base station cell site
Coherent RAKE reception	
Signal-to-Interference (SIR) based adaptive power control	Used to resolve near/far problems that arise when a mobile station is closer to the base station than other mobile stations thereby swamping the signals from other mobile stations
Orthogonal variable multi-rate transmission	Up to a maximum of 2 mbps per stationary subscriber and 384 Kbps for users that are walking and 144 kbps for users that are moving rapidly such as riding in a car or train.
Adaptive active antenna arrays and interference cancellers	

Fourth Generation Mobile Communications where it highlights the following technologies:

- Micro- and millimeter wave bands (5 GHz and upwards)
- Software-radio technology
- Spatial-division multiple access
- Adaptive array antennas
- Adaptive interference cancellers

Do any of those sound familiar?

Figure 20.11
NTT and NTT DoCoMo's strategic supplier relationships

Equipment Type	NTT East, NTT West, NTT Com	NTT DoCoMo
ATM Switches	NEC, Fujitsu	NEC
Routers	Cisco, Fujitsu	Cisco
Digital PTSN Switches	NEC, Fujitsu, Oki, Mitsubishi	
PDC D60/70 Switches		NEC, Fujitsu, Ericsson
PDC Base Stations		NEC, Fujitsu, Japan Radio, Matsushita, Lucent, Ericsson, Motorola
PHS Base Stations		Matsushita
i-Mode Handsets		Fujitsu, Matsushita, Nokia
W-CDMA NS-8000 Switches		NEC, Fujitsu, Lucent
W-CDMA Base Stations, Radio Network Controllers, and Multimedia Processors		NEC, Fujitsu, Lucent, Nokia, Ericsson, Motorola
Fiber Optic Access and Transmission Systems	Sumitomo Electric, Lucent, Matsushita	

Source: William Benton & Associates, Pyramid Research.

DoCoMo's Shift to 4G Will Affect United States and European Telecom Makers

If one takes a look at the list of suppliers for DoCoMo's 3G network (see Figure 20.11) one has to wonder what they must all be thinking now that DoCoMo has shifted gears. If the North American and European telecom makers want to participate in DoCoMo's 4G development, they are going to have to demonstrate their commitment to 4G. China, too, will be affected by DoCoMo's announcement, and the Ministry of Information Industry will need to reassess its adoption of the Siemens-led TD-SCDMA system in China.

Not surprisingly, the media went into a feeding frenzy with DoCoMo's change of direction; the way the authors of *Brave New Unwired World* (BNUW) see it, 4G has already become a change agent at NTT DoCoMo! In fact, DoCoMo is now talking about realizing its "Vision 2010" in 2006, four years ahead of schedule.

Notes

1. For those who wonder where the name Sony came from, some say it actually stands for "Standard Oil of New York," a direct consequence of the close business connections that Morita had with the Rockefeller family post–World War II.

2. For a detailed analysis of the Japanese telecom market we refer readers to a report written by one of the BNUW authors with Pyramid Research, an Economist Intelligent Unit company, called "Communications Markets in Japan 2000."

3. Goldman Sachs, "Wireless Data—Issues and Outlook 2000."

4. "Wireless Data: Issues and Outlook 2000," *Goldman Sachs Research Report* (Winter 2000).

CHAPTER 21

WHY CHINA WILL ADOPT 4G

21.1 EXECUTIVE SUMMARY

Why will China adopt 4G? Very simply because 4G represents the natural path from where China is trying to go with its vast telecom build-out. More specifically, our conclusion is based on the following arguments:

1. *China has a broadband infrastructure.* 4G cannot be realized without an underlying broadband fiber infrastructure, which China is feverishly building out in the form of four license-fixed national carriers with a combined 125 million main phone lines and over 1.2 million km of fiber-optic cable, over 8,000 very small aperture terminal (VSAT) terminals, over 170 satellite transponders, two nationwide mobile-cellular carriers, and over 300 cable television (CATV) operators with a total of 86 million subscribers.

2. *Phenomenal wireless subscriber growth.* Wireless growth in China has been spectacular to say the least. In 1999 the number of fixed-line subscribers was 108 million (24% year-year growth) or 8.58% of the population and the number of mobile subscribers was 43.29 million (73% year-year growth) or 3.42% of the population. By the end of 2000, the number of fixed users had increased to 144,407 (32% Y-Y growth) while the

number of mobile users had sky rocketed to 85 million (97% Y-Y growth) or 6.7% of the population.

3. *Wireless subscribers will overtake wireline.* This will happen by year-end 2002 in China to reach 200 million mobile users, which when combined with Internet-enabling mobile technologies will position wireless networks to become the main medium for most people in China to get access to e-mails, carry out e-commerce transactions, and receive news. The PRC authorities have completely embraced the Internet but with the negative caveat of continuing a rather restrictive censorship policy against socially "destructive" content (e.g., pornographic sites and politically sensitive web sites). China has a difficult balancing act to pull off with the Internet: On the one hand, without the Internet the country's educational and engineering system cannot progress, but on the other hand, progress will occur at the risk of influence from outside China—influence that only the Internet can bring in large volumes.

4. *Opportunity to develop its own intellectual property.* 4G provides a chance for China to develop its own wireless engineering and manufacturing know-how because with the 2G and 3G systems China has had to rely almost entirely on outside technical expertise and standards. Only recently, with the development of China's homegrown TD-SCDMA standard for 3G CDMA, has China had the opportunity to show its capabilities in wireless commercial telecom systems.

5. *Wireless LANs will be a big hit in China.* 4G provides a unique opportunity for China to take advantage of high-speed wireless LAN and in-building systems. In spring 2001 a number of cities including Beijing and Shanghai have announced plans to install 4G 802.11b base stations in various places across cities to complement the public GSM GPRS networks.

6. *4G could help the rural areas as well.* 4G presents a crucial opportunity in developing China's rural population which is over 75% of the entire population of 1.2 billion people. Another way of saying that is to say that without 4G China cannot possibly hope to maintain economic growth without a good wireless infrastructure that combines voice, data, and Internet access at an economically feasible price for both the handset and for usage.

In the rest of this chapter, we are going to present analysis of the nonmilitary telecom industry in China, including regulatory structure and policy, and once the reader comprehends the sheer size and depth of infocommunications in China, he has no choice but to conclude that the 4G wave will hit China, albeit with unique Chinese attributes adapted for that marketplace.

21.2 TELECOM INFRASTRUCTURE OVERVIEW

Convergence of the information, communications, and media sectors is a phenomenon reaching virtually into all markets around the globe. The convergence is beginning to sweep the People's Republic of China (PRC) also. China has the daunting and exciting task of building-out its fixed and wireless networks at the same time, unlike Western Europe or the United States which completed construction of the basic telephone services to every home and office over two decades ago.

It is said, for example, that over 60% of the latest and fastest ATM switches that Lucent Technologies manufactured and sold in 1997 were shipped to China. China Telecom, China Unicom, China NetCom Corp. and the Ministry of Railways through its China Railways Network (CRNET), are planning to provide much greater bandwidth than is available today on the terrestrial fiber optic networks. In the next three to five years, China is planning to invest some US$30 billion in communications technologies including further deployments of GSM 900/1800 MHz mobile cellular, DWDM optical fiber for local and long-distance trunking, synchronous digital hierarchy (SDH) transmission, CATV access, Internet access, voice over IP telephony, 3G W-CDMA mobile, and intelligent networks. According to Pyramid Research (October 1998) China has invested over $15 billion from 1990 to 1998. However, the total amount spent in that five year period is being spent on an annual basis—in 2000 the MII reported that renmenbi (RMB) 132 billion ($15.75 billion) was spent on telecom infrastructure with China Telecom, which already manages one of the world's largest telephone networks with over 125 million main lines, accounting for 60% of the capital expenditure. China Mobile Telecom manages the single largest cellular network in the world with over 85 million mobile subscribers and is adding 3 million new subscribers each month (see Figure 21.1). China Unicom is the second licensed mobile carrier in China and is expected to have 20 million subscribers by the end of 2001.

The PRC's declared target is 1 billion wireline and mobile lines by 2020, but by the end of 2002 mobile subscribers will have caught up with wireline subscribers. Our educated guess is that China will meet those targets a lot sooner based on the phenomenal investments in telecom infrastructure in the past eight years. Net of the story: China is going on-line big time!

China has been constructing public telecommunications networks at a frantic pace. Most of those networks can be classified into carrying one of the following types of information:

- Voice
- Data that includes graphics, Internet, and file transfer
- Cable TV and broadcasting video

There is virtually no advanced telecom technology that China is not using:

- Microwave PDH and SDH links—Guangdon province alone has over 17,000 km of microwave links.

Figure 21.1
China: Telecoms market at a glance

	1998 YE	1999 YE	2000 YE	2001 YE
Population (millions)	1,232,000	1,260,000	1,290,000	1,310,000
Main lines (thousands)	86,984	108,715	144,407	183,000
International internet capacity (Mbps)	130	351	470	3,257
No. of international gateway facilities	3	3	5	6
ISPs	100	200	400	450
Leased lines (millions)	312	416	686	1,063
Internet users (thousands)	1,980	8,900	12,905	28,000
CATV subscribers (millions)	77,583	86,504	95,545	106,399
Paging subscribers (millions)	47,200	61,300	73,700	79,000
No. of mobile users (millions)	25,000	43,296	85,300	137,500
No. of IP ports (millions)	250	1,000	3,577	4,200
No. of broadband ports	1,000	10,000	37,000	50,000
No. of VSAT terminals	7,000	7,500	8,000	8,500
Kilometers of fiber-optic cable	800,000	1,100,000	1,252,000	1,500,000

Source: ITU, Pyramid Research, Nomura International, William Benton & Associates.

- DWDM-based fiber-optic long-haul trunks with capacity per fiber strand of between 20 Gbps and up to 160 Gbps. Next generation telecommunication technologies such as IP terabit switches with direct DWDM interface to the fiber-optic transport will enable the raw transmission systems to carry integrated voice, data, and video.
- Wireless Local Loop (WLL) and Broadband Fixed Wireless Access (BFWA).
- VSATs: Terrestrial fiber-optic SDH-based cable TV transmission systems with frequencies ranging from 300 to 750 MHz.
- Satellites (Ku-band and C-Band).
- Gigabit submarine fiber-optic cables for international communications.
- Paging, mobile cellular, and trunked radio.

Regardless of the physical transmission system used, the high-bandwidth and advanced IP- and TDM-based switching systems that Chinese telecoms operators are incorporating into most of their major long-distance trunks suggests that each of these networks will be capable of transporting all sorts of digital information including voice, data, and even video (see Figure 21.2).

China's telecoms infrastructure will grow to reflect the dynamics of social and technological change in China. Multimedia will become prevalent on both fixed and wireless networks.

21.3 REGULATORY ENVIRONMENT

The regulatory regime for public telecoms in the PRC is complex but has been helped by the recent merging of three former ministries into the newly formed and powerful Ministry of Information Industry (MII) described in the next section. China Telecom through the Directorate General of Telecommunications (DGT) is now being run as an operator, and the regulation role belongs to the MII.

China is currently in the process of drafting a Telecom Act that will presumably include a legal framework for direct foreign investment. In the following list, we summarize the major governmental bodies that get involved in the regulation and policy making for the telecoms sector.

1. State Council is made up of many of the senior figures including the Premier, Vice Premier, and Ministers. It acts as China's legislative body and is responsible for overall policy in a wide variety of areas including telecommunications policy. With regards to the telecoms sector, the State Council approves all major laws (promulgation), and these laws act above

Figure 21.2
Planned capital investment in China's telecom infrastructure

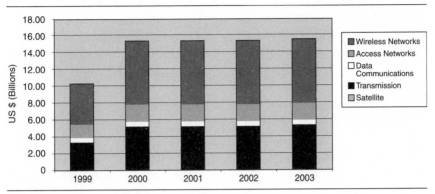

Source: William Benton & Associates.

the control of the MII's regulatory authority. Any subsequent disputes that arise among ministries would be appealed to the State Council.

2. State Development Planning Commission (SDPC) is responsible for economic planning and for financial allocation for all large investment and infrastructure projects; "large" is presently defined by Chinese law as projects requiring sums of 30 billion RMB ($3.5 billion) or more.

3. Ministry of Public Security (MPS), in the context of telecoms, assists the MII in administering and enforcing regulations and imposing penalties relating to network (including the Internet) access, network security, registration, and licensing.

4. State Science and Technology Commission (SSTC) is responsible for research and development and for raising the level of technological expertise in the country.

5. State Economic and Trade Commission (SETC) is responsible for economic and trade development. It also operates the State Information Center and is the sponsor for a national project called the Golden Enterprise Project, which is chartered to develop an intranet and commercial databases service to the top 1,500 and later 10,000 state owned enterprises (SOEs).

6. State Radio Regulation Commission (SRRC) has been merged into the newly formed MII. Formerly, it controlled the radio spectrum and its allocation jointly with the PLA and the State Security Bureau, which is responsible for police and emergency services.

7. Ministry of Information Industry (MII) is now the merged MPT and the MEI (Ministry of Electronics Industry) and part of the MRFT (Ministry of Radio, Film and Television). The MRFT has been involved in building local cable TV networks in virtually all major cities in China. The MRFT also operates the China Film Import and Export Corporation. The former MEI had been operating the first four Golden Projects: Golden Bridge, Golden Card, Golden Tax, and Golden Customs.

8. China Telecom is 100% owned by the central government and operates 31 provincial subsidiaries which formerly were the Posts and Telecommunications Administrations (PTAs), and local Posts and Telecommunications Bureaus (PTBs). China Telecom, who is expected to publicly list by the summer of 2002, is the incumbent national long distance, local public telephone company, and international telephony operator. Its only real competition is China Unicom, also under the regulatory authority of the MII, and China Netcom, of which 20% is owned by the MOR. China Telecom is also engaged in leasing long distance lines, issuing calling cards, and providing basic international and domestic telephone services including data and fax services as well as satellite and VSAT communications. China Mobile operates China Telecom's former mobile GSM and analog cellular networks in China. China Mobile through the DGT is the parent of China Telecom Hong Kong, which completed a dual listing in the United States and Hong Kong in 1998.

9. Ministry of Foreign Trade and Economic Cooperation (MOFTEC) is responsible for approving foreign joint ventures and consults with the other relevant ministries when reviewing applications for foreign joint ventures.

Industry Restructuring and Introduction of Competition

The area where China is lagging developed nations is telecom liberalization, specifically as relating to foreign investment in telecom service providers, censorship of the Internet, licensing requirements, and so forth. The leadership in Beijing understands this all too well and consequently in February 1999, the State Council approved a restructuring plan for the telecommunications industry in the PRC. As part of the restructuring plan China Telecom was split into four operating business lines: mobile, fixed line, paging, and satellite. Paging has been already consolidated (in the form of a company called Guoxin) and has been injected into China Unicom, in an effort by the MII to beef up China Unicom's balance sheet. The fixed line business will consist of six regional divisions, while the satellite business is under the name of China Satellite Communications Co. and the mobile business will assume the name China Mobile Communications Co.

In 1999 the Ministry of Finance (MOF) injected RMB 5.9 billion ($710 million) into China Unicom, China's second national operator, to assist it in buying many of the foreign Chinese-Chinese-Foreign (CCF) paging and mobile partners.[1] China Unicom mandated Morgan Stanley Dean Witter (MSDW) and China International Capital Corporation (CICC) to carry out a dual listing (Hong Kong and New York) in June 2000, which ended up raising approximately $4 billion. A third operator was also created and given a full telecom license, China Netcom.[2]

Late last year the Ministry of Railways, which already operates a nationwide fiber-optic network of thousands of kilometers of fiber-optic cable, was granted a full telecom service provider license. Other entities also very interested in entering the telecoms market in China would include the State Power Administration.

The WTO Agreement

Direct foreign investment in telecommunications operators is not allowed by the present Chinese laws, although direct investment in value added services appears not to fall under the current restrictions.[3] Some foreign investors and operators have bypassed the ban on direct equity investment by using alternative structures such as revenue sharing agreements and build-operate-transfer schemes. In 1999–2000, the MII announced that the Unicom CCF joint ventures (JVs) were irregular and as a result must be dissolved. In 2000, after considerable negotiation, China Unicom decided to buy-out most of the CCFs and negotiated particular terms and conditions for buying out each CCF foreign partner.

On 24 May 2000 the U.S. House of Representatives voted to grant China permanent normal trade relations (PNTR) after a lengthy review process. Already, as a result of the WTO agreement, China has indicated the willingness to allow foreign investors to own up to 49% of certain categories of value-added telecoms service companies. Following the U.S. congressional vote, a number of U.S. corporations announced plans to increase investment in the Chinese market. For example, Motorola released details of its plans to invest an additional $2 billion in China, contingent on China trade policies. Motorola has already invested $1.1 billion in its production and processing base in Tianjin and has filed application to the MII to establish a new base in Tianjin for semiconductor and telecommunications production. If Motorola's application is approved it envisions investing another $2 billion, bringing its total China investment to $3.5 billion. Motorola is hoping to have success in China with its new lines of Internet-enabled cellular phones.

We expect that by late 2002 or early 2003 China will complete a draft of a Telecoms Act similar to the U.S. Telecoms Act of 1996 or Japan's 1997 revisions to the telecommunications business and NTT laws. We are already seeing a number of global Internet companies beginning to establish a presence in China such as Lycos, which recently announced plans to open Lycos China.

A lot of pressure was put on China during the WTO negotiations, and it looks like the tough stance has paid off. In the first quarter of 2000, China completed negotiations with the United States for entry to the WTO. Now that China is part of the WTO, some industry watchers believe that China will further relax the restrictions of direct foreign investment in the future once a telecoms law is drafted and ratified, but we would conjecture that it will probably be in the form of special experiments in selected geographies, similar to trials that have been conducted in the insurance sector: Select foreign insurance companies have been allowed to have limited operating licenses in Shanghai and Guangzhou.

Below are the salient features of the WTO agreement reached with the United States:

Value-Added (incl. Internet) and Paging Services
- Foreign investors will be able to provide e-mail, voice mail, on-line info and data base retrieval, electronic data interchange (EDI), enhanced value-added facsimile services (including Store and Forward, Store, and Retrieval), code protocol conversion, on-line info & data processing (including transaction processing), and paging.
- Ownership: 30% upon accession, 49% after one year, 50% after two years.
- Foreign-invested service providers limited to certain geographic region initially until after five years.

Mobile Voice and Data Services
- No limitations on type of service offered
- Ownership: 25% foreign equity share one year after accession, 35% after three years, 49% after five years

- Foreign invested service providers limited to certain geographic region initially until after 5 years

Domestic and International Services
- Includes domestic and international voice and data and facsimile
- Ownership: 25% foreign equity after three years, 35% after five years, and 49% after six years
- Foreign-invested service providers limited to certain geographic region initially until after five years

Satellite:
- no special restrictions

The issue of management control, though, will be a sensitive one for quite some time. In the case of China Telecom Hong Kong (CTHK), China Telecom holds the majority of shares, so the actual free float is relatively small, especially with the recent purchase of CTHK shares by the Hong Kong Monetary Authority. However, we should note that in certain cases, such as VAS network projects, it may be possible to have foreigners (defined here as non-PRC citizens) on the special advisory board of directors.

Regardless of whether we adopt democratic language or socialist language to describe China's future society, China will need lots of information; it will have to process huge amounts of information; and it will need to process that information efficiently, quickly, and with robust network security.

21.4 BUILDING THE INTERNET INFRASTRUCTURE

The growth of telecoms infrastructure is fueling rapid growth in the data communications sector. According to Liu Yunjie, Director of the Data Communications Bureau of the former MPT, China's data communications industry beginning in 1996–1997 entered a stage of rapid development. In 1993, China only had about 1,700 data communications users, but that figure climbed to over 100,000 by July 1996. There are several major non-broadband networks in China described in following sections, but many of the largest users are actually state entities such as the State Economic Trade Commission, the State Administration of Taxation, the Chinese Academy of Sciences, the State Education Commission, MOFTEC, China Travel Services, securities exchanges, futures trading departments, public security departments, universities, and railway departments.

Latest statistics from China, which were compiled by the official Internet agency—China Internet Information Center (CNNIC)—suggest over 26.5 million registered Internet users based on a total of 8.9 million host computers of which over 1.3 million were using leased lines. Unofficial users probably are twice the registered users. We forecast that after 2003 the majority of new accounts will be wireless Internet accounts (see Figures 21.3 and 21.4).

China Telecom, which currently operates the nation's three terrestrial international gateway facilities (IGFs), has dominant influence on the ISP market in China because ISPs must lease the international capacity from China Telecom. We estimate that China Telecom's own ISP/data service, ChinaNet, accounts for over 73% of the total 3.257 Gbps of international Internet access presently available in China.

The Internet is defined as a publicly accessible network comprising, at the time of this writing, ten major networks each managed and operated separately, including:

1. ChinaNet
2. ChinaGBN (Golden Bridge Network)
3. CSTNet (China Science and Technology Network)
4. CERNET (China Educational and Research Network)
5. Uninet (China Unicom)
6. China Netcom (planned)

Figure 21.3
Internet host and subscriber growth in China, 1996–2005

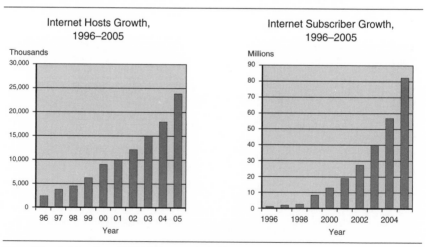

Note: Historical data from CNINC; forecasts by William Benton & Associates.

Almost all of China's public Internet traffic goes over ChinaNet, CNCNet, and ChinaGBN with ChinaNet transporting the majority of the traffic. Since CSTNet and CERNET are not commercial networks they have to rely on government spending in order to expand their capacity and improve their service. Until March 1997, there was virtually no interconnectivity between the above four networks, and today there is limited connectivity via low bandwidth (128k) leased-line connections between the four backbones. These links are already said to be saturated. In late 1998 Cisco Systems signed a joint-venture agreement with the Beijing City Information Office and China Information Highway Corporation to construct the Capital Public Information Platform (CPIP), which will be China's first Internet exchange and will connect the four major networks listed above and also the China Financial Network. CPIP will run over fiber-optic cabling owned by

Figure 21.4
Internet growth at a glance in China, 1997–1999

	As of Oct 1997	As of 30 June 1998	As of 31 Dec 1998	As of June 2001
No. of computers with Net access (dial-up and or direct)		542,000	747,000	10,020,000
No. of computers with dial-up access		460,000	630,000	8,390,000
No. of computer with direct access		82,000	117,000	1,630,000
No. of Dial-only users	620,000	850,000	1,490,000	17,930,000
No. of Dial-up & Direct		N/A	210,000	4,030,000
No. of Directly Connected Users		325,000	400,000	4,540,000
No. of Web sites				242,739
International Internet Bandwidth (Mbps)		50	140	3,257
• CSTNET				55
• CERNET				117
• ChinaNet				2,387
• ChinaGBN				151
• Uninet (China Unicom)				100
• CMNET (China Mobile)				N/A
• CNCNET (China Netcom)				355

Source: CNNIC.

the Bureau of Radio, Film, and Television (BRFT) of the MII. CPIP will also connect to BRFT's planned ATM backbone network.

The entire Internet in China currently has approximately 3,257 Mbps of capacity on international links as compared with less than 20 Mbps one year ago.

China Public Computer Network (ChinaNet)

The Beijing Telecommunications Agency, a branch of the recently formed MII, operates ChinaNet, which is China's primary commercial data communications network connecting more than 230 cities in all 31 provinces and municipalities. ChinaNet was first launched in 1995, and by February 1998 it had signed up over 800,000 users. ChinaNet's expansion plans call for more than 360 cities to be connected nationwide by late 1999 or early 2000. ChinaNet's long term plans are to link all government offices, over 360,000 state enterprises in more than 600 cities, and over 8 million other industrial and commercial enterprises throughout China. ChinaNet is actually a merging of several predecessor networks including ChinaDDN (China Digital Data Network) and ChinaPac.

The kernel of ChinaNet originates from the National Computing and Networking Facility of China (NCFC), which began in 1989 with financing from the World Bank and the SPC and finished in 1993. NCFC was originally set up for the Chinese Academy of Sciences, Beijing University, and Qinghua University, and today connects with other universities and research institutes in China.

ChinaNet is managed by a body composed of representatives from the State Education Commission, the State Science and Technology Commission, and the SPC and professors from universities (see Figure 21.5).

ChinaDDN was launched in October 1994 and is owned and operated by the MII. ChinaDDN now plays the role of the backbone for ChinaNET and has been recently upgraded to support E1 links between major nodes and is now connected to the global Internet via at least 14 gateways for a total international bandwidth of 2.3 Gbps.[5] Funding came partially from several foreign country and overseas loans. The backbone consists of a total of 22 fiber trunk lines covering some 32,000 km. The fiber network also connects to 20 interprovincial microwave satellite links. The network extends to 31 municipalities and provincial capitals.

The network comprises 140,000 ports with some but not all running at 2,048 Mbps. The transmission architecture is currently PDH (plesiochronous digital hierarchy) equipment but has plans to migrate to SDH (synchronous

Figure 21.5
Map of CERNET

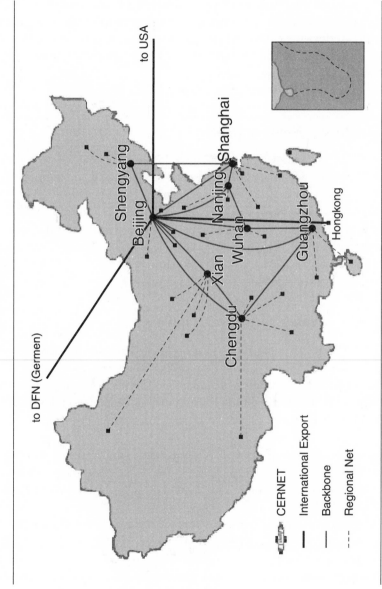

CERNET

—— International Export

— Backbone

--- Regional Net

Source: Hualin Qian, China Computer Network Information Center and Chinese Academy of Sciences Presentation, May 19, 2001, "Internet Development in China and its community activities."

digital hierarchy). Network equipment has been supplied by Newbridge Co. (Canada) and AT&T with its DACS II 200 cross-connecting switch.

International gateways and trunks (total of 14) are located in Beijing, Shanghai, and Guangzhou with direct connections to Hong Kong and also to several submarine cables including those connecting Japan, the Republic of Korea, Taiwan, and the United States (via international cable systems).

The local Public Information Bureaus (formally known as the PTAs) have also built private DDNs to link to ChinaDDN.

Golden Bridge Network (GBNet)

ChinaGBN is Jitong Communication's ISP service that uses the Golden Bridge network, which consists of a series of 256 kbps trunks provisioned over VSAT channels between 14 provincial capitals (see Figure 21.6). The VSAT channels are complemented with frame relay PVCs leased from China Telecom. Jitong maintains two international links from its Beijing gateway with a current capacity of 151 Mbps. As a reference, as of June 30, 2001, the total international Internet capacity was 3.257 Gbps of which China Telecom's ISP service "ChinaNet" accounted for 2.39 Gbps.

CERNET (China Education and Research Network)

CERNET is the first state-funded nation-wide education and research computer network in China similar to the DARPA network set up in the United States in the mid-1970s for the universities. CERNET is funded by the SPC and is directly managed by the State Education Commission. The project is broken into two phases:

> Phase I: Connecting some 1,075 universities and research institutes in China
> Phase II: Connecting high schools, middle schools, and primary schools

CERNET uses ChinaNET (ChinaPac and ChinaDDN) for the physical connections and is administered by the MII in terms of network management and planning.

China Unicom's Uninet and Wireless Internet

China Unicom's long-distance network currently consists of 23 Lucent circuit switches, 90 ATM Lucent switches and routers, and other IP equip-

Figure 21.6
Map of Golden Bridge Network

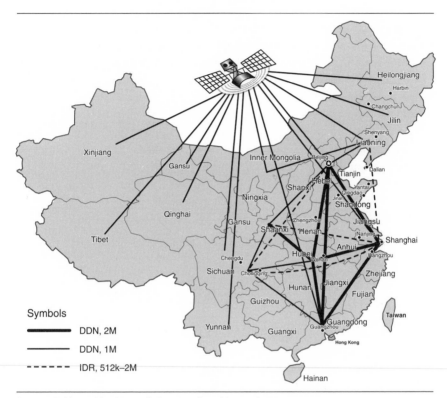

Source: Golden Bridge Network Company, http://www.gb.com.cn.

ment from Cisco Systems. China Unicom has also built a trial voice over IP (VoIP) network in 12 cities in China and hopes to have by the end of 2000 up to 220 cities connected on its long-distance network and 30 circuit switches. China Unicom is also trailing a Wireless Application Protocol (WAP) enabled Internet service for its mobile cellular subscribers in 20 large Chinese cities including Beijing, Shanghai, Tianjin, and Chongqing.

China Netcom CNCNet

China Netcom was established in 1999 as a partnership between the Shanghai Municipal Government, the Chinese Academy of Sciences, State Administration of Radio, Film, and Television (SARFT), and the MOR. Each partner has an equal 25% share. It is our view that the State Council tolerated a certain amount of favoritism that occurred in the formation of China Netcom because it was eager to create more domestic players. China Netcom is planning to utilize the MOR's existing telecommunications networks and also possibly the SARFT's CATV network as a supplement to constructing a large 17-city POP network. Current plans call for deployment of DWDM along with most of the major long-haul trunks. AsiaInfo Holdings (which incidently was founded by Edward Tian, the current CEO of China Netcom) has been awarded a lead systems-integration contract to build an IP over DWDM architecture that will utilize terabit routing and multiprotocol label switching (MPLS) for prioritization of traffic. China Netcom has announced plans to offer a number of services including:

- VoIP telephony
- Internet access
- VPN
- Virtual ISP
- Web-hosting

In May 2000, the company announced that it was budgeting for up to $2 billion for its network build-out; it hopes to raise most of the funds through a dual listing in Hong Kong and NASDAQ.

21.5 OTHER NATIONAL VALUE-ADDED SERVICES NETWORKS

Golden Enterprise Network

The SETC has planned and is in the process of building a nationwide information network, known as the Golden Enterprise Network. The Network will comprise several subnetworks, the first being an industrial commerce information network that will provide domestic and overseas enterprises with industrial commerce information and will engage in various value-added services with domestic state-owned enterprises (SOEs) and overseas companies and organizations. The information network was incorporated as a company in 1997, the Zhongjing International Industrial Commerce Network Limited (ICNL) and will be implemented with open systems standards.

The China Machinery Industry Computer and Technology Corporation (MICT), a state-owned company associated with the Ministry of Machinery and based in Beijing, has been entrusted with the mission of setting up ICNL to connect up to 14,000 SOEs in the first several years of operation and eventually connect up to 100,000 SOEs around the year 2001. ICNL will operate a large data center in Beijing, which will connect to the State Information Center's national databases. Eventually, ICNL is envisioned to become a sort of Intranet for the SOEs.

21.6 REGULATION OF THE INTERNET IN CHINA

Prior to the formation of the MII, Internet policy was being developed by the Leading Group on Economic Informatization, but the newly formed MII has not completely sorted out which department will be responsible for the Internet. With respect to Internet Telephony, we expect that the Department of Policy and Regulations will assume responsibility for its regulation.

We should also note the role of MPS with respect to the Internet. New regulations that were put forth in early 1998 confirmed the role of the MPS in policing Internet services in China. With respect to voice over IP we do not anticipate any problems because once the voice calls are de-compressed and de-aggregated they are then connected to the PSTN network of China Telecom, which presumably has appropriate arrangements with the MPS.

Internet Pricing

The majority of commercial users access the networks via dial-up accounts via 33.6 kbps links. ChinaNet account holders dial the same number throughout the country and several choices of payment plans. Access charges have been steadily dropping. The cheapest plan offers three hours of monthly access for just 20 RMB ($2.50). Users can get 75 hours a month for 300 RMB ($36). In addition, users must pay local phone access charges of about 4 RMB per hour ($0.50). We expect communications prices relating to the Internet to continue to be reduced in the next several years following the rate cuts that took place in 1998:

- Domestic private line charges for Internet operators were cut 50%.
- International private line charges for ISPs were cut 30%.
- Frame relay tariffs were cut 65%.

However, for a 2 Mbps link to the Internet in the United States, PRC ISPs are still having to pay high prices: approximately $95,000 per month.

21.7 VOICE-OVER IP AND INTERNET TELEPHONY

Internet telephony is currently not regulated, but according to sources at China Telecom and the MII, that means that it is not legal either: Until the PRC laws say that something is legal, one can never be certain that is legal.

However, some analysts have suggested that the provincial administrations PIBs may pose a threat to China Telecom's international telephony revenues. Voice-over IP would enable the provincial operators to retain all the revenues from international calls, rather than handing the proceeds over to China Telecom in Beijing.

Another competitive threat to China Telecom comes from the numerous cable TV operators, which would like to offer data/IP telephony services over their cable networks. Currently, only China Unicom and China Telecom have domestic voice telephony licenses. Clearly, the PRC authorities will have to sort out what types of services the cable operators will be allowed to participate in.

Even though voice-over IP is not legal, strictly speaking, it has not prevented the government from approving a joint venture to manufacture IP telephony products. In November 1998, NetTrue Communications of the United States announced that it had entered into a JV with Tangsheng Investment and Development Co. Ltd., an affiliate of Shanghai Bell Telephone Equipment Manufacturing Co., for the development of a carrier-grade, large-port capacity, scalable IP switch based on NetTrue's IP telephony technology. Shanghai Bell is a JV between China's MII and Alcatel Bell of Belgium and the Belgian government. It is one of the largest manufacturers of telecom equipment in China, supplying its products mainly to the provincial China Telecom bureaus.

As of this writing, no solid regulation exists on the provision of voice-over IP services in the PRC. There are stories of certain government departments that are actually using voice-over IP gateways to reduce their international call bills. In March 1998, NetTrue Communications Inc. carried out an official demonstration of Internet telephony services in China at a seminar for provincial telecom operators, ISPs, and senior telecom officials in Beijing. NetTrue is claiming to have shipped two of its systems to the PRC for trials. A number of provinces have expressed keen interest in voice-over IP, including Zhejiang, Jiangsu, Hainan, Fujian, Guangdong, Beijing, and Shang-hai.

21.8 BUILDING THE BROADBAND INFRASTRUCTURE

As China forges ahead with its vast construction of a modern telecommunications infrastructure, the proliferation of broadband networks and subnetworks can be expected to follow suit. SDH/SONET connected over microwave and fiber-optic links have formed the backbone of China Telecom's PSTN long-distance trunks, which has also been complemented by satellite in the more remote areas. Many of China's CATV networks also have advanced SDH backbone networks with up to 2.5 Gbps transmission capacity. In the future it might be possible that the SARFT and the MII can come to an agreement to allow the CATV networks to carry Internet and voice traffic.

Huge Investments Still Needed

The amount of investment needed to implement broadband widely among the largest cities is immense. China has announced its targets of achieving 25% fixed line teledensity by 2020 with a total of 1 billion lines of switching capacity (mobile and fixed) and a national ATM-switched backbone connecting to local networks. In 1996 the State Council, in a study commissioned by its Joint Conference for National Economic Informatization, has estimated that China needs to invest $200 billion between 1996 and 2020 in order to realize a national broadband infrastructure.

Recently, ChinaNet, China Netcom, and Jitong announced that they were planning to invest $1 billion to convert their networks to broadband (155 Mbps).

Fiber-Optic Backbone Networks and the Introduction of DWDM in China

China is at the beginning of a period of unprecedented growth in its converged data and voice communications networks and services as it transforms itself into a networked economy.

China has an extensive and growing fiber-optic infrastructure for its data and voice networks connecting major and minor cities throughout the nation. As of this writing, there were over 1 million kilometers of fiber-optic cable in China's telecom networks. In 1994, China Telecom and the PTAs started installing SDH transmission systems in both the telephone, data, and CATV networks; today, China's fiber-optic networks are among the most advanced in the world with digitalization approaching 100%.

China was the first country after the United States to deploy, on a large scale, DWDM systems when it installed a wave division multiplexing (WDM) fiber-optic trunk line between Wuhan and Xian in the fourth quarter of 1998. The national telecommunications infrastructure comprises three layers:

1. National backbone
2. Provincial networks
3. City, rural, VSAT and mobile cellular networks

DWDM is used in the national backbone, usually at transmission rates of OC-192 (10 Gbps) or greater and already is connecting over 60 major and smaller cities. Provincial rings usually are operating at OC-48 (2.5 Gbps) rates. China cannot build the network fast enough: According to Lucent Technologies, the annual compound annual growth rate (CAGR) growth rates for data and voice traffic in China are 80% and 10%, respectively. The current state of the art in single-fiber transmission is 10 Gbps, but according to vendors such as Nortel and Lucent Technologies, advances in silicon transistors, opto-electronics, and software will enable 160–320 Gbps on a single fiber in the next three years.

Although DWDM has been used principally for the tandem networks in China, we expect that it is just a matter of time before DWDM will find its way into major metropolitan networks. One of the challenges for China's planners will be the attraction of IP over fiber and the replacement of ATM switches with gigabit or terabit IP + ATM or IP only switches. Quality of service (QoS) will become an important requirement as demand for multimedia and real-time data services begins to emerge in China. On the mobile cellular side, the aggressive push by European and Japanese cellcos is giving impetus to China to accelerate its 2.5 and 3G mobile upgrades and new construction.

Below is a list of the operators which either already have or are constructing national, high-capacity fiber-optic backbone networks for public use:

- China Telecom and the PTAs (Chinanet): Nationwide 8x8 PSTN and data network; regional broadband networks and metropolitan area networks
- China Unicom: Nationwide IP-based backbone
- China Netcom CNCnet (will utilize a DWDM backbone network)
- Ministry of Railways CRTC (CRCN)
- Citic Pacific/Citic Beijing[6] (DWDM backbone, the dark fibers of which are planned to be purchased from the PLA)

In late May 2000, China Telecom announced that it had selected Alcatel to supply DWDM equipment for two national network projects, Shendahu and Xichengyu. China Netcom meanwhile has earmarked in its midterm construction budget of $2.5 billion to construct its nationwide broadband network (see Figure 21.7). The company in planning, according to its vice president, Mr. Fan Xingcha, a dual listing in Hong Kong and NASDAQ in order to raise the funds to build out its network.

Figure 21.7
List of some of the major broadbend telecoms investments in China

Customer/ Location	Date	Vendor	Contract Value	Comments
Shangdong PTA	Oct 1999	Alcatel	US$20	16-λ (2.5 Gbps per channel), DWDM for two national China Telecom links (470 route km) connecting Jinan to Qindao
China Telecom	Mar 1999	Alcatel		8-λ DWDM for a national link connecting Chongqing to Chengdu
China Netcom	May 2000	Pirelli		Purchasing fiber–optic cable for 100,000 km or G.652 single-mode and 50,000 km of Freelight G.655 II zero-dispersion shift single-mode fiber optic cable
China Netcom	Mar 2000	AsiaInfo		AsiaInfo is the lead systems integrator for China Netcom and is planning to utilize MPLS for QoS and IP Over DWDM at rates of 2.5 Gbps per λ for up to 16 wavelengths.
Guangdong PTA	Apr 1999	Newbridge		Purchased 128 MainStreetXpress 36170 Multiservice Switches in order to connect banks and other financial institutions in more than 100 counties in the province.

Provincial Metropolitan Broadband Network Projects

A number of municipal and provincial governments are building broadband public networks using the local PTA's license or the cable TV operator's network (which currently are technically not licensed for telephony). Below we provide a brief overview of several exemplary network projects.

Shanghai Infoport. Shanghai's Infoport project follows in the footsteps of aggressive construction in the last decade of a number of municipal infrastructures including the Yanan Road Viaduct (Elevated Road), the Shanghai Oriental Peral TV Tower, the Nanpu Bridge, and the Yangpu Bridge. A number of companies are involved in the Infoport project including Shanghai Telecom, Shanghai Radio and Television, China Unicom, China Netcom, and dozens of specialized companies. The total investment for Phase I is estimated to be RMB two billion ($242 million). The objective of the project is ultimately to provide an information-dedicated pipeline network running across the whole city.

A number of miniprojects fall under the umbrella of the Infoport initiative. For example, Shanghai Cable TV Network, which had 2.2 million subscribers by the end of 1999, upgraded its network in 1999 to enable up to 300,000 two-way subscribers. As part of the Infoport initiative, Shanghai Cable TV Network will expand its upgrades to enable up to one million two-way subscribers.

The Infoport projects is being led by a newly formed JV, Shanghai Information Network Company, which is joint effort between the Shanghai Municipal Government and Shanghai Telecom. The JV is responsible for developing a communications platform for the Infoport. Presently, the platform will comprise eight core 40 Gbps ATM switches, 41 1.6 Gbps ATM edge switches with 622 Mbps (OC-12) fiber optic links. OC-3 (155 Mbps) secondary optical links are being provided at the edge, which in effect means that the network is of a two-star topology. The 622 Mbps links will be upgraded to 2.5 Gbps and the number of edge switches will reach 89.

The Infoport will also cooperate with the Shanghai Information Interactive Exchange Network (SIHX), which has its roots with a number of organizations including Shanghai Online,[7] Shanghai School of the China Academy of Sciences. A super-computer data center is also planned to be built in the Zhangjiang Hi-Tech Park in Pudong. The Shanghai Municipal government is actively promoting the Hi-Tech Park and recently opened the Shanghai

Pudong Software Park Phase I inside the Zhangjiang Hi-Tech Park. The software R&D building occupies some 30,000 m² and is fully booked.

Shanghai Telecom's OFSnet and the Shanghai Cable Fiber-Optic MAN Network.   The incumbent telecom operator in Shanghai is Shanghai Telecom, but perhaps the most aggressive competition comes from Shanghai Cable Network, which boasts the largest metropolitan area network in the world with 2.8 million subscribers, 4000 km of fiber-optic cable, and 2,200 optical nodes. Shanghai Cable Network is now converting its network to two-way Internet capable and expects by year-end 2000 to have 1 million IP two-way subscribers.

Shanghai Telecom, of which 90% of its revenues comes from voice circuit switching, is responding to the competition from Shanghai Cable Network by constructing its own city-wide broadband services networks called OFSnet. OFSnet is based on an underlying backbone ATM over SDH and IP over DWDM fiber-optic physical layer and intends to offer a wide range of narrowband and broadband services including video on demand (VOD) and multipoint video conferencing. The metro network will utilize several broadband last mile technologies including xDSL and FTTB.

Shekou Information Island.   The Shekou Industrial Zone in Shenzen, Guangdong has earmarked an additional RMB 280 million ($34 million) for the Shekou Information Island; RMB 70 million has already been invested in the project, which also involved China Telecom and the Guangdong PTA. China Telecom has laid fiber-optic cable across the Shekou Industrial Zone connecting to many of the buildings, referred to as fiber-to-the-building (FTTB). The project calls for an ATM-based network and IP-based multiservices. Approximately 20 residential zones are to be equipped with broadband access by the end of 2000. By the end of 2001, 33 zones will have broadband access with VOD planned to go operational in late 2001.

The MOR China Railway Telecommunications Center (CRTC).
The Ministry of Railway (MOR) owns and operates the second largest public telecommunications network after China Telecom. The MOR operates its telecommunications network through its wholly owned subsidiary, China Railway Telecommunications Center (CRTC).

The MOR network connects over 5,000 railway stations through a network of 120,000 kilometers of communications links spanning the entire nation (42,000 kilometers of fiber-optic cable and 78,000 kilometers of satellite, microwave, and coaxial transmission systems). The CRTC has invested approximately RMB 10 billion in the existing network. The CRTC voice network has 800 PTSN switches and a capacity of 1.4 million toll-quality voice lines and presently has approximately 1 million users (not commercial subscribers). Only 20% of the available capacity is being used for railway-related telecommunications services. The CRTC also operates video conferencing and VSAT connection services. The MOR has received financing from a number of financial institutions including the World Bank, the Bank of China, the Construction Bank of China, and the Industrial and Commercial Bank of China.

A wholly-owned subsidiary of the CRTC, the China Railway Telecommunications Network Technology Company (CRCN) has been licensed by the MII as an Internet service provider with the added provision that it can use seven major cities including Beijing and Shanghai as international Internet gateways.

- Plans to obtain the operating license and relevant frequency bands to operate a GSM-R network along the nation's railway lines
- Owns and operates a data separate logical data communications network, China Railway Network (CRNET)
- Planning to construct a domestic long distance (DLD) automatic voice switching (S-12J) network called CRTTN. The switched network will support broadband services such as image transmission, television broadcast, and multimedia transmission
- Planning to construct and operate by the end of the ninth five-year plan (2004) a satellite communication network system reaching to all 13 railway telecom bureaus and all sub-bureaus that will encompass 70 mobile ground stations and 69 satellite ground stations.

21.9 THE BROADCAST MEDIA INDUSTRY

Regulation and policy regarding broadcast media is spearheaded by the State Council and the former Ministry of Radio, Film, and Television (MRFT), which has been merged into the MII. In order to understand China's evolving broadcast media policy it is important to realize that already some 81% of the country have access to television (i.e., 900 million people). By some accounts China is already the second largest TV market in the world in terms of

Figure 21.8
Satellite communications in China

Fixed Line Satellite	Mobile Communications

• Direct Broadcast satellite (DBS)
• Direct-to-Home Services (analog and digital cable TV)
• VSAT
   • Voice and data
   • Video broadcast
	• Pagers
	• Mobile phones
	• Airplane mobile phones
	• Mobile automobile systems

units. Industry sources estimate that China's TV advertising expenditures have surpassed $2.0 billion, and with the rise of living standards in China, TV has thus become indispensable for many households. Civilian satellite communications systems fall into two main categories as presented in Figure 21.8.

Direct-to-Home Satellite (DTH)

In 1993, the State Council issued regulations to control the installation and use of TV satellite dishes. The regulations deal with minimum capital requirements for companies that sell and install satellite TV reception equipment, as well as requirements for registration and government licenses for manufacturers and owners of the satellite dishes.

Several high profile satellite communications ventures targeted for the Chinese market have been formed. For instance, China Defense and Science Technology Industries Association, MPT, China Aviation Industries Co., and two Singaporean telecom companies have taken majority stakes in a mobile satellite project valued at between $500 million and $800 million.

In a separate development, China Aerospace International Holding (CAIN), the Hong Kong subsidiary of China Aerospace Corporation (CASC), announced in 1997 that it is forming a joint venture with the then MFRT, the State Education Commission, the SSTC, and a computer company, Beijing Wan Yuan. The joint venture, called the Beijing Sat-Way Information System, plans to deliver up to 100 high-quality DTH satellite TV channels; the company will also manufacture some ground equipment. If successful, this would be the first DTH satellite business to homes in China because under the current regulation satellite reception dishes for domestic use are prohibited.

By the end of 1997 or early 1998, there were six satellites with signals specifically covering China including the Apstar 2R satellite built by Space Systems Loral and launched by the APT Satellite Co. in late 1997. By mid-2001 there were over 170 C-band and Ka-band transponders in use in China. More DTH projects can be expected in China and various consortia to be formed as both domestic and foreign parties wait for China to liberalize the DTH market.

Satellite regulation in China appears, however, to make a distinction between urban and rural areas. Because of the rugged topography in many rural areas, the restrictions regarding satellite dishes are much more relaxed in the rural countryside. In fact, Asiasat is used by the China Central Television (CCTV) to deliver its broadcast across the nation.

Cable TV

There are over 86 million CATV subscribers in China. Cable TV has been in China since the 1960s and 1970s when manufacturing companies set up corporate (and therefore private) systems as part of their employee benefits. In 1980, the State Council approved a proposal to have all new buildings include an accommodation for Master Access Television (MATV). Moreover, in 1988, the government allowed operators to connect all of the MATV buildings with coaxial cable and a headend, thereby creating what is referred to in China as an urban network. These networks are typically 300 MHz and consist of 12 to 13 channels. Ownership of urban networks is governed by the state and only one network is allowed in any one city.

As of the time of this writing over 3,000 cable TV licenses have been issued along with the establishment of over 200 urban networks and over 400 private networks. In 1997 the MRFT placed a moratorium on new cable operator licenses in an attempt to get better control over the expansion of and quality of the programming. The pace of cable TV rollout in China is impressive, and it is worth noting that China intends to provide subscription TV to all of its 2,900 cities (see Figure 21.9).

Very Small Aperture Terminal (VSAT)

The VSAT market is another field that is growing by leaps and bounds in China at an annual rate of some 50%. The market leaders in terms of terminal equipment and hub stations are Hughes Network Services, Gilat Satellite Network, NEC, and Scientific Atlanta.

A number of large VSAT networks have been established in China. Some examples would include the following:

- Shanghai Stock Exchange is one of the largest VSAT networks in China and connects to over 1,000 data and 1,000 audio terminals receiving securities information.
- Ministry of Water Resources is constructing a nationwide VSAT network comprising over 3,000 terminals. The network is to be used to collect data and manage water resources including flooding and water level monitoring.
- Inner Mongolian Coal Corporation (IMCC) installed in 1991, a VSAT-based voice telephony system using equipment from Hughes Network Systems. Prior to the launch of the VSAT network, IMCC was forced to link its coal fields in Northeast China with a terrestrial network that used different transmission media like twisted pair connecting to underground cables connecting back to twisted pair and so forth. Each link was owned by a different entity, Ministry of Posts and Telecommunications (MPT) or People's Liberation Army (PLA). The average availability was only 50% to 60% prior to the installation of the VSAT system. The VSAT supplier had to overcome many obstacles including a requirement for different PBX signaling in different locations and large fluctuations in power supply.
- MOFTEC, as part of the Golden Customs Project, awarded a supplier contract to Scientific Atlanta to supply 60 remote CSAT sites and two master earth stations in Beijing and Shenzen and has plans to add another 140 remote sites. MOFTEC is using the VSAT network to provide voice and data communications between its regional facilities and provincial foreign trade and cooperation bureaus. The network utilizes Ku-band transponder space leased on Asiasat-2. MOFTEC may also use transportable stations in the future.

21.10 DEVELOPMENT OF CORE TECHNOLOGY COMPETENCIES

Foreign participation in the telecom market is closely regulated and is carried out principally through the issuance of joint venture licenses and tax laws. As China seeks to develop its technology sectors including telecoms, it has to carefully weigh the pros and cons of only buying and installing foreign equipment and not developing core engineering and manufacturing competencies. In the area of integrated circuits, China has begun to encourage some foreign firms such as Motorola and NEC to establish chip fabrication facilities inside China, which fits in the framework of trade access agreements with very specific technology transfer demands.

Telecommunications is particularly a strategic sector with respect to integrated circuit technology because, for example, according to some estimates, 50% of the cost of digital cellular handsets is from the integrated circuits. Increasingly, custom VLSI, large scale integration (LSI), and application specific integrated circuit (ASIC) chips are becoming integral components of telecommunications switching and end-user devices, such as set-up boxes for cable TV and satellite TV, mobile phones, modems, routers, and so forth.

In 2001 the MII and the Chinese Academy of Sciences set up a research program similar to the U.S. DARPA to focus on microelectronics research with the goal that China can develop its own chips and patents.

One example of an IC development company that has been quite successful is Huawei Technology Ltd., based in Shenzen, which boasts an IC design center with the ability to design 0.35 micron ASICs. The company is developing ASICs for ATM, SDH, and video conferencing.

Another example is Zhongxing Telecom Ltd. (Shenzen), a startup, that has actually established its own R&D center in Silicon Valley and has formed a joint DSP-technology laboratory with Texas Instruments Inc. Zhongxing is also working with IBM subsidiary ComQuest Technology Ltd., to develop a GSM-based dual-band cellular phone and expects to ship handsets in early 1999.

Software is another strategic area for China, and in our opinion, it will take time before China will be able to compete on the world market for core software and applications. If the rest of Asia is an example, it might be a long time before core software from Asia can compete with the likes of Microsoft. Nevertheless, with respect to applications programming for particular industries, China has made much progress in terms of EDI, shipping, train control systems, credit card transaction processing, and network management.

21.11   3G AND THE PROSPECTS FOR 4G

The Chinese Academy of Telecommunication Technology (CATT) has developed its own home-grown 3G technology that it calls TD-SCDMA (described in more detail in the earlier chapter on 3G), which China subsequently submitted and lobbied hard to get accepted as one of the three CDMA standards for the IMT-2000. Siemens was also involved in the development of the specifications for TD-SCDMA, which is a TDD-based wideband CDMA system similar to the UTRA standard in Europe. Although the

Chinese government has showcased TD-SCDMA as its own home-grown brew, it appears unlikely that the other IMT-2000 standards will be completely locked out of the Chinese market. China Unicom is installing cdma-One IS-95 networks in various cities and China Telecom Mobile has not yet decided, given that its install base is 900 MHz and 1800 MHZ GSM. Both China Telecom Mobile and China Unicom are upgrading certain locations to include GPRS services, and it will take another one to two years before wireless Internet services begin to gain significant momentum in China.

And that is where the problem with 3G lies in China. By the time that GPRS or EDGE services really take off in China, 802.11 W-LANs will have become quite popular and 4G wireless mobile cellular technologies will have made significant strides in the development labs of the major telecom equipment makers and some of the large service providers such as NTT DoCoMo and Telecom Italia Mobile. Thus, Chinese researchers and planners are already gearing up for 4G. In a telling paper, Li Zhengmao, deputy chief engineer and director general of China Unicom, published a paper in December 1999 entitled "The 3G Mobile Communications: Ideal and Reality"[8] in which he cited the disparities of the different "harmonized" 3G standards and concluded that the continuous development of wireless technologies will not stop and that 4G technologies such as spatial division multiple access (SDMA), adaptive antennas, and wearable computing can be expected to arrive before the end of the decade.

China does not intend to auction any of its 3G spectrum, which removes some of the financial pressure on China Unicom and China Telecom Mobile. However, the cost of upgrading to 3G IMT-2000 systems simply cannot be justified on wireless data forecasts that do not provide genuine broadband capabilities to users. Until 4G is available, we predict that China mobile carriers will concentrate on getting their wireless data users up and on developing IP broadband backbones to support 4G systems. By the year 2003, 802.11 W-LANs will be popping up everywhere in China, albeit they will still require licensing from the government because they will be classified as public telecom networks if they charge for their services.

NOTES

1. According to public press releases from China Unicom, the total value of its CCF's was $1.4 billion.

2. China Netcom is the newest operator and received approval from the State Council in February 1999. It is constructing a DWDM-based fiber-optic backbone and will be initially linked by the MOR's trunk network. China Netcom is seeking to become an all-IP network and will provide support for voice, data, and multimedia. Its initial capital is estimated to be approximately $300 million.

3. Under the present laws, the PRC can make exceptions if the project falls under a list of special high-tech areas that MOFTEC and the former MPT jointly identified.

4. CNNIC, formed in 1997 and headquartered in Zhongguancun hi-tech zone in Beijing, was created by the Chinese Academy of Sciences, which is a research group that tries to keep track of demographics statistics relating to the Internet in the PRC.

5. ChinaNet's total international bandwidth jumped significantly with the late March 1998 opening of an AT&T 45 Mbps submarine cable from Shanghai to the United States.

6. On 16 March 2000 Citic Pacific (HK) announced that it was acquiring 32,000 km of fiber-optic cable, presumably dark fiber, that had been laid by the PLA. Citic plans to combine that fiber optic network with CATV assets that Citic Beijing has to provide data communications services to CATV users if and when the regulations allow it.

7. China Online is owned by high-tech firm Shenzen Rayes Group. China Online uses GBNetVSAT connections as well as ChinaNet for backbone provision.

8. Li Zhengmao, "The 3G Mobile Communications: Ideal and Reality," http://tdscdmaforum.org/english/articles/article2.htm (December 1999).

CONCLUSION

Readers who have gone through the entire book, even if they've skipped sections here and there, generally take away one or more of the following 19 points:

1. The computer industry is undergoing rapid evolutionary change caused by the exponential improvement in chips and storage, with further changes waiting hidden in the wings.
2. The telecommunications industry is experiencing a wrenching and revolutionary shift caused by the multiple impacts of government policy, new government demands (such as for license fees via auctions), the competition for spectrum, the awkward transition from a focus on wireline voice to blurred or divided focus on wireless voice, broadband data, and, in fits and starts, wireless broadband.
3. 4G is, at its simplest, mobile wireless broadband, and it is truly the "next big thing" and the "killer app" because it makes use of most of the technology advances that are proven, though not yet implemented on a national or global scale.
4. There is a convergence of computers and communications, and it appears that computer companies are better positioned to be left standing when the convergence is complete because of their better and broader R&D strengths in an era where new science and technology can completely change the world.
5. The assumption that telecom companies will always be able to charge by the minute is not justified by technology. Just as there is no marginal cost for using walkie-talkies or car radios, there may eventually be one-rate subscriptions, or even one-time purchases for an increasing fraction of all communications.
6. There will be another major convergence, which is just appearing, between the converged computer and communications industry, with aspects of the biotechnology industry. Surprisingly, the biotech industry

may end up having the advantage, especially when nanotechnology takes off.

7. Upgrades in the computer business are relatively easy because it's a more modular, standardized industry. However, this also makes it easier for a newcomer, perhaps with a lower-powered CPU chip, to come along and shake up the entire industry.

8. Upgrades in the communications industry are very, very hard, and are made harder by the incredible complexity and long lead times required, as well as by the need to deal with internal bureaucracy in a typically nonentrepreneurial culture and external bureaucracy from regulatory agencies, as well as unfair competition from the military and television broadcasters, as well as historical precedents from amateur radio that mean that logic and efficiency—the drivers of the computer revolution—are not allowed to be the major influences of telecommunication progress.

9. Despite the major investments in 2G and 3G, the stakeholders of the telecommunications industry—especially those like Sony and other nontelecom companies without much investment in the past—should admit that the emperor has no clothes, that 3G is not good enough to serve as the standard for the 2001 to 2010 decade as analog and digital wireless did for the 1980s and 1990s.

10. Wearable computers and augmented reality, along with small wireless sensors, are going to change first the computer and communications industries, and then the entire world.

11. There is a four-way race for the future between Europe, the United States, Japan, and China. Amazingly, each has a unique strength and a unique weakness, and any one area could end up as the regional home of companies that are the leaders in 4G. Being the seller of 4G rather than the buyer could, over time, make a bigger difference than any other major economic change in years to come.

12. Europe's governments are the most harmful to their companies, and America's government is the most neutral. In 4G, governments will matter more than ever before, and can help their companies win or lose without even knowing why.

13. Japan is the first country to have near universal acceptance of wireless Internet. 4G is Japan's best, and possibly only, chance to reverse its decline and again move back into a position of technology and business leadership, after six years during which its economy shrank while America's grew almost 25 percent.

14. China, the dark horse, has all the elements to make a surprise move into leadership in 4G, and thus to turn the conventional wisdom of the competition between developing and developed countries upside down. China already has a strong trade surplus with the United States, and one day China could even have a hardware and telecommunications surplus with America, changing the world's balance of power. China's telecom revolution will, in the future, be seen as unexpected, but it is entirely predictable from the statistics in this book.

15. Over a dozen new technologies and policies are needed to make 4G happen, and no one country or continent has even half of all these elements, making for a wide-open competition that will go to the smartest and swiftest builders of alliances.

16. Making 4G happen before 2010 will require the creation, or restructuring, of companies so that all key executives, employees, and influential investors know most if not all of the information in Brave New Unwired World, as complex as all of this material can be. Even more difficult, building a 4G industry will require governments, the technology media and later the mass media, corporate buyers, and even the general public—first regionally and then globally—to become at least somewhat conversant with the issues and companies mentioned in this book.

17. The opportunity to take one or more pieces of 4G and bring them to market is surprisingly massive, making this current period in the very early part of 2002 possibly one of the very best times to be in business, when expectations for technology have just fallen very low, and while technology capabilities that are not yet implemented are getting exponentially higher, setting the foundation for another boom that may be bigger than the one in the 1990s.

18. All of this combines to make a "smart world" that has the potential to function much more efficiently and supportively, particularly with respect to human creativity

19. The authors invite communication, brainstorming, and collaboration and hope to inspire bold, visionary actions to bring about this, our brave new unwired world, in which anyone anywhere can get any information in any media, almost instantly and at almost no cost. This is the future to which we hope to give momentum, and we invite the reader to join our efforts to make this book come to life.

INDEX